How to Study Lingu

D0106426

Palgrave Study Guides

A Handbook of Writing for Engineers   *Joan van Emden*
Authoring a PhD Thesis   *Patrick Dunleavy*
Effective Communication for Arts and Humanities Students   *Joan van Emden and Lucinda Becker*
Effective Communication for Science and Technology   *Joan van Emden*
How to Manage your Arts, Humanities and Social Science Degree   *Lucinda Becker*
How to Write Better Essays   *Bryan Greetham*
Key Concepts in Politics   *Andrew Heywood*
The Mature Student's Guide to Writing   *Jean Rose*
The Postgraduate Research Handbook   *Gina Wisker*
Professional Writing   *Sky Marsen*
Research Using IT   *Hilary Coombes*
The Student's Guide to Writing   *John Peck and Martin Coyle*
The Study Skills Handbook   *Stella Cottrell*
Studying Economics   *Brian Atkinson and Susan Johns*
Studying History (second edition)   *Jeremy Black and Donald M. MacRaild*
Studying Mathematics and its Applications   *Peter Kahn*
Studying Psychology   *Andrew Stevenson*
Teaching Study Skills and Supporting Learning   *Stella Cottrell*

Palgrave Study Guides: Literature

General Editors: John Peck and Martin Coyle

How to Begin Studying English Literature (second edition)   *Nicholas Marsh*
How to Study a Jane Austen Novel (second edition)   *Vivien Jones*
How to Study Chaucer (second edition)   *Rob Pope*
How to Study a Charles Dickens Novel   *Keith Selby*
How to Study Foreign Languages   *Marilyn Lewis*
How to Study an E. M. Forster Novel   *Nigel Messenger*
How to Study James Joyce   *John Blades*
How to Study Linguistics (second edition)   *Geoffrey Finch*
How to Study Modern Drama   *Kenneth Pickering*
How to Study Modern Poetry   *Tony Curtis*
How to Study a Novel (second edition)   *John Peck*
How to Study a Poet (second edition)   *John Peck*
How to Study a Renaissance Play   *Chris Coles*
How to Study Romantic Poetry (second edition)   *Paul O'Flinn*
How to Study a Shakespeare Play   *John Peck and Martin Coyle*
How to Study Television   *Keith Selby and Ron Cowdery*
Linguistic Terms and Concepts   *Geoffrey Finch*
Literary Terms and Criticism (third edition)   *John Peck and Martin Coyle*
Practical Criticism   *John Peck and Martin Coyle*

www.palgravestudyguides.com

How to Study Linguistics

A Guide to Understanding Language

Second Edition

Geoffrey Finch

First published 1997
Second edition 2003
Published by
PALGRAVE MACMILLAN
Houndmills, Basingstoke, Hampshire RG21 6XS and
175 Fifth Avenue, New York, N.Y. 10010
Companies and representatives throughout the world

PALGRAVE MACMILLAN is the global academic imprint of the Palgrave Macmillan division of St. Martin's Press, LLC and of Palgrave Macmillan Ltd. Macmillan® is a registered trademark in the United States, United Kingdom and other countries. Palgrave is a registered trademark in the European Union and other countries.

ISBN 1–4039–0106–6

This book is printed on paper suitable for recycling and made from fully managed and sustained forest sources.

A catalogue record for this book is available from the British Library.

Library of Congress Cataloging-in-Publication Data
Finch, Geoffrey.
  How to study linguistics: a guide to understanding language / Geoffrey Finch.—2nd ed.
    p. cm. — (Palgrave study guides)
  Includes bibliographical references and index.
  ISBN 1–4039–0106–6 (pbk.)
  1. Linguistics—Study and teaching. 2. Linguistic analysis (Linguistics) I. Title.
  II. Series.

P51 .F544 2003
410'.71—dc21   2002035261

10   9   8   7   6   5   4   3   2   1
12   11   10   09   08   07   06   05   04   03

Printed in Great Britain by
Creative Print & Design (Wales), Ebbw Vale

For Marion, who also loves language

Contents

Acknowledgements

The author and publisher wish to thank the following for permission to use copyright material:

Blackwell Publishers for Figure 2 from G. Hughes, *Words in Time* (1986); and Figure 9 from Peter Trudgill, *The Dialects of England* (1991).

Every effort has been made to trace the copyright holders but if any have been inadvertently overlooked the publishers will be pleased to make the necessary arrangement at the first opportunity.

General Editors' Preface

If you are studying linguistics the chances are that you are looking for a book that will not only help you come to grips with the basic principles of linguistic study, but also a book that will help you understand the ideas behind linguistics in a clear, sensible way. The aim of *How to Study Linguistics* is to offer you guidance on how to gain both of these important skills by providing the sort of vital information you need to understand linguistics as a discipline and also by providing approachable discussions of the main aspects of linguistic analysis.

The first chapter offers a straightforward introduction to linguistics and the way in which language works and how we can describe it. Then come a series of chapters dealing with the major aspects of linguistic study, starting with the context of linguistics – what we do with language, how we use it, and its various functions. Following this come three chapters dealing with the central aspects of all linguistic study: sound, syntax, and meaning. Each of these topics is approached from a common-sense point of view, with each chapter slowly building into a full discussion of the topic. The emphasis throughout is on relating linguistics to our own experience as language users.

The final two chapters of the book deal with how to take the study of linguistics further, exploring its diverse strands and aspects, and also offer advice on how to write an essay on an aspect of linguistics. As with all the chapters of the book, these can be read separately or dipped into for information or guidance. In the first instance, however, it may well repay you to read quickly through the book as a whole, so that you gain a sense of what linguistics involves and how the essays you are asked to write relate to the wider study of language as the most distinctive feature of human beings. At once a guide to current ideas about linguistics and a practical textbook that will develop your skills as a student of language, *How to Study Linguistics* is designed to help you get the most out of your course and to achieve excellent results.

1 Beginning Linguistics

If you are just starting your studies in linguistics the first piece of advice I have may seem rather odd. It is this: **beware of all books on linguistics**. And that includes the one you are now reading. A healthy scepticism is not a bad thing. Most books on linguistics raise expectations of understanding which they cannot fulfil. This is not entirely their fault, of course. There is an undeniable technical and theoretical base to the subject, and negotiating through this whilst still remaining reasonably coherent is not easy. But in spite of all the technical terminology, linguistics is not a science. It's a pity that the subject doesn't have a different name. We tend to think of disciplines ending in 'ics' – e.g. statistics, mathematics, physics – as having a precise scientific core consisting of unchallengeable facts. Linguistics is not like that. Neither, of course, strictly speaking, are mathematics, statistics, or physics. Indeed, many scientists, nowadays, would question this view of science. Nevertheless, it's important to bear in mind that the subject matter of linguistics, language, is made up. Words do not grow out of the ground, they haven't evolved like matter from the interaction of natural elements. And whilst there is much to suggest that the structures and processes which enable language to develop are inborn, there is still a very important sense in which language is human-made. It is our possession in a way that nothing else is. And the process of making up, or inventing, never stops.

It's as well to remember this when government bodies go on, as they periodically do, about 'bad' English and the importance of maintaining standards. The question we should be asking is 'whose language is it anyway?' Language is one of the few truly democratic forces left to us. It may be used as an instrument of oppression, when one nation colonises or annexes another, but it has an unerring ability to turn on its handler. We have only to look at how international varieties of English are flourishing around the world in former colonies, from the Indian sub-continent to the Caribbean, to see the democratising influences of the language. And even in England, although it is sometimes argued that the combined forces of the media and public schools are producing a uniform pronunciation, the truth is that conservative speech patterns are themselves subtly changing under the influence of newly emergent accents. Despite institutional pressure and manipulation, language is ultimately a law unto itself. Samuel Johnson, the eighteenth-century writer, and one of the first people to attempt to control linguistic behaviour, reflects soberly in the preface to his *Dictionary of the English Language* on the failure of nations to 'fix' their languages:

> With this hope, however, academies have been instituted, to guard the avenues of their languages, to retain fugitives, and repulse intruders; but their vigilance and activity have hitherto been vain; sounds are too volatile and subtile for legal restraints; to enchain syllables, and to lash the wind are equally the undertakings of pride unwilling to measure its desires by its strength. (Johnson, 1958, pp. 233–4)

Despite Johnson's lament about 'the boundless chaos of a living speech' (p. 219), however, language is not chaotic. There are rules governing linguistic behaviour just as there are everything else in life. They may not be the rules which people might wish to impose on us, but they are rules none the less. It is these rules which linguists are concerned with studying. Perhaps an analogy might help here. Imagine that I am attending an important function at my place of work. One of the things I have to do is decide what to wear. If there is a dress code I have to find out what it is in order to avoid embarrassing myself along with everybody else. Let's say it's a suit and tie affair. Now I may of course decide that wearing a suit and tie is rather stuffy and turn up instead in jeans and a tee-shirt. The reaction of people to this will inevitably vary. Some will think it refreshingly informal, whilst others will consider it 'bad form'. But no one will think me undressed. I have clothes on in all the right places even if some people don't like what I am wearing. If, however, I were to arrive with my underpants around my head, my trousers round my neck and my shirt tied round my waist I could be accused of being undressed, as well as running a serious risk of being locked up. There are two sorts of rules here. One is a rule about which part of the body, trousers, for example, are worn on, and the other is about what kind of trousers are worn. The first we could consider a clothing rule, and the second a social rule. The first one is not likely to change; it is doubtful that we will ever get a situation where it is considered normal to wear trousers around one's neck. The second, however, is changing all the time. There are many more occasions now when people dress casually where previously they would have dressed formally.

And it is similarly the case with language. Sometimes you will hear people object that certain expressions or constructions are 'not English' or 'ungrammatical'. Some teachers still like to say this about *ain't* or the use of the double negative, as in *I ain't got no money*. But this is not so. Something is only ungrammatical if it fails to follow a rule in the way it is formed. *I ain't got no money* doesn't follow the same rule in its construction as *I haven't any money* but it's not without one. People who use this construction wouldn't dream of saying *got I have money n't no*, which would be uninterpretable. Someone who produced that would be like the hypothetical person mentioned above, wearing his clothes in all the wrong places. And, as in the clothing example, there are two sorts of rules here: a linguistic sort and a social sort. This is an important distinction to make because it's easy to mix them up. We mustn't confuse linguistic judgements with social ones. Of course, some people will attempt to prove that the double negative is ungrammatical by saying it's illogical, 'two negatives make a positive'. But no one in the entire history of its use has ever understood it in that way. Up until the end of the Middle Ages it was a regular feature of English, as anyone who has studied Chaucer knows. Here is Chaucer, for example, in *The Wife of Bath's Tale*, bemoaning the fact that people can no longer see fairies: 'But now kan **no** man se **none** elves mo' ('but now no one can see no more elves'). The double negative was simply an emphatic way of negating something. What we have done in standard speech over the centuries is to weaken it. Other languages, like French, have resisted this, except in colloquial speech, where, ironically, it is the single negative which is non-standard.

The second piece of advice I wish to give therefore is this: **learn to think linguistically**. This doesn't mean ignoring social rules. They obviously have their place. We might want to argue about what that place is but they are an undeniable fact of life. There are some occupations where using forms like *ain't*, or double negatives, or saying *I done that* instead of *I did that*, could cost you your job. Oddly enough we have become a little more tolerant of certain accents than we have of non-standard grammar. It is quite common nowadays to hear the weather forecast in a regional accent on television, although more prestigious accents are still reserved for the main news. We need to know about social rules, therefore, but it is important to recognise that they are simply conventions. What weight we give to them is entirely relative. In ten or twenty years time, they could be less or more important. There is nothing to stop the Queen giving her Christmas broadcast in jeans, just as there is nothing to stop her saying *me and my husband*. No clothing, or linguistic rule, would be broken. The publishing world, except in the case of creative writing, sticks rigorously to standard grammar, and one can see why. Using a uniformly accepted style is clearly convenient and runs less risk of offending anyone. In writing this book I have used standard forms although you will find many more contractions, *haven't, mustn't, isn't, it's*, than were acceptable some years ago. And I have several sentences which begin with *and* – like this one. The nature of social rules, and the way in which they operate, is itself a fascinating study and some areas of linguistics, notably sociolinguistics, are more concerned with them than others. But compared with linguistic rules they are only of fractional significance. The rules which enable us to produce either *I haven't any money*, or *I ain't got no money* are far more complex and profound than those which would discriminate against one in favour of the other.

The best place to start an investigation of the differences between social and linguistic judgements about language use is with your own speech habits. Try making a list of things you say which people object to and see if you can categorise them in terms of the nature of the objections and the contexts in which they are made. Some objections might be purely on grounds of politeness, like saying *what?* instead of *pardon?* when something is misheard. Others might concern the use of non-standard forms, as for example, *mine's better than what yours is* or *he done it very nice*. And some might entail a fine point of grammar quite impenetrable to all except those making the objection. Like most people, I can remember as a child being told to say *may I leave the table?* not *can I leave the table?* and failing to see the difference, let alone its importance. Picking others up on minor points of language use is very much a national pastime. People seize with glee on any deviation in spelling, pronunciation, or expression as if it were some failure of character or intelligence. This is partly because in England, at any rate, language use is unfortunately bound up with issues of class. Using 'incorrect' forms is frequently considered an indication of being lower class, and no one wants to be thought that.

If you do this exercise you will find that part of the problem of categorising your 'deviant' speech habits lies in the terms 'correct/incorrect' themselves. Apart from being very vague, they inevitably suggest social approval or disapproval and as such blur any distinction we might want to make between social and linguistic judgements. The whole notion of correctness is too prescriptive to be of any use linguistically. Not surprisingly, therefore, you will rarely find linguists referring to it, except in a social sense. They prefer to talk instead of usages being **well-formed** or **ill-formed**. A particular usage is only ill-formed if it is not generated by a grammatical rule. Using this criterion, all the examples above are perfectly well-formed even though at first glance they might not appear to be so. Those who regularly produce forms such as *he done it very nice*, for example, are not ignorant of the existence of *did*. They will continue to say *he* **did** *do it* not *he* **done** *do it* (unless they are speaking Caribbean English). It is simply that a different rule is operating about when to use the past participle (*done*), as opposed to the past tense form (*did*). And as for the use of an adjective instead of an adverb, *nice* rather than *nicely*, this also occurs sometimes in **Standard English** – *come quick*, not *quickly*, and *open the window wide*, not *widely*. We can find frequent similar uses in Shakespeare: 'How sweet [not "sweetly"] the moonlight sleeps upon this bank' (*The Merchant of Venice*, V.i.54).

'Well-formed' and 'ill-formed' are terms which encapsulate linguistic judgements. We need another set of terms, however, to encapsulate social ones. In 1965 the linguist Noam Chomsky introduced the terms **acceptable/unacceptable**. The notion of 'acceptability' offers a much better way of coping with variant forms than that of 'correctness'. Using it as a criterion we could say that all of the expressions in the last but one paragraph,

> *what?*
> *mine's better than what yours is.*
> *he done it very nice.*
> *can I leave the table?*

are of varying acceptability depending on individual taste and conventions of politeness and context. Any usage which is ill-formed must of necessity be unacceptable whereas the reverse is not the case. The consequence of this is that we can categorise *he done it very nice*, for example, as well-formed, but unacceptable, if used in a BBC news broadcast. Between friends, however, it is both well-formed and acceptable.

The difference between concepts of well-formedness and acceptability on the one hand, and correctness on the other, is that the former are descriptive, rather than prescriptive, in character. That is, they seek to establish rules, whether of the social or linguistic kind, from actual use rather than from the pronouncements of some external authority. But, if that is the case, the question arises 'in what sense are they rules?' If they are merely describing what exists, how can that constitute a set of rules? In the case of social rules a better term, as suggested earlier, would probably be 'conventions'. We could argue that it is a matter of social convention that newscasters avoid non-standard grammar. Conventions operate by a kind of unconscious agreement between the parties involved. The matter is more complicated, however, with linguistic rules, to which we have said that the terms well/ill-formed apply. What gives a linguistic rule its authority? A linguist might well reply, 'the language', in that a sentence like *got I have money n't no* is linguistically impossible, but we are entitled to probe a little further I think.

To begin with, linguistic rules are not immutable; they do change over time and across dialects. Consider, for example, the sentence *they disappeared him*, and ask yourselves whether it is well- or ill-formed. I am guessing that you would judge it to be ill-formed, that is, not linguistically possible, and many conservative grammars would agree with you. They would do so on the grounds that *disappear* is an intransitive verb, in other words, it can't take an object – you don't disappear something. Verbs are quite frequently classified into transitive and intransitive according to whether they have objects; so the verb *hit* is transitive – something has to be hit. Verbs such as *fall* and *die*, on the other hand, are intransitive, in that they cannot take an object – you don't *fall* or *die* something. According to this grammatical account, *disappear* is a similar kind of verb: *he disappeared* is complete, whereas *he disappeared him* is nonsense. However, it isn't nonsense to an increasingly large number of people. In some parts of the world *to disappear someone* means to make them vanish, usually in highly mysterious circumstances. It's a usage which has been popularised by the media, in particular the American film industry. So, we are faced with a dilemma here. We either pronounce the American usage incorrect and seek to outlaw it, which is the approach a prescriptive grammar might take, or, because we are taking a descriptive approach, we decide it is well-formed but then are faced with having to alter the rules and declare it transitive. And the problem doesn't end there, because there are other verbs which have this slippery habit of crossing over. If we look again at *fall*, for example, it's possible for that to be used transitively in Nigerian English. A Nigerian can say *don't fall me down*, meaning don't cause me to fall over. We should have to say *don't push/knock me over*, but the meaning there is subtly different.

If it is the case that particular communities can change the way in which words behave, is there any real point in talking about linguistic rules? Isn't it just a free for all? The answer to this is 'no', and we must realise why this is so. What we are witnessing in these innovations is the grammar of English growing with use. There's an important point here and one which, as students of linguistics, we have to keep hold of. The popular view of grammar sees it as something mechanical, the learning of which is akin to learning the laws of thermodynamics. But in reality grammar is organic, it resembles a living thing in its ability to produce fresh matter apparently without end. What we term 'rules' are not so much laws, as linguistic patterns of behaviour governing the operation of English. Every speaker of English contributes to these, for not only do we speak the language, but in a more subtle sense, the language speaks through us. Rules are open to interpretation and negotiation, whereas laws, being immutable, are not.

But you're probably wondering where this leaves the issue of transitive and intransitive verbs. Well, the important thing about innovations is that they make us look more closely at the rules to see how they can be modified in order to take account of the new evidence. And what we begin to discover when we look more closely at verbs is that being transitive or intransitive is an operation potentially open to the great majority, and possibly all, of them. In other words, rather than classify them into transitive and intransitive, it's better to talk of transitive and intransitive *uses*. Those which we class as intransitive are simply the ones for which we have not yet discovered a transitive use. In the case of *disappear* we now have done this. The sinister process by which some governments cause people to disappear without trace has led to the verb developing a transitive sense. And just as some verbs can extend their grammatical range, others may contract theirs. Today, the verb *like* is only used transitively, the sentence *I like* is incomplete – we must like something or someone. In Shakespeare's time, however, it was quite normal for the verb *like* to be used without an object. In his preface to *The Devil is an Ass*, the seventeenth-century playwright Ben Jonson writes 'if this play do not like, the Devil is in it'. The verb *like* is being used here with our modern sense of 'please', a sense it has since lost. Because of this, the intransitive construction is no longer usable.

What I am suggesting, then, is that the linguistic rules which we extrapolate from actual use are inevitably provisional. Every time the language changes it offers us the chance to interpret them more accurately so that we have a more precise understanding of the way in which language works. Let me try another analogy here. Linguists like to compare language to a game, usually a board game because there are pieces which can be moved around, and usually chess, because it's arguably the most complex of the board games. It's quite a good analogy because in chess each piece moves in a specified way, but its power to do so at any particular moment in the game depends on the place it occupies on the board and its relationship to the other pieces. Similarly with words, their value is constantly changing depending on their freedom to manoeuvre. In the case of *disappear* an obstruction has been removed and its range increased because the state of play has changed; whereas with *like*, however, an obstruction has been imposed and therefore its range has been limited.

But there is one important difference between chess and language. If you want to learn how to play chess you study the book of rules and these tell you exactly what you can and can't do. This is not, of course, how native speakers of English learn to use their language. We do not expect children to know the rules for forming questions or negating statements. And yet they must know them otherwise they couldn't frame questions or denials properly. They know them, but yet they don't know that they know them. And it's the same with a majority of adults. Try asking someone what the rules are for forming a question in English and you're likely to be met with a blank stare. Understandably so, after all it's not something you need to know unless you are studying linguistics. So there's a paradox at the heart of the subject which it's necessary for anyone starting out to be aware of. In studying linguistics we are trying to articulate what we already know; we are, in a sense, studying ourselves: the rule book exists inside us. Linguistics then is about discovery. Going back to the chess analogy, imagine trying to establish the rules of chess by watching an actual game in progress, rather than by looking at the rules in advance. What you would have to do in this case would be to observe the progress of the play, describe the moves being made, and from that description formulate a set of rules that the players were following. This is exactly the process that Chomsky elaborates for studying linguistics: linguists observe, describe, and explain. This is where linguistics does have something in common with science, namely that its method of enquiry is empirical. It assumes nothing in advance except the possibility of arriving at a principled description, and explanation, of the way in which language operates.

There is an important corollary to this method, however. You would have to watch a lot of chess games before you could be sure that you knew all the rules players were following. And in a sense you could never be completely certain about this. There would always be the possibility of two players making a move you hadn't thought allowable from your observations thus far. You would then have to decide whether they were using a little-known rule you simply hadn't come across, whether they were playing a new variety of the game, or whether they were simply ignorant of the rules. But what you couldn't do is pull out the book of rules and say 'you can't do that because it's not permitted'. You could only appeal to common practice and say 'that's not how everyone else plays it' and wait to be proved wrong. The final authority has to rest with the players, or in the case of language, with its users. 'The meaning of a word,' said the philosopher Ludwig Wittgenstein, 'is its use in the language' (Crystal, 1987, p. 102). If this is so, then there are some important points for us, as budding linguists, to take note of. Firstly, we should see ourselves, and indeed others, as linguistic resources; the rules are internalised in us as native speakers of the language. Secondly, we should trust our intuitions about language. If someone tells us that a particular construction which we instinctively feel to be well-formed is not so, we should credit our instincts until we are shown otherwise; they are, after all, a form of knowledge. Thirdly, we should develop a spirit of enquiry towards all language phenomena, taking nothing on trust and being willing to alter or amend our views in the light of fresh information and new knowledge.

What I have principally been urging on you as beginners in linguistics is the necessity of developing the right mental attitude towards the subject, seeing it as an open-ended and participatory pursuit. The structure of English is constantly evolving, bits wither away as new possibilities emerge. Thinking linguistically means viewing language as a dynamic entity, constantly changing, alive on the lips and on the pens of its users. If you begin with the right image of the subject you are much more likely to succeed in mastering it. 'That's all very well,' you may say, 'but the real difficulty I have is understanding the terminology which linguists use: if only they could write more simply.' This is a complaint which everyone makes at some time or other, so you are not alone. The problem is that for many people the terminology is the first thing they encounter when studying linguistics. As a consequence they think the only way to understand the subject is to decode the terms. They consult glossaries and book indexes hoping for enlightenment only to find they don't understand the explanations. This is trying to run before you can walk. There are no short-cuts here. Glossaries can be useful, and I'll recommend one in a moment which I have found particularly good, but there's a sense in which a new term will only have any meaning for you at the point at which you need to use it. I find myself needing one now: I need a term to describe all this new terminology which has evolved around linguistics, and the one which is most useful here is **metalanguage**. Metalanguage is language about language, it consists of words, usually of a technical variety, which enable us to comment on, and describe more accurately, our everyday use of words.

Take for example the term **lexeme**. When I first encountered it I couldn't really see why the writer didn't simply use the term **word**. The glossary I used defined it briefly as a 'dictionary item', but since that was my understanding of 'word' it didn't help much. It wasn't until I realised that 'word' is itself a very vague term that light began to dawn. If you think about it, any simple word exists in a variety of different forms. The word *dogs*, for example, has a written form and a spoken one – 'dogz' – which are different from each other. None the less we still feel that they're the same word. We would feel odd describing them as two separate items. Not only that, but the word exists in a singular and a plural form – *dog(s)*. Our intuition here would be that there's still an important sense in which we are talking about the same word; there is a change in number but not meaning. However, by now the term 'word' has become hopelessly overworked. It's at this point that 'lexeme' becomes useful. We can think of *dog* as a lexeme, or underlying word, and the different versions of it as word forms. It has a singular and a plural form of which there are written and spoken forms. 'Word' thus becomes a term to describe the word as actual substance and 'lexeme' a term to describe the word as concept, or more accurately, as sign (see Chapter 5: 'Studying Meaning'). This is an important distinction because, of course, a lexeme may be realised in any number of ways including morse code, semaphore, or sign language. But what if we use *dog* in an entirely new way and with a completely different meaning, if, for example, we turn it into a verb *to dog* as in *to dog someone's footsteps*? Well, once again, the lexeme/word distinction helps. Instead of having the same lexeme realised by different words as before, here we have a new lexeme realised by the same word. Words can thus be seen to have an abstract and a physical dimension. This is something which we shall discover to be true of language generally. What I hope we shall see by the end of the book is that grammar is ultimately a mental phenomenon. It's a fundamental part of the Chomskyan tradition of linguistics that what linguists are studying is the human mind. If I have not made this clear enough yet, hang on to it for the time being and we shall return to it later.

What I'm suggesting to you then is, firstly, that terminology is not being used by linguists simply to put obstacles in your path, or to make a simple point seem more complicated than it is. Linguists are no more or less bloody-minded than anyone else. Secondly, only worry about the meaning of a term if not understanding it is preventing you from being able to read on. In other words, don't stop reading at every unfamiliar term you come across and start consulting dictionaries or glossaries. You will only find it frustrating and lose the thread of what you are reading. What you can do, however, is to make a note of all the terms which are unfamiliar to you and then at a later point look them up. One of the best sources of information is *A Dictionary of Stylistics* (1989), by Katie Wales. There are substantial entries for all the linguistic terms you are likely to come across, sometimes a page long, and it also tells you if there is any difference of opinion about their meaning or use.

And finally, bear in mind that language is both a spoken and a written phenomenon. This may sound supremely obvious but it is still the case that people tend to judge spoken language by its written counterpart, as if one were simply a translation of the other. For a long time writers about English tended to regard the written form as the ideal model for the language. People were encouraged to speak as they wrote. Even today you may sometimes hear complaints about sloppiness of speech because people are not pronouncing the words as they are written. Like me you probably say *India rand Pakistan*, and *the idea rof it*. There is nothing unusual in this, most people do. It is in fact part of a regular process called **liaison**, but there are some who would find this unaccept- able. I shall have more to say about this in Chapter 3, but the important thing to bear in mind is that speech is not writing in another form, nor vice versa. There is no punctuation in speech, for example. Speaking and writing are separate but related mediums through which language is expressed. They have their own procedures and rules of behaviour, both of the social and linguistic kind. Indeed modern linguistics has largely arisen from the realisation that speech is not a debased form of writing but a highly structured activity in its own right.

So, having primed yourself to think linguistically about language, the question is 'where to begin?' And as always, the best starting point is your own experience. Before plunging into the mysteries of **phonology** (the sound system) or **syntax** (word order), it's a good idea to reflect on what you use language for and how much you already know about some of the linguistic processes involved. Only in this way can you put some of the ideas you will come across later into a workable and relevant context. I propose, therefore, that we begin by considering language as an experi- ential phenomenon, in other words, as something we encounter as an intrinsic and essential ingredient of our everyday lives, and from that develop a way of describing the kinds of knowledge which linguists seek to explore. This is the subject of the next chapter.

2 The Linguistic Context

2.1 Language and competence

One of the extraordinary things about language is the way in which we take it for granted as though it were a given fact of life like being able to breathe. In a sense this is inevitable and to a certain extent, perhaps, even desirable. If every time we spoke or wrote anything we were struck not only by the strangeness or oddness of the words we were using, but also by the fact that we had the capacity to speak or write at all, we should probably never get anything done. Knowledge advances by making certain processes automatic, but in so doing it also hides from us their nature and operation, and even their very existence. We learn by taking things for granted or, to put it more bluntly, we learn by forgetting. In order to carry with us the knowledge of how we learnt things as well as what we learnt we should need brains of considerably greater capacity to deal with the additional mental load. Once we have passed the barrier of language acquisition and become experienced users of our native language, the processes by which we learnt to identify words in the apparently undifferentiated stream of sound, or first learnt to associate that sound with marks made on a piece of paper, pass out of view.

And yet language can never become so automatic as to be entirely instinctive. Whilst there is much to suggest that our capacity for language is innate, it is still the case that speaking and writing are significantly different from bodily functions such as breathing or eating which we do without conscious thought. Everyone has had the experience at some time of not being able to find the right words to express what they are feeling or thinking. Indeed, this is one of the chief frustrations of language. If only, when we are angry, the right words would come automatically to our mouths instead of occurring to us afterwards, when it is usually too late. In fact, such linguistic situations usually involve the suppression or displacement of instinct rather than its release, since our natural response might be to lash out or simply yell incoherently. Instead, we often end up saying the wrong thing. As T. S. Eliot, the twentieth-century poet, laments in his poem *Four Quartets*:

> One has only learnt to get the better of words
> For the thing one no longer has to say, or the way in which
> One is no longer disposed to say it.
>
> ('East Coker', ll. 5–7)

Let's begin thinking about language, then, by considering the unnaturalness of what we take to be an entirely natural function – in other words, by **defamiliarising** it. The sense of the unfamiliarity of language is one of those hidden bits of knowledge which we carry with us to some degree all our lives. We only become fully aware of it when we are engaged in an activity which foregrounds the medium itself; such as, for example, writing an essay or giving a speech, or indeed, preparing a book like this. At such times we become acutely aware of the intractability of language, of its resistance to the ideal shapes we envisage in our minds. The fact that words have to be in linear order, for example, is frequently frustrating since we normally experience things as a totality: our ideas are concurrent not consecutive experiences. Language forces us to pay attention to one thing after another. It imposes a discipline on us which every speaker/writer negotiates individually. But like all useful disciplines it also creates possibilities which could not exist without it. It is the nature and extent of those possibilities that this chapter is primarily intended to explore.

As a starting point for our 'defamiliarising' strategy, you might try listing some of the activities where you use language in which language itself seems problematic. And then see if you can account in any way for the difficulties you characteristically encounter. My own list would include the following:

(a)   giving street directions to someone;
(b)   telling jokes;
(c)   leave-taking;
(d)   writing on a transparency;
(e)   writing poetry.

Commentary
This is a fairly miscellaneous list of things and, quite clearly, the problems are not all down to language, although that may be the medium in which they manifest themselves. (b) and (c), for example, depend on personal

and social factors such as confidence and, in the case of telling jokes, an awareness of audience and a good sense of timing. Similarly, of the difficulties which are language specific, some may seem more trivial than others. Writing on a transparency, for instance, is a mechanical problem. It is a result of what handwriting specialists term **motor difficulty**. My physical control of the letter shapes is not very good so that my handwriting at the best of times is, to say the least, wayward. With the added complication of a slippery surface such as a transparency the result is usually a mess. Having said that, however, mechanical problems account for a significant number of language difficulties. All the forms of language activity – speaking/listening, writing/reading – depend on the successful performance of certain mechanical processes. To a large extent they are automatic but on occasions they become problematic. It is then that we become aware of just how much mental energy they consume. Most people will write out an important letter twice or say their name extra carefully over the phone. This is because slips of the tongue can be very annoying to make and sometimes result in the speaker becoming a figure of fun.

Mechanical skills, then, may be marginal to our consideration of language hurdles (except, of course, in the case of those with severe linguistic handicaps), but they are not insignificant even for competent language users. At a different level of linguistic analysis it is interesting how these skills can become indicators of class, education, and even personality. Just why this should be so is not obvious and it is in itself an important question to consider. People who pronounce words in a certain way are commonly thought to have an accent. These accents are grouped regionally so that we can talk of a Tyneside or Mancunian accent. But there is no regional manner of writing. No one ever says 'He has Geordie handwriting'! Everyone's handwriting is perceived to be individual. Speech is an interactive and corporate activity whereas writing is inherently less so. There is no real equivalent in writing to **received pronunciation** (r.p.) – the term given to the standard BBC way of pronouncing words. It's true that a recognised standard shape does exist for each letter, in the form of print, but anyone who tried to write in that way would be thought of as odd. Clarity is not a high priority in socially approved styles of handwriting as we see daily in the flourishes and twirls of publicly successful people. Generally, it seems, society values conformity in pronunciation and individuality in writing. This is evident from the way some specialists see personality and character traits reflected in handwriting.

It's important to bear in mind that mechanical skills (that is, the 'motor' skills involved in language activity) are the means by which the higher-order skills of understanding are realised. When we hear someone speaking to us there is the physical reception of the sound in our ears, but in addition to that, we hear what is said to us as words. We make the mental act of endowing the sound with meaning. The difference is immediately apparent if we compare listening to something in a language we know with something in one we do not. In the latter case we would have no idea where words began or ended, or even what constituted a word. Indeed, listening to a foreign language can be an unsettling experience because it seems to be just a meaningless gabble with no discernible pattern and no natural boundaries, except in the occasional pause for breath. This, of course, is how we sound to foreigners. The problem does not lie with our, or their, hearing: it is not a motor problem. The real difficulty is that the patterns or mental shapes created by the sounds within the system of the particular language are not discernible to us (that is, we are unable to connect the sounds to words). Once we know the shapes we experience the language differently. This ability of sounds to function as carriers of meaning is referred to as **duality of patterning**. Later on we shall look at how English utilises this capacity of sound (see Chapter 3).

We can say, then, that the boundaries between words in spoken English are in the ear of the listener. There's a humorous poem by Eugene Field, called 'A Play on Words', which draws attention to this. Can you make sense of the following lines? If not, the solution is immediately below:

> Assert ten barren love day made
> Dan wood her hart buy nigh tan day;
> But wen knee begged she'd marry hymn,
> The crewel bell may dancer neigh.

(from Aitchison, 1987, pp. 134–5)

Standard written version:

> A certain baron loved a maid
> And wooed her heart by night and day;
> But when he begged she'd marry him,
> The cruel belle made answer nay.

It would be perfectly possible, given the spelling system of English, for this verse to sound to a native English speaker as Field represents it. The fact that native users wouldn't hear it like that is because they confer meaning on what they hear. They know, first of all, that certain sounds make up certain words. But it's more than that. Being able to recognise the word boundaries isn't simply a matter of knowing what words there are in the language. All the words in Field's poem are English words; it's just that they don't make sense in those sequences. 'Assert ten barren' is not a meaningful sequence in English. In other words, word recognition depends on grammatical knowledge. As a consequence of this, the mechanical skill of hearing becomes transformed by the mental skill of understanding. It is this mental ability which is characteristically the concern of linguistics, and the term which I shall use from now on to describe it is 'cognitive'.

So far we have really been looking at various kinds of abilities in language in relation to different sorts of language difficulty. In the case of the mechanical skills we have been looking at we could say we are considering the **performance** of language. As we have already noted, however, the way in which we perform these activities is often taken as an indicator of a wide range of personal and social attributes. Nothing in language is ever innocent. But more importantly, performance is only significant in relation to the more cognitive activities involved in language, whether we are receiving it as listeners and readers, or producing it as speakers and writers. This ability to discern and interpret shapes both in sound and letter form as meaningful we could call **grammatical competence**.

Competence and performance are the terms which Noam Chomsky uses to distinguish two types of linguistic ability. As I have said, performance is concerned with the mechanical skills involved in the production and reception of language, that is, with language as substance. So, for example, the ability to form letter shapes correctly when writing, or to make the right movements with our speech organs when speaking, are aspects of performance. And some kinds of reading difficulty – notably the problem of distinguishing between letter shapes, commonly called dyslexia – are performance related. Grammatical competence, on the other hand, covers a range of abilities which are broadly structural. It entails two kinds of cognitive skills: firstly, the ability to assign sounds and letters to word shapes distinguished from each other by meaning – we can call this lexical knowledge: and secondly, the ability to recognise larger structures such as phrase and clause to which individual words belong – we can call this syntactic knowledge. And as we have seen from looking at the poem by Eugene Field, they are both necessary elements in the determination of meaning. The distinction between competence and performance, however, is not unproblematic since performance can itself be represented as a kind of competence, and indeed, deciding whether a particular language difficulty is a matter of performance or competence is not always easy. But what Chomsky wants to emphasise by this distinction is that the mechanical skills of utterance or writing only have any value linguistically if they are a representation of grammatical competence. It would be perfectly possible for someone to be trained to write or speak a passage in a foreign language without them having any idea of the words they were producing let alone their meaning. Performance does not necessarily imply competence, but without it, it is linguistically uninteresting.

But what of the other difficulties I confessed to earlier – giving street directions and writing poetry? The first is something which many people find problematic. Imagine the scene: a business man in a hurry stops his car and asks you the way to the A12. You know the route off by heart since you drive it every day. But suddenly the problem of having to describe it throws you into confusion. Why? If you had a pen and could draw the route there would be no problem. In fact most people accompany their directions with body language meant to represent the route. The problem seems to be peculiarly linguistic. Part of the difficulty is in translating a spatial dimension into a verbal one and there are particular cognitive problems associated with that. But in a larger sense it is bound up with problems of communication. There is an interesting and amusing literary counterpart to this in Laurence Sterne's eighteenth-century novel *Tristram Shandy*. Sterne's novel is all about problems of communication and the multitude of ways in which language seems inadequate at crucial moments. One of the main characters, Uncle Toby, has been wounded at the siege of Namur during the Wars of the Spanish Succession. His injury is in the groin, the result of a large stone falling off a parapet, the true extent of which is shrouded in mystery throughout the book. His recovery is impeded by the fact that well-wishers will insist on asking him where exactly he was when he got his wound. Although he knows the answer to this backwards, he cannot articulate it clearly. As Tristram says:

> the many perplexities he was in, arose out of the almost insurmountable difficulties he found in telling his story intelligibly, and giving such clear ideas of the differences and distinctions between the scarp and counterscarp, – the glacis and covered way, – the half moon and ravelin – as to make his company fully comprehend where and what he was about. . . .
>
> What rendered the account of the affair the more intricate to my uncle Toby, was this – that in the attack of the counterscarp, before the gate of St Nicholas, extending itself from the bank of the Maes, quite up to the great water-stop – the ground was cut and cross cut with such a multitude of dykes, drains, and sluices, on all sides – and he would get so sadly bewildered, and set fast amongst them, that frequently he could neither get backwards or forwards to save his life; and was oft-times obliged to give up the attack upon that very account only.

(Sterne, 1967, pp. 103–4)

Fortunately for Uncle Toby, he is saved by the simple expedient of a map, which allows him simply to point to the place where he received his wound. As Sterne makes clear, Toby's problem is one of communication. He is overwhelmed by detail. Obviously his listeners are not interested in the exact metre of ground where he was wounded. All they want is some approximate indication. What Toby lacks here is not grammatical competence – he can string words together in meaningful sequences – but communicative competence. The same sort sort of anxiety besets us when someone requires accurate instructions in a hurry. 'If I say the third turning on the left will s/he know that doesn't include the small track?' Or, 'if I say carry on to the next traffic lights do I need to mention the small roundabout first?' It's the equivalent of poor Uncle Toby's counterscarps and ravelins. In giving the information we have to balance clarity and speed against the need for sufficient detail. And of course we have to take into account the listener: elderly people, the hard of hearing, inexperienced drivers, and so on.

So it's not enough to be grammatically competent, we also need to know what counts as an appropriate utterance. It's perfectly possible to speak clearly and meaningfully but fail to give the listener what s/he needs. If you asked someone the time of day and received the reply 'you take the third on the left' the fact that the reply was grammatically competent would be of no help to you. Communicative competence, then, is a distinct linguistic ability. The difference between the two competences is important in learning a foreign language. Take the following exchange for example:

Q: *Where are you going?*
A: *I am going to the pictures.*

This is a perfectly competent reply grammatically and it's the kind of exchange you could find repeated in traditional language learning books. But it's not very realistic as an actual exchange. In real life the normal reply would probably be 'to the pictures' or, possibly, just 'the pictures'. Communicative competence is the concern of discourse analysts and its primary interest is in the way we negotiate the interactive processes of language whether in speech or writing.

As for my last 'problem' area, writing poetry, a different set of issues is involved here. Perhaps I should have said *composing* rather than *writing* since it is the creative process which is the problematic bit. I am aware in composing of a new set of constraints in addition to those we have already considered. There are problems of form involving rhyme, rhythm, and length of line. These are special difficulties which are not encountered in other uses of language. Even so they are not the principal problem. Most people would find it fairly easy to write a poem which embodied all of these features but the result would simply be an imitation. The real difficulty is in producing something original, which uses the surface features of the form in a way that has not been done before. This may involve the creation of new words or a new arrangement or combination of words in fresh syntactic or rhythmic patterns. Every poem is an innovation. Major innovations result in the creation of entirely new forms, such as the innovation which generated the sonnet, or blank verse. Minor ones create new possibilities within the established form.

We could describe the set of abilities I have been talking about as *creative competence*. But we need to be careful here. Creativity is basic to all language production. To be grammatically competent means, as Chomsky has pointed out, to have the ability to formulate new and original sentences. *An elephant fell out of the sky yesterday* is a sentence which I have never written myself or come across elsewhere before. I am using my knowledge of the syntax and lexis of English to create a new sentence. And yet I am not so foolish as to think anyone would wish to preserve it as a valued piece of writing. Clearly there are degrees of creativity. Arguably, writing poetry is an extension of abilities which we all have and exercise every day of our lives without thinking about it. But in what sense then is it distinct from other linguistic activities? Most poets report that they have to struggle with the language sometimes over a considerable period of time in order to arrive at the finished poem. If that degree of difficulty were present in everyday writing and speaking, civilisation would collapse. Poets struggle not simply to find a different or new way of saying something but to find the way of saying it. They pursue uniqueness of utterance. To use language uniquely is not simply to use it in a new way – many new utterances are totally unmemorable – but to use it in a way which is felt by both speakers and listeners to be especially meaningful. It is the difference between 'The question is, to be, or not to be', a fairly bland generalisation, and Hamlet's 'To be, or not to be, that is the question', which has the force of revelation.

Creative competence, then, as I am using it here, is the ability to use language in a uniquely valuable way such that a community will want to preserve the particular form of the utterance. It is here that much of the anxiety of composition lies. In the novel *La Peste* (English edition: *The Plague*, 1948) by the twentieth-century French writer Albert Camus, there is a character called Grande who spends most of his time trying to write a novel. The difficulty is that he wants everything to be perfect down to the last syllable. Here he is explaining his dilemma to the main character in the novel, Dr Rieux:

> 'What I really want, doctor, is this. On the day when the manuscript reaches the publisher, I want him to stand up – after he's read it through of course – and say to his staff, 'Gentleman, hats off!' . . .
> 'So you see,' Grand added, 'it's got to be . . . flawless. . . . '
> Grand went on talking, but Rieux failed to follow all the worthy man was saying. All he gathered was that the work he was engaged in ran to a great many pages, and he was at almost excruciating pains to bring it to perfection. 'Evenings, whole weeks, spent on one word, just think! Sometimes on a mere conjunction!'   (Camus, 1948, p. 99)

As Camus' novel makes clear, the pursuit of perfection is illusory and perhaps, in the light of the plague which is devastating the city, an indulgence: none the less writers are continually tinkering with their works seeking the magic formula which will match utterance with meaning. Creative competence, however, is not the preserve of great literature alone, it can be found in all memorable uses of language, ranging from witticisms and jokes to the latest novel. It is a productive not a receptive competence. Most people have a general literary competence which enables them to appreciate creativity without feeling able to write poems and plays themselves. If, however, we see it, as I have suggested, as an extension and development of a competence which is present in all language activity then it is something which is there *in potentia*. In this sense uniqueness of utterance is the ultimate linguistic aim of the creative impulse.

This section has been concerned with looking at a range of language issues in order to discern some of the abilities, both mechanical and cognitive, which are part of our native inheritance as users of a language. We can list the principal kinds of linguistic knowledge we possess as follows:

- *Linguistic performance.*   Mechanical/motor skills necessary for the production and reception of language.
- *Linguistic competence.*   Cognitive skills necessary for the construction and understanding of meaningful sequences of words, and consisting of:

    1. grammatical competence;
    2. communicative competence; and
    3. creative competence.

We began by looking at the mechanical skills involved in performing the language. We saw that these enable the realisation of a range of competences: grammatical competence, which is our ability to recognise and use lexical and syntactic patterns; communicative competence, which is our ability to use our grammatical competence to communicate effectively; and creative competence, which is our ability to exploit the other competences uniquely. We need now to consider in more detail some of the functions which these competences enable, in other words, what we use language for. This is the concern of the next section.

2.2   The functions of language

We use language for an almost infinite number of purposes, from writing letters, or notes to the milkman, to gossiping with our friends, making speeches and talking to ourselves in the mirror. However, if you think about it, there are a number of recurring functions which, despite the many different uses we make of language, are generally being served. Some are apparently so ordinary as almost to pass unnoticed as functions, whilst others are more lofty and almost abstract. But the important thing to recognise is that, linguistically speaking, they are all of equal importance. Whatever social significance we may give to various functions, language itself does not discriminate.

It's useful first of all to distinguish between the micro and macro functions of language. Micro functions, as the name suggests, cover the particular individual uses whilst macro functions relate to the larger, more general purposes underlying language use. Let's begin by looking at some of the micro functions.[1]

2.2.1   Micro functions
(i)   *To release nervous/physical energy (physiological function)*
This may seem a rather trivial function but in fact a good deal of language use has a physiological purpose. If you are a sports fan watching your favourite sport on television you may well feel the overwhelming urge at certain exciting moments in the match to shout instructions to the players: *Go on, don't mess about, for God's sake shoot!* The instructions are perfectly useless; they serve no communicative purpose, but they allow us to release pent-up energy which otherwise would be quite intolerable. A great deal of what we say when angry, in the heat of the moment, is said simply to relieve the physical and nervous energy generated by emotional distress. It's often a mistake to take what is said in such moments literally. The distress, of course, is real enough but the language we use is really the equivalent of flailing about. Indeed, language is frequently not

adequate enough to relieve our feelings fully and we may need to find other ways of finding relief – bursting into tears, for example.

A great deal of so-called 'bad language' or swearing fulfils this function. If you hit your thumb with a hammer you need some way of expressing your anger. One way would be to throw the hammer through the window. Parents frequently tell children *to smack the naughty door* when they have bumped into it. The impulse here seems to be to punish the object for hurting you. But hitting and throwing things is only likely to cause more damage, either to yourself or another object. For most people the usual outlet is a volley of oaths, the more violent the better. Clearly, words like *fuck, bloody, bugger, shit*, and so on, are not being used for any conceptual content they may have. They are essentially meaningless. They are being used because they are socially taboo and because at such moments we need a vocabulary of violence to match that of our feelings. The origin of many of these words is the curse and in a way we are perhaps ritually cursing the object which has hurt us.

(ii)   *For purposes of sociability (phatic function)*

It is surprising how often we use language for no other reason than simply to signal our general disposition to be sociable. The technical term for this is **phatic communion**. The word 'phatic' comes from Greek and means 'utterance'; it's the same root from which we get 'emphatic'. So literally this is speech for its own sake. The term itself was coined by Malinowski, the anthropologist, who was struck by how much of what we say is essentially formulaic and meaningless. He did most of his research on the Pacific islanders and found that the same was true of their languages. His description of this function is worth quoting in full:

> A mere phrase of politeness, in use as much among savage tribes as in a European drawing-room, fulfils a function to which the meaning of its words is almost completely irrelevant. Inquiries about health, comments on weather, affirmation of some supremely obvious state of things – all such are exchanged, not in order to inform, not in this case to connect people in action, certainly not in order to express any thought. It would be even incorrect, I think, to say that such words serve the purpose of establishing a common sentiment, for this is usually absent from such current phrases of intercourse; and where it purports to exist, as in expressions of sympathy, it is avowedly spurious on one side. What is the *raison d'être*, therefore, of such phrases as 'How do you do?', 'Ah, here you are,' 'Where do you come from?' 'Nice day today' – all of which serve in one society or another as formulae of greeting or approach.

I think that, in discussing the function of speech in mere sociabilities, we come to one of the bedrock aspects of man's nature in society. There is in all human beings the well-known tendency to congregate, to be together, to enjoy each other's company. Many instincts and innate trends, such as fear or pugnacity, all the types of social sentiments such as ambition, vanity, passion for power and wealth, are dependent upon and associated with the fundamental tendency which makes the presence of others a necessity for man.   (from Quirk, 1962, p. 58)

Malinowski is suggesting that language acts as a form of social bonding, that it is the adhesive which links people together. According to the psychiatrist Eric Berne (*Games People Play*, 1968), such language is the equivalent of 'stroking', and acts as an adult substitute for the considerable amount of cuddling which we receive as babies. Clearly it would be inappropriate to expect the formulas which perform this function to be particularly sincere. Too many people are linguistic puritans and want everything to have a precise and clearly definable semantic meaning. But the point is that we need language at times to be imprecise and rather vague. Semantically empty language can none the less be socially useful. Greetings and leave-takings are often especially problematic. When you pass an acquaintance in the street by chance you can't ignore them because to do so would be unfriendly but at the same time you may not wish to start a lengthy conversation. Both parties need a set of ready-made phrases to negotiate the encounter without either being offended. So it might run:

> *Hello. How are you?*
> *OK but I can't take this heat. What about you?*
> *Oh, bearing up.*
> *I know how you feel.*

No one expects in reply to *How are you?* a detailed medical history. Phrases like these are the verbal equivalent of waving. They are also subject to fashion. *Have a nice day* is now fairly well established but when it first was used in England many people responded like the American humorist S. J. Perelman, *I'll have any kind of day I want*, but it's not really so different from the more traditional *Have a good time*. Down South the usual greeting currently is *Alright?* and fairly popular in leave-taking is *Take care*. The phatic use of language is mainly spoken but there are some written equivalents. The most obvious examples are the conventionalised phrases for starting and ending letters: *Dear Sir/Madam . . . Yours faithfully, sincerely, truly*. In one of the *Monty Python* episodes, John Cleese played a senior civil servant investigating a subordinate over allegations of homosexuality. The evidence for the allegations lay in the letters he had written: what did he mean by addressing a man as *Dear* or declaring his faithfulness and sincerity, and what of *Yours truly* or, even more incriminating, just *Yours*?

Phatic language, then, fulfils important contact uses: it helps us negotiate the start and end of exchanges whether in spoken or written form. Failure to observe these social courtesies can cause considerable embarrassment and even bad feeling, as this account by Samuel Johnson of a stage-coach ride in the eighteenth century demonstrates:

> On the day of our departure, in the twilight of the morning I ascended the vehicle, with three men and two women my fellow travellers. . . . When the first ceremony was despatched, we sat silent for a long time, all employed in collecting importance into our faces, and endeavouring to strike reverence and submission into our companions.
>
> It is always observable that silence propagates itself, and that the longer talk has been suspended, the more difficult it is to find anything to say. We began now to wish for conversation; but no one seemed inclined to descend from his dignity, or first to propose a topic of discourse. At last a corpulent gentleman, who had equipped himself for this expedition with a scarlet surtout, and a large hat with a broad lace, drew out his watch, looked on it in silence, and then held it dangling at his finger. This was, I suppose, understood by all the company as an invitation to ask the time of the day; but nobody appeared to heed his overture: and his desire to be talking so overcame his resentment, that he let us know of his own accord it was past five, and that in two hours we should be at breakfast.
>
> His condescension was thrown away, we continued all obdurate: the ladies held up their heads: I amused myself with watching their behaviour; and of the other two, one seemed to employ himself in counting the trees as we drove by them, the other drew his hat over his eyes, and counterfeited a slumber. The man of benevolence, to shew that he was not depressed by our neglect, hummed a tune and beat time upon his snuff-box.
>
> Thus universally displeased with one another, and not much delighted with ourselves, we came at last to the little inn appointed for our repast, and all began at once to recompense themselves for the constraint of silence by innumerable questions and orders to the people that attended us. . . . Thus we travelled on four days with malevolence perpetually increasing, and without any endeavour but to outwit each other in superciliousness and neglect; and when any two of us could separate ourselves for a moment, we vented our indignation at the sauciness of the rest.
>
> (Johnson, 1958, pp. 163–4)

Johnson's humorous story makes clear just how important the phatic use of language is in creating and maintaining social links. At the same time, however, it has its limitations. An entire conversation made up of ritualised exchanges would be tedious. As a consequence most play-wrights use phatic language sparingly and then only to establish a sense of realism. The exception to this is Harold Pinter, the twentieth century dramatist, for whom the phatic function of language is its most important characteristic. He explores the failure of people to make relationships and our obsession with hiding behind repetitive phrases. More than any other dramatist his plays recall the philosopher Kierkegaard's claim that not only do we use language to conceal our thoughts but to conceal from ourselves that we have no thoughts:

Last to Go

A coffee stall. A BARMAN *and an old* NEWSPAPER SELLER. *The* BARMAN *leans on his counter, the* OLD MAN *stands with tea. Silence*

MAN: You was a bit busier earlier.
BARMAN: Ah.
MAN: Round about ten.
BARMAN: Ten, was it?
MAN: About then.
Pause

           I passed by here about then.
BARMAN: Oh yes?
MAN: I noticed you were doing a bit of trade.
Pause
BARMAN: Yes, trade was very brisk here about ten.
MAN: Yes, I noticed.
Pause

           I sold my last one about then. Yes, about nine forty-five.
BARMAN: Sold your last one then, did you?
MAN: Yes, my last *Evening News* it was. Went about twenty
           to ten.
Pause
BARMAN: *Evening News*, was it?
MAN: Yes.
Pause

           Sometimes it's the *Star* is the last to go.
BARMAN: Ah.
MAN: Or the . . . whatsisname.
BARMAN: *Standard.*
MAN: Yes.

> *Pause*
>   All I had left tonight was the *Evening News.*
> *Pause*
> **BARMAN:** Then that went, did it?
> **MAN:**   Yes.
> *Pause*
>   Like a shot.
> *Pause*
> **BARMAN:** You didn't have any left, eh?
> **MAN:**   No. Not after I sold that one.
> *Pause*

(Pinter, 1968, pp. 129–30)

It's the sheer inconsequentiality of the dialogue with its repetitions and banal phrases combined with the total lack of dramatic action that makes the technique so novel. Where other dramatists load speeches with images, significant ideas, or themes, Pinter offers seemingly bland statements that carry no weight. But underlying the technique is the recognition of just how much everyday discourse is made up of phatic language. In a sense, Pinter is dramatising what is *not* said rather than what *is*.

(iii)   *To provide a record (recording function)*
This is a more obviously 'serious' use of language than the previous two, although not necessarily more significant even so. We are constantly using language to record things we wish to remember. It might be a short-term record, as in a shopping list or a list of things to do, or a long-term record, as in a diary or history of some kind. It's the most official use of language; bureaucracies thrive on exact records and modern commercial life would be impossible without up-to-date and accurate files. Indeed, it's probably the most significant function behind the development of language from being simply an oral medium to becoming a written one. Archaeological evidence from around 4000 BC suggests that the peoples of the Middle East were using an early writing system to record business transactions. Clay shards from the Sumer valley with pictures of animals, and scratches indicating numbers, suggest that a primitive form of trading script flourished there. This is obviously a long way from writing as we know it in the shape of a modern alphabet, but once pictures are used to represent material transactions it's only a small step to the development of further expressive possibilities. A pictogram of an animal can easily develop into a phonogram, or rebus as the puzzle game is often called, in which the picture represents the sound of the object rather than the thing itself, so a

picture of a mill, a wall, and a key can represent Milwaukee, or it could develop into an ideogram in which the picture represents an idea associated with the object – for example, a picture of a sheep to represent rural life.

All these uses of pictures can be found in Egyptian hieroglyphics which is one of the most complex of surviving scripts from the ancient world. But the difficulty with all pictographic systems whether ancient or modern is that they are enormously wasteful. A huge number of characters would be necessary to represent all the words in an ordinary person's vocabulary. The Chinese system has about 40,000 characters, of which most people only know a few thousand. Writing systems which use pictures, despite their various sophistications, and indeed, in the case of Chinese, their elegance, are all linked at some point to the view of writing as a representation of the real world, the root of which lies in the power of the system to record transactions and objects in as literal a way as possible. The alphabet represents an advance on such systems in that the link with the real world has vanished completely. There is no connection between the letter and the sound it represents. The relationship is totally arbitrary, that is, we could quite easily use another shape to represent a given sound provided everyone else agreed. The alphabet has no connection with things as such; what it does, as Walter Ong points out in *Orality and Literacy* (1982), is to represent sound itself as a thing.

If you look at Figure 2.1 you can see the process by which this most probably happened over a period of some centuries. First of all the picture of the object is used to represent the word, so an ox yoke represents the

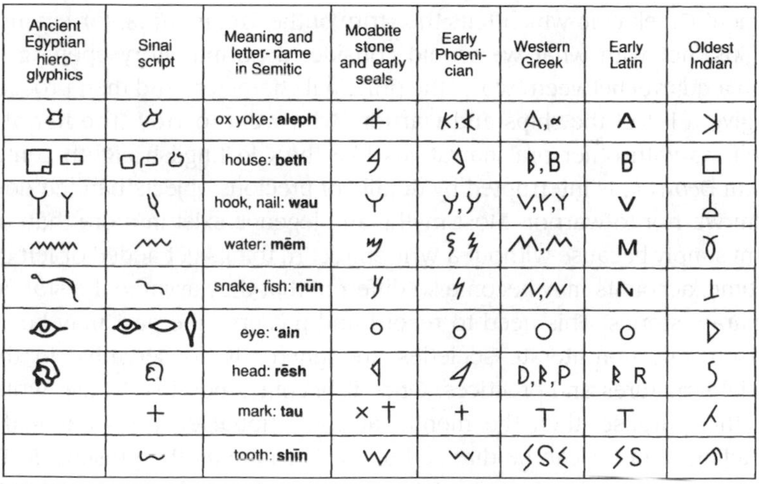

Ancient Egyptian hiero-glyphics	Sinai script	Meaning and letter-name in Semitic	Moabite stone and early seals	Early Phoeni-cian	Western Greek	Early Latin	Oldest Indian
੫	੪	ox yoke: **aleph**	∠	K,𝖐	A,α	A	㣺
☐ ▭	▢▭ ☉	house: **beth**	�“4	𝟇	฿,B	B	☐
Υ Υ	𝟇	hook, nail: **wau**	Υ	Υ,Υ	V,Υ,Υ	V	⊥
ＭＭ	Ｍ	water: **mēm**	ᵐᵞ	𝟇 𝟇	M,Ｍ	M	ठ
⌐	⌐	snake, fish: **nūn**	𝒴	𝟇	N,N	N	⊥
◎	◎ ◔ ◖	eye: **'ain**	o	o	O	o	▷
𝕊	𝔈	head: **rēsh**	⟨	⌁	D,ℝ,P	ℝ R	⟩
	+	mark: **tau**	✕ †	+	T	T	∧
	⌐	tooth: **shīn**	W	⋀	⟨S⟩	⟩S	⋀

FIGURE 2.1   The development of the alphabet (Firth, 1937, p. 45)

word 'aleph' in Semitic script (the name given to a form of writing which developed along the eastern Mediterranean between about 1800 and 1300 BC). Then over time the picture becomes more stylised and less recognisable as an ox yoke, and at the same time it comes to stand for the first sound of the word rather than the word itself. But, clearly, the point about writing is not so much that it makes it possible to record things, but that it enables us to do so accurately and permanently. Imagine the difficulty of recording things without a writing system of some kind. Most non-literate societies expend an enormous amount of time and energy on preserving their links with the past either through the re-enactment of rituals or the recitation of time-honoured formulas. Much early oral poetry contains devices for recording things from the past. Here is a passage from the Old Testament which utilises a simple repetitive pattern for recording genealogy:

> And Sheshan gave his daughter to Jarha his servant to wife;
> and she bare him Attai.
> And Attai begat Nathan, and Nathan begat Zabad,
> And Zabad begat Ephlal, and Ephlal begat Obed,
> And Obed begat Jehu, and Jehu begat Azariah,
> And Azariah begat Helez, and Helez begat Eleasah.

(1 Chronicles 2: 35–9)

It has only been relatively recently that anthropologists and literary historians have appreciated to what extent oral narrative is shaped by the need to provide a record of the past in memorable form. *The Iliad*, the ancient Greek epic which tells the story of the Trojan Wars, for example, begins, not with what we would consider a normal story opening but with a quarrel between two of the principal characters and then proceeds to give a list of the ships and warriors who went to Troy. The narrative itself, as with other oral narratives like the Old English eighth-century poem *Beowulf*, is interrupted by details of precious objects handed down from warrior to warrior. Most myths and legends exist in more than one form simply because without a written record things get added or left out. In time, accounts may become so different that they assume the status of separate stories. This need to record and preserve the past may be one reason why non-literate societies are inherently conservative in their social structures and practices. Once it becomes possible to use writing for this purpose, then the mental and emotional energies devoted to recalling the past can be directed towards changing the present. In this way we can see that learning to read and write involves not simply the acquisition of another set of skills but an important change in the human

psyche. Literacy is dynamic. Part of this may have to do with the different
senses involved; the poet W. H. Auden has suggested that the ear enjoys
repetition whilst the eye enjoys novelty. He illustrates this by referring to
the way in which people tend to listen to their favourite music repeatedly
and like to tell and hear the same stories over again, but will rarely read
the same novel twice. When we look back at the way in which writing
first developed out of the need to record things, we can see the first steps
taken by our ancestors in exchanging a linguistic world dominated by
sound for one dominated by sight. The consequences of that exchange
have been profound, and are a reminder of the necessary relationship
between linguistics and other related fields of enquiry, such as communication and media studies.

(iv)   *To identify and classify things (identifying function)*
Language not only allows us to record, but also to identify, with considerable precision, an enormous array of objects and events, without which it
would be very difficult to make sense of the world around us. Learning
the names of things allows us to refer quickly and accurately to them; it
gives us power over them. Many non-literate societies believe that names
are sacred; once you know the name of someone or something you can
manipulate it magically by means of a spell or special ritual. In some
cultures the special name of god is sacred and not allowed to be spoken
except by priests because that name is enormously powerful and could be
used for evil purposes. This is the origin of many taboo words. The Bible
warns against using God's name 'in vain', or indiscriminately, and a
special value is attached throughout the New Testament to the name of
Jesus.

Our own culture is enormously confused about the naming function of
language. On the one hand we feel that the uniqueness of names is a
piece of superstition. How can a mere word have any intrinsic power let
alone be sacred? Juliet's argument, in Shakespeare's play *Romeo and
Juliet*,

What's in a name? That which we call a rose
By any other name would smell as sweet.

(II.ii.43–4)

makes logical sense since we know that names are made up and essentially arbitrary. To call a lion a 'mouse' would not alter the reality of the
animal. And yet most people spend a considerable amount of time
deciding on the right name for their child or pet. We persist in feeling that
the name confers some special quality, that it is, in some indefinable way,

powerful. In Sterne's *Tristram Shandy*, for example, Tristram's father, Walter, believes that part of his son's misfortune in life is due to his being given the wrong name. He believes that names influence personality and individual destiny, a theory which he supports by asking 'Your son! – your dear son . . . would you, for the world, have called him JUDAS?' Unfortunately for Tristram, because of a mistake at the christening ceremony, he ends up with a name which his father absolutely detests.

Walter is a victim of **nomenclaturism**, the belief that words represent the true essences of things, and that everything has its own right and proper name. It's a belief about language which has had a long and influential history. In Genesis, for example, Adam is given the authority to name everything which God has created, 'And whatsoever Adam called every living creature, that was the name thereof' (2:19). In this way, he confers a unique importance on each animal. The concept of the true name is not limited to Christianity, however; in Plato's dialogue *Cratylus*, a philosophical work about the nature of language, one of the principal participants holds that:

> everything has a right name of its own, which comes by nature, and that a name is not whatever people call a thing by agreement, just a piece of their own voice applied to the thing, but that there is a kind of inherent correctness in names which is the same for all men, both Greeks and barbarians.
>
> (Harris, 1988, p. 9)

Nomenclaturism still persists; the natural assumption of children is that things have their own real names which express what they are. The realisation that other languages have different names can at first be confusing, as James Joyce demonstrates in his twentieth-century novel *A Portrait of the Artist as a Young Man*:

> It was very big to think about everything and everywhere. Only God could do that. He tried to think what a big thought that must be; but he could only think of God. God was God's name just as his name was Stephen. Dieu was the French for God and that was God's name too; and when anyone prayed to God and said Dieu then God knew at once that it was a French person praying. But, although there were different names for God in all the different languages in the world and God understood what all the people who prayed said in their different languages, still God remained always the same God and God's real name was God.   (Joyce, 1960, p. 16)

Like all powerful instinctive beliefs, however, nomenclaturism is not simply to be dismissed; as the Romantic poet William Blake reminds us, 'Everything possible to be believed is an image of truth' (*The Marriage of*

Heaven and Hell). Names are important to us – otherwise we should not feel so affronted when someone gets ours wrong or admire so highly someone who can correctly distinguish an arctic from a common tern.

Half the mystique of new disciplines comes from the hidden power suggested by a new terminology. Mastering a fresh concept means mastering the terms in which it is encoded, which in turn allows us to control and manipulate reality. This applies, incidentally, as much to learning card games as it does to a discipline such as linguistics. The mistake is to think that the terms mean anything outside the system to which they belong. In other words, it's the system which endows the individual word with meaning and which relates it to the real world rather than the other way round: words don't exist on their own but are always part of a larger network. That is why I have referred to this function as classifying as well as identifying things, for we can only identify things within a classificatory system. The linguist most associated with this approach to meaning is Ferdinand de Saussure, whose work we shall be looking at later. But, to take a fairly simple example, let's consider all those terms which classify types of residences: *house, maisonette, flat, bungalow, caravan, castle, mansion, palace* – to mention only a few. These all belong within the linguistic system known as English, and outside of that they are essentially meaningless. This is stating the obvious, but even within English they belong to various subsystems, or fields, of meaning. For the moment, until we come to Chapter 5, we can think of a 'field' simply as an area of meaning of some kind, within which the individual word belongs. It's important to establish the correct field as the majority of these terms will belong to more than one. *Castle*, for example, as well as being a residence also belongs to the field of chess, whilst *flat* belongs to the field of shape, both of which have their own classificatory groupings. In this case the field we are considering is that of residences. Clearly all these terms relate to things in the world but according to Saussure they do not derive their meaning simply from the real world. Rather, the meaning of any one of them is the sum of its similarities to and differences from the other terms. For Saussure, then, the meaning of a word is dependent on the relationship it has with other words in the same field. This will change according to how many terms there are in the system. If the word *maisonette* did not exist, for example, then either *flat* or *house* or possibly both would have to expand in meaning to absorb it. Similarly, someone who did not know the word would have to use one of the others to include it. In this way each term derives its meaning from its place in the classificatory system through which it is related to the real world. Its meaning is determined by the space it occupies, fewer terms means greater space, more terms means less; it expands or contracts accordingly. Terms may overlap, but no single item is completely identical with another, otherwise one of them would soon become redundant. You might say what about *flat* and *apartment*? To which I would reply that *apartment* belongs to a different system or variety of the language – American English. We shall return to this again in Chapter 5, 'Studying Meaning'.

In a sense we could say that language puts its own blueprint over reality, and many of the arguments which people have about words are about the way in which the blueprint either matches or fails to match. We would all agree that *flat* and *maisonette* mean something different but may still disagree on whether a particular residence is one or the other. Rivers, streams, and brooks are all different but at what precise point does a stretch of moving water change from one category into another? When does a branch become a twig? Nature is a continuum which language can only approximately represent. It is still a contentious issue within linguistics as to how far a particular language influences our view of the world but at the very least we can say that languages do differ in the way they classify things, and this means that certain distinctions are possible in one language which are not possible in another. We need to consider some of these issues later on and, in particular, to look more closely at the variety of classificatory relationships which operate in language, because they bring us to the heart of modern approaches to the way in which words carry meaning.

(v)   *As an instrument of thought (reasoning function)*
All of us have a running commentary going on in our heads during our waking hours. For most of the time we are not aware of it; like breathing, it's automatic. Schizophrenics are acutely conscious of it and imagine it to be coming from someone else. But the voices they hear are really parts of themselves which they are unable to acknowledge. Running for the bus or the train we are constantly talking to ourselves in a form of continuous monologue. Sometimes it takes the form of a dialogue with some imagined 'other', but more often than not it is simply a form of silent thinking. As an exercise you might try thinking about something, making a conscious effort not to use words. Making your mind blank is one of the most difficult things to do because the brain is in a state of constant activity; its principal concern is with enabling us to survive, and language is an essential part of that survival process.

A majority of our thinking is done with words or, to be more precise, in words. A common view of language is that it is merely a tool of thought, in other words, that we have ideas forming in our minds for which we need to find the appropriate words: the words are simply the expression of the ideas. In practice, however, the words are the ideas because our ideas are generated in language, they come to us already linguistically encoded. Speaking and writing are forms of thought. This is why most people feel that they have not really understood something until they have been able to express it in language. Language doesn't just express thought, it also creates it. A simple example of the way in which it can do this is given by the well-known linguist Randolph Quirk:

> Most of us can remember passing through stages like the following. Let us suppose we have attained, in early childhood, the distinction between 'round' and 'square'. Later on, 'round' is further broken down into 'circular' and 'oval', and it becomes easier to see this 'obvious' difference between shapes when we have acquired the relevant labels. But then we come to metaphorical extensions of the terms. We grope towards a criticism of arguments and learn to follow a line of reasoning; we learn to exercise doubt or be convinced according to how the argument goes. Some arguments may strike us as unsatisfactory, yet they have nothing in common except their tendency to give us a vague lack of conviction and some discomfort. Then we hear someone discussing a line of argument and we catch the word 'circular' being used. At once everything lights up, and we know what is meant; the idea 'clicks', as we say. There is of course nothing about an argument which resembles the shape of a circle, and we may never have thought of 'circle' except in terms of visual shapes. Yet in a flash we see the analogy that the metaphor presents, and thereafter we are able to spot this type of fallacious agument more speedily, now that we have this linguistic means of identifying it.   (Quirk, 1962, p. 55)

What exists in terms of thought prior to its emergence linguistically is difficult to determine. Like the chicken and the egg each seems to be contained within the other. In recent years, however, a number of studies have been carried out of deaf adults who lack any kind of language whatsoever and these have shown that an ability to understand mathematical processes and logical relations exists independently of language. The linguist Steven Pinker (1995) labels this ability 'mentalese' and argues that it is a reasoning faculty which we all possess. Clearly, not everything in our mental life depends on language. At the same time, however, it still remains that the gap between mentalese and linguistic competence is huge. And we might still wonder how a languageless society would communicate. In his novel *The Inheritors*, William Golding tries to imagine a race of pre-historic neanderthals who have a very limited form of language. Their thought processes are made up of images of the outside world by means of which they communicate telepathically to the rest of the group. But their world is static, and dominated by sensations which they are unable fully to understand. Eventually they are destroyed by a 'superior' race with far more developed language skills which is able to reason about the outside world in a more sophisticated way, but in the process an alternative manner of communicating and existing vanishes. It may be, therefore, that whilst language enables certain mental processes to develop, it also inhibits others.

A principal problem, however, of this reasoning function of language is that the meanings of many words are not stable and as a consequence it is difficult to think with any precision. People are often told in developing an argument to define their terms, but how can we define words like *civilisation*, *culture*, *democracy*, and *liberty*? They seem to be subject to what has been called the law of accelerating fuzziness by which words expand in meaning and decline in precision. Because many nouns (like *table* and *chair*) refer to real substantial things, there is a tendency as the nineteenth-century philosopher Jeremy Bentham pointed out, to think that other nouns like *democracy* and *crime* are also real in the same way. We call them **abstract** nouns but often treat them as **concrete** nouns. We know of course they are not but, nevertheless, the 'thing' view of language is pervasive.

Attempts to make language logical and precise, like George Orwell's Newspeak in his novel *Nineteen Eighty-Four*, usually entail trying to get rid of ambiguity and nuance in language. The slipperiness of language is something that has been bewailed by philosophers for centuries. In his *Essay Concerning Human Understanding* the seventeenth-century philosopher John Locke moans that: 'every man has so inviolable a liberty to make words stand for what ideas he pleases, that no one hath the power to make others have the same ideas in their minds as he has, when they use the same words as he does' (1964, p. 262). Words mean different things to different people, they are laden with connotations and subject to the influence of fashion. They are rarely neutral in meaning. We have only to think of the debate about colour prejudice to see how difficult it is to find a vocabulary which is truly non-discriminatory. A few years ago the term *black* was considered discriminatory because in European culture it is associated with evil and death, and *white* with purity and goodness. As a consequence the term *coloured* became fairly common, but that of course entailed regarding white as not a colour and therefore more statusful. At the same time, however, in many non-European cultures, and to a certain extent in European, the term *black* was often associated with vitality and power, whilst *white* suggested frigidity, coldness, and death.

This reversal of values allowed the term *black* to be rehabilitated as a positive instead of a negative term. People of an older generation, however, who are not aware of this movement in the language, will still use the term *coloured*. To them *black* remains an offensive term. Perhaps, as T. S. Eliot laments in *Four Quartets*, we expect words to carry too much meaning:

> . . . words strain,
> Crack and sometimes break, under the burden,
> Under the tension, slip, slide, perish
> Decay with imprecision, will not stay in place,
> Will not stay still.

('Burnt Norton', ll. 149–53)

Eliot's lines can also serve as an important reminder to us that language is not the preserve of linguistics. The struggle with words, and the ways in which they 'mean', is the concern of all of us: not least, the poet.

(vi)   *As a means of communicating ideas and feelings (communicating function)*

This is probably the function that most people would select first as the principal purpose of language. And clearly it is an extremely important function. But as we have just seen, the relationship between language and meaning can be problematic. Communication is a two-way process. On the one hand we need to be able to use language to express ourselves to others, and, conversely, we need it in order to understand what they are communicating to us. There are of course a variety of reasons which may prompt the act of communication. We use language for requesting, informing, ordering, promising, and reprimanding, to mention just a few. In all these cases we could say that language is being used to perform certain speech acts, or, more specifically, 'direct' speech acts.

   Speech act theory is associated with two linguistic philosophers, J. L. Austin and J. R. Searle. They developed a functional view of language based on the notion that the social use of language is primarily concerned with the performance of certain communicative acts. The problem is to determine what those acts might be. If, for example, I say to you, *it's cold in here*, I am presumably performing an informing or announcing act, but I may also be doing other things as well. I could be indirectly asking you to close the window, or perhaps complaining because you have turned off the heating, or indeed both. Speech act theory copes with this indeterminacy by distinguishing between direct and indirect speech acts. We frequently find that people convey their wishes indirectly and it is an important part of communicative competence to be able to decode these. We rarely find that employers *tell* their workers to see them, they invariably *ask* them. But although the direct speech act might be a request, *can I see you?* or *could I see you?*, the indirect act is interpreted as a demand of some kind since to refuse is not permissible. In this instance indirectness is a form of politeness and, indeed, the greater the indirectness the more polite it is. *Could* is more indirect than *can*, since it uses the past tense. Past here has no connection with time, it simply indicates mood. Even more polite would be *do you think I could see you?* or even more obsequiously, *I couldn't see you, could I?* These are colloquially known as 'whimperatives'. Indirectness is not simply a feature of politeness, however. It also is an important element in irony. Calling out *nice one* when someone does something stupid is clearly performing an act of derision, even though on the surface it is performing one of praise.

Speech act theory provides a useful framework for analysing the personal and social purposes which language fulfils, and we shall be returning to it in Chapter 5. Meanwhile, we could say that any utterance performs two essential macro – that is, general – acts: a message act and a communicative act. The message act comprises the total message made up of both direct and indirect acts. The communicative act conveys the intention to communicate. That is to say that in any interchange the listener assumes that the speaker is attempting to communicate to him/her so that even if the message part fails and the listener completely misunderstands what is being said, s/he is still aware of the intention to communicate. If this were not the case the listener would not bother to pay attention. In other words, the process of communication involves cooperation. A great deal of work has been done on the importance of cooperation in speech acts by the American philosopher Paul Grice. He elaborated the **cooperative principle** together with its associated maxims of quantity, relation, manner, and quality. Basic to the principle is the belief that communication involves an ethical imperative to cooperate. We go a long way before we abandon the attempt to make sense of what someone says to us simply because the idea that they may be speaking to us without wishing to communicate seems nonsense. This is reinforced by the phenomenon known as **accommodation**, or **convergence**. It is interesting that when two friends are speaking to each other they will tend to copy each other's speech patterns. They will accommodate by converging in terms of **accent** and **dialect**. This is often an unconscious process, and allows them to switch from speaking to their friends, to their boss quite easily. On the other hand, one way of stressing our difference from someone we do not like is by diverging. In this case we deliberately adopt a different speech pattern in order to stress the mental, or emotional, distance between ourselves and the person(s) with whom we are communicating.

Clearly the need to understand and be understood, to have our feelings and ideas recognised and acknowledged, is an important one for most human beings. Language has become especially well equipped to perform this function because the dominance and survival of the human race depend on it. When the system breaks down we employ counsellors or therapists to re-establish the communicative ability. Much of the success of counselling comes not from any message delivered by the counsellor but from the client's sense of achievement in having been able to communicate successfully to a wholly disinterested party. All human achievement is bound up in some way with successful acts of communication. Language is obviously not the only way in which these acts can be performed, but it is the most developed and the most subtle, and it is the natural inheritance of us all as 'talking animals'.

(vii)   *To give delight (pleasure function)*
There are various kinds of pleasure which we derive from language. At the simplest level there is the sheer enjoyment of sound itself and the melody of certain combinations of sounds. Most poetry exploits this function. Devices such as **onomatopeia, alliteration**, and **assonance** all draw on the pleasure we find in **euphony**, as do rhythm and rhyme. This pleasure is important in language learning. There is considerable evidence to suggest that children respond as much to the melody of the language as to any cognitive content. Indeed, spoken English is rhythmically organised around the syllable. The syllable is the smallest rhythmic unit in the language. Derek Attridge in his book *The Rhythms of English Poetry* (1982) compares it to the step in dancing. If you say the following line, emphasising the rhythm of it, you will find yourself separating the words into syllables:

Ma-ry, Ma-ry, quite con-tra-ry

We perceive some syllables to be stronger than others, and it is this pattern of strong and weak syllables which gives us the rhythm of speech. If we gave every syllable equal weight we should end up talking like the Daleks, whose non-human condition was indicated, amongst other things, by their syllabic method of speaking: 'you-will-be-ex-ter-min-at-ed'. At the heart of the syllable, its **peak**, is the vowel, and vowels are the most sonorant or resonant of all the sounds of English. They are produced without any restriction in the mouth and simply use the interior of the mouth as a kind of echo chamber (see Chapter 3). English is a musical language – all that poetry does is to make us more aware of that.

At the syntactic level – the level of word order and word classes – there is the pleasure we gain from the rearrangement by inversion or ellipsis of normal phrase or clause order and from the conversion of words from one class to another. These changes play against our normal expectations from the language and create a sense of novelty. In his poem *Ode to a Nightingale*, Keats describes the nightingale as singing in 'Some melodious plot/Of beechen green, and shadows numberless'. We would normally expect 'green beeches' and 'numberless shadows' but by inverting the order Keats creates a minor surprise for the reader. But he does so in a way which seems wholly appropriate since the emphasis of the line is very different. And turning 'beech', a noun, into an adjective 'beechen', and vice versa with 'green', is another linguistic surprise. Keats not only inverts word order but normal word classification, that is, nouns and adjectives, as well. Some poets do this more startlingly than others. The American poet e. e. cummings begins one of his poems 'anyone lived in a pretty how town', where instead of 'how pretty', we find 'pretty how', with 'how' in the unusual position of an adjective. Suddenly we find a complimentary term becoming its opposite since a 'how town' in American slang is a dump.

How can we justify, as readers, such syntactic novelties? After all, poets who employ such devices are demanding more attention from us. We can only do so, I suggest, if we feel that there is some compensating gain in meaning for the extra effort involved in processing these syntactically eccentric phrases. Part of the pleasure, then, will lie in discovering precisely how, and why, the effort has paid off. As a consequence, we could say that an essential ingredient of the creative competence which we looked at earlier is the ability to manipulate language in exactly these sorts of ways. At the level of meaning (the semantic level), most creative uses of language provide considerable pleasure through the generation of puns, paradoxes, ambiguities, and metaphors. With these the oddness is not necessarily syntactic but lies in the capacity of the language to generate a plurality of possible meanings. Advertisers exploit this capacity just as much as poets and novelists. When cash dispensers first appeared, Lloyds bank advertised this facility with the slogan 'The bank that stays open even when it's closed.' In one sense this is a contradiction, but if we take 'open' to mean 'open for business', then a bank can be open even if its doors are closed (see Chapter 5 for further discussion of plural meaning).

There is much to suggest, then, that a large part of the pleasure we derive from language comes from the successful exploitation of linguistic novelty at different levels of the language. The most memorable examples are those where the manipulation of sound, syntax, and semantics works to provide a pleasing density of novelty.

Initial summary

We have identified seven main functions of language:

(i)	To release nervous/ physical energy	(physiological function)
(ii)	For purposes of sociability	(phatic function)
(iii)	To provide a record	(recording function)
(iv)	To identify and classify things	(identifying function)
(v)	As an instrument of thought	(reasoning function)
(vi)	As a means of communicating ideas and feelings	(communicating function)
(vii)	To give delight	(pleasure function)

This is not an exhaustive list and you may well have thought of other functions which we could add. Notice, however, that I am making the following broad distinctions which I think are necessary to delimit the area of enquiry. First, we should distinguish between functions which are 'linguistic' and those which we can consider 'extra-linguistic'. All of those which I have listed above I would argue are of the first kind in that they are fundamental to language activity. It is possible, however, to think of all kinds of functions which involve language but which are not part of its *raison d'être*, such as, for example, as an instrument of colonial rule. It is the first kind that I am concerned with here. Second, it is important to distinguish between function and use. This is a necessary distinction since the range of possible uses is potentially infinite. I may use language to get people to do things for me, like fix my car or make my breakfast, and I may employ a variety of tactics such as persuading, cajoling, or threatening. But rather than see these as separate functions it is better to see them as uses to which the communicative function can be put. It is here, as I suggested earlier, that speech act theory can be enormously helpful. Similarly with the recording function. We may use language to record the minutes of a meeting or a recipe for a meal. They are different uses of the same function. It is also important to bear in mind that a specific use of language may fulfil more than one function. A recipe, for instance, may be used to record something but if it is inventive in its choice of expressions it can give delight as well. Indeed, the more functions something fulfils the more complex it usually is. And last, we can distinguish between overt and covert uses, or following speech act theory, direct and indirect acts. A recipe written with a great deal of flourish may overtly be performing an informing act, but we may also feel that covertly it is showing off. Clearly these kinds of judgements are socially and culturally constructed and depend on individual responses, but it is important for any functional framework to take account of the indeterminate nature of human motivation.

2.2.2　Macro functions

If instead of going below the level of individual functions we go above it, it is possible, as I suggested earlier, to identify several macro functions. But perhaps a better way of describing them would be to follow the linguist Michael Halliday and call them 'metafunctions'. A metafunction is one which is capable of describing one or more other functions. Let's see how this might work out.

(i)　*The ideational function*

With a number of the micro functions identified above we can see that there is a common mental or conceptualising process involved. In using language to identify things, or as an instrument of thought, or to provide a record, we are using language as a symbolic code to represent the world around us. The ideational function, then, is that function in which we conceptualise the world for our own benefit and that of others. In a sense we bring the world into being linguistically.

(ii)　*The interpersonal function*

Several of the micro functions are concerned with the relationship between ourselves and other people or things. Clearly, in addition to using language to conceptualise the world we are also using it as a personal medium. We gain much of our sense of identity, of who and what we are, from our relationships both with animate and inanimate things, and language is an essential part of that personalising process. We could say that rather than bringing the world into being, this function is concerned with the way we bring ourselves into being linguistically. Using language as a means of communication, for purposes of phatic communion, or to release nervous/physical energy, involves activities in which we are prioritising the interpersonal function of language. And it is possible for people to be able to perform this function very well without necessarily being able to perform the ideational function so well. There are those whose interpersonal skills and general ability to project themselves are quite developed but whose conceptual powers and level of understanding may be limited. And vice versa, of course.

(iii)　*The poetic function*[2]

Any functional account of language must take into consideration that side of our nature in which rather than conceptualising the world or interacting with it we are simply playing with it. In this sense the word 'poetic' doesn't mean the ability to write poetry. It means the ability to bring the world into being as an area of play. It is by such means that we bring delight to ourselves and others, but we also do much more. We render the world safe and less threatening because we can manipulate it linguistically for our own individual pleasure. Through metaphor, jokes, and rhythm we express our own creative freedom. All utterances or writings of whatever kind are by this criterion 'poetic' in so far as they appeal to our fundamental instinct for play.

We can see that these three functions, the ideational, the interpersonal, and the poetic, relate very broadly to the competences outlined earlier: grammatical, communicative, and creative. I am suggesting, then, that linguistic competence is a mix of competences which all individuals possess and which are basic to the fulfilment of a few overarching and central functions.

Developing a framework such as this enables us to put linguistics, as a subject of enquiry, into some perspective. We can see that its scope is extremely large; it's as extensive as language itself. But its fundamental concern is with relating the many individual ways in which we use language to the linguistic abilities of native users – with mapping function on to competence – and with developing a systematic way of describing that relationship. Some approaches, as we shall see, concentrate on the competence level and, in particular, on grammatical competence. This is the kind of linguistics which is often thought of as 'formal' linguistics, in that its overriding purpose is with describing the mental rules which govern linguistic behaviour. Other approaches, for example discourse analysis and stylistics, concentrate on the functional level and are more concerned with the specific use we make of language. But whether we approach language from the angle of competence or function, it's important, from the outset, that we should see them as complementary (see Figure 2.2).

(iv) *The textual function*

There is, finally, however, one function of language which I have so far ignored. It is in a way the most purely linguistic function in that it relates to our ability to construct texts out of our utterances and writings. Michael Halliday calls it the 'textual function'. We can see it as using language to bring texts into being. When we speak or write we don't normally confine ourselves to single phrases or sentences, we string these together to make a connected sequence. And there are words in our language which are particularly designed to enable us to do that. Consider, for example, the following piece: *One day a lady came into our*

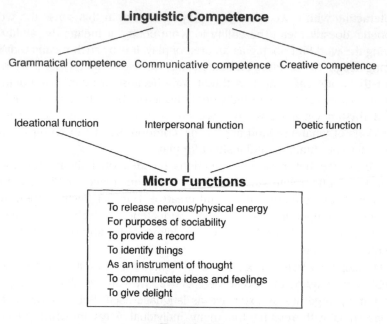

Linguistic Competence

Grammatical competence   Communicative competence   Creative competence

Ideational function   Interpersonal function   Poetic function

Micro Functions

To release nervous/physical energy
For purposes of sociability
To provide a record
To identify things
As an instrument of thought
To communicate ideas and feelings
To give delight

FIGURE 2.2

*street. She had on a brightly coloured bonnet which seemed out of place
there. It had three feathers and a broad blue ribbon which fluttered gaily in
the breeze.*

There are a number of words and phrases here which indicate that
these sentences belong to the same little story. In the second sentence,
the word *She* clearly refers back to the phrase *a lady*. Similarly, *there* looks
back to *our street* and is only comprehensible because of that link. In both
the second and third sentences *which* relates to the much longer phrases
a brightly coloured bonnet and *a broad blue ribbon* respectively, and in
each case it enables the grafting of a second clause onto the main one.
These words ensure that the sentences are cohesive and form a recognisable text. The study of **textual cohesion**, the way in which words refer
backwards and forwards, or substitute for others, is now quite developed
and there is every indication that people are able to negotiate a very wide
array of cohesive devices effortlessly. Even those suffering from quite
severe mental disorders frequently speak cohesively, though they may
not always make sense. Consider the following, which uses the cohesive
device of substitution unexceptionably but is still nonsense: *a castle is a
piece in chess. There's one at Windsor.* In the second sentence *one*
substitutes for *castle* but, of course, a completely different kind of castle

from the first sentence. This utterance is cohesive but not coherent. We obviously need more than cohesion to form a successful text.

And where should this important function fit in our scheme of things? We could see it as an aspect of communicative competence since the purpose of most texts is to communicate, and devices such as reference and substitution are helpful communicative aids. But there is more to it than that. Many of these devices are not essential to communication. We could manage without them, but our communications would be more long-winded and boring. A good deal of the problems we face in drafting material are precisely because we like to avoid repetition by finding alternative words and phrases. The concern for 'elegant variation' is as important as communicative efficiency, particularly in written style. In other words, an element of creative competence is important here. Arguably, then, we are looking at a distinct skill which involves a range of linguistic competences. It is perhaps best understood as textual competence. Approaching something as a text means perceiving it in quite a different way from a series of utterances or a string of sentences. Fundamental to a text is the principle of unity whereby everything is perceived to hang together. Preserving that unity over long stretches of language is a considerable achievement and it is not surprising that rhetoric, the study of effective forms of speaking and writing, was for centuries the principal subject pursued in Western universities. So a revised scheme might look something like Figure 2.3.

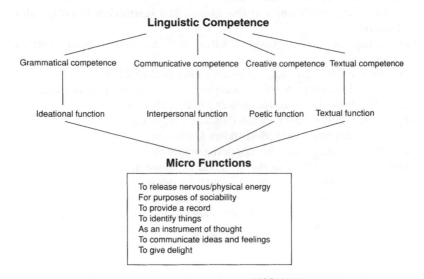

FIGURE 2.3

2.3   Final summary

In this section we have tried to identify and categorise some of the principal functions of language. We have identified seven individual, or micro functions, which can themselves be related to four broader, or metafunctions. These functions are in turn related to a range of competences which are the natural inheritance of a native speaker of English. We must now turn our attention to looking in a closer fashion at some of the ingredients of these competences.

Further reading

Aitchison, J. (1992) *Teach Yourself Linguistics*, 4th edn (London: Hodder & Stoughton).
Blake, N. (1993) *Introduction to English Language* (London: Longman).
Bolinger, D. (1980) *Language – The Loaded Weapon* (London: Longman).
Burgess, A. (1992) *A Mouthful of Air* (London: Hutchinson).
Crystal, D. (1985) *Linguistics*, 2nd edn (London: Penguin).
Doughty, P., Pearce, J. and Thornton, G. (1972) *Exploring Language* (London: Edward Arnold).
Finegan, E. (1994) *Language: Its Structure and Use*, 2nd edn (New York: Harcourt Brace Jovanovich).
Fromkin, V. and Rodman, R. (1980) *An Introduction to Language*, 5th edn (New York: Harcourt Brace Jovanovich).
Graddol D. and Goodman, S. (1996) *English in a Postmodern World* (London: Routledge).
Greenbaum, S. (1988) *Good English and the Grammarian* (London: Longman).
Kenworthy, J. (1991) *Language in Action* (London: Longman).
Milroy, J. and Milroy, L. (1991) *Authority in Language* (London: Routledge).
Pinker, S. (1995) *The Language Instinct* (London: Penguin).
Quirk, R. (1962) *The Use of English* (London: Longman).
Quirk, R. (1986) *Words at Work* (London: Longman).
Quirk, R. (1990) *English in Use* (London: Longman).
Thomas, G. (1990) *Linguistic Purism* (London: Longman).
Todd, L. (1987) *An Introduction to Linguistics* (London: Longman).
Trask, R. L. (1995) *Language: The Basics* (London: Routledge).
Trudgill, P. and Anderson, L. (1990) *Bad Language* (Oxford: Blackwell).
Wardhaugh, R. (1993) *Investigating Language* (Oxford: Blackwell).

Notes

1. My list is based on a traditional one compiled by A. Ingraham (Swain School Lectures, 1903), which is frequently used as a starting point for discussing the uses of language.
2. Halliday identifies three principal metafunctions, namely, ideational, interpersonal, and textual. The concept of the poetic function comes from the linguist Roman Jakobson and describes a centrally important function not adequately accounted for by the other three.

3 Studying Sound

3.1 Introduction: the nature of sound

Most introductory books on linguistics will have a section on the sound structure, or **phonology**, of English, which will aim to tell you how sounds are formed and what the principal symbols of the International Phonetic Alphabet are. At some point you will need to come to grips with this alphabet and learn to use its symbols confidently, but it's probably a mistake to begin studying phonology by trying to acquire what can seem rather dry and difficult information, rather like learning to play a musical instrument by memorising scales. We need to have a sense of what the instrument is able to do first. Similarly with the human voice, which is a form of instrument: it's important to understand its significance in a more general sense before tackling some of the technical ways in which we can describe its linguistic properties. I suggest we start, then, by using the method we began with in Chapter 2, that is, by defamiliarising the subject we are considering. Let's start with sound.

Sound is arguably the most elusive of the senses. 'It exists', as the writer Walter Ong says, 'only when it is going out of existence' (1982, p. 32).[1] If you say a word out loud, the beginning of it has vanished by the time you get to the end. It's impossible to freeze sound in the same way you can vision. If you press the pause button on your video recorder the frame is fixed on the screen, but if you attempt to pause your tape recorder all you get is silence. There is no way, in other words, 'to stop sound and have sound' (Ong), and as a consequence its relationship to time is quite special. We can write the word 'permanence' backwards and preserve the sequence of letters in reverse order, but a recording of our saying it, played backwards, would completely destroy any semblance of the original sequence.

So sound is ephemeral; it seems to lack substance. After all, in physical terms speech sounds merely consist of breath. It's no accident that people who speak a lot are colloquially called 'windbags'. Writing, on the other hand, seems more prestigious. We tend to think of it as an activity reserved for specially gifted people. To refer to someone as 'a writer' is automatically to confer on them a considerable measure of distinction, whereas to call someone 'a speaker' would be merely to state the obvious. This hasn't always been the case, however. In oral cultures the activity of speaking was endowed with considerable authority, and even reverence. It's the development of writing, and, in particular, the superior technology connected with its reproduction, which has altered our perspective. Nevertheless, at the same time, we still recognise, in all sorts of ways, the special power attached to speaking. The oath has to be taken orally in the court of law, and couples still have to declare themselves orally in order to get married.

Our attitude towards spoken language, then, is ambivalent: on the one hand, it seems a fairly trivial, transitory, medium, and on the other, potentially powerful and life changing. Part of its power, and the special aura which surrounds it, is due to the place which sound occupies in our sensory system. Despite its ephemeral nature sound is the best sense at registering the interiority of an object. Imagine that you wish to know whether the wall in front of you is hollow or solid. The easiest way to find out would be to tap on the surface and listen to the noise. You could, of course, bore a hole and feel or peer inside, but this would be to violate the space – it would no longer be an interior. Musical instruments all produce sounds from inside, and the precise sort of sound comes from the space that is enclosed and the way in which the instrument is structured. As I suggested earlier, the human voice is a kind of instrument. Sounds are produced by a stream of air which comes up from the lungs and passes through the vocal cords into the mouth and nasal cavities (see Figure 3.1, p. 70). The noises we make come from deep inside us and will vary in pitch and volume according to the way in which we manipulate the air with our lips, tongues, and other vocal organs. With speaking, as in playing an instrument, we have to learn to synchronise a number of different activities to produce a smooth sequence. In this sense, speaking is like following a score.

By contrast with sound, the world of sight is concerned with surfaces. We can't see through objects unless they are transparent. Sight gives us the impression of the world laid out before us; we see ahead of us but not behind us. If we want to survey our surroundings we have to move our heads. Spectators at a tennis match move their heads to follow the flight of the ball because they can't take in the entire action in one go. Sound, on the other hand, is not subject to the same restrictions. We can hear all sorts of things going on around us, from any direction. And we can hear them simultaneously: someone talking behind us, a fly buzzing, the rain falling outside. With sound we seem situated at the centre of things, experiencing life stereophonically, as opposed to sight, which makes us into observers, looking on. Sound is also the less tidy sense of the two. We have only to consider the way in which spoken language makes use of grunts, mumbled words, and half-finished phrases to see this. When we write, however, we normally make a more determined attempt to set things out clearly, and in a standard fashion. We write <yes>, for example, where, in fact, we would probably say *yeh*.[2] Sight is more orderly than sound: we tend to see things sequentially, one after another. We read from left to right, top to bottom (unless we are reading Arabic or Chinese); and whereas in speech, individual words are run together, in writing they are separated from each other on the page by a little space, as indeed are those representatives of sound, the letters.

A subtle change overtakes words when they move from the domain of sound to that of sight. They become objects occupying space, things which can be moved around on a word processor, anonymous bits of type detached from their author. As we saw in Chapter 2, the view that words are really things is perennial, and it is reinforced by the visual medium in which language is mechanically reproduced and stored. Sound is more mysterious, less tangible, than sight; it's not surprising that non-literate cultures view words as magical and supernatural in origin. The effect of reproducing words in print is to detach them from a particular source; they could come from anyone and anywhere. They seem, in essence, anonymous. We can see the difference from spoken language if we compare the way in which we approach the problem of meaning. When we do not understand an utterance we are more likely to ask '*what do you mean?*' rather than '*what does it mean?*', as we might with something in print. In speech, meaning is personalised in a way that is difficult to achieve in writing. We could say that writing is more **decontextualised**, that is, the kind of clues to meaning which we get from spoken language such as tone, rhythm, and intonation pattern, are missing. We have to supply them ourselves, and imagine someone talking to us. By contrast, spoken language normally exists in a rich context. Apart from rhythm and intonation, it's accompanied by non-verbal signals, that is, gestures, facial movements, and expressions. As a consequence, written words are far more likely to be misunderstood than spoken ones. Speech doesn't need to be as tidy as written language precisely because it provides many more aids to interpretation than simply the words themselves.

We can see, then, that sound is a deeply social sense. It serves to unite living things – animals as well as humans – although only humans have the ability to talk, in any meaningful sense of the term. In the wild, mating calls and warning cries serve as signals to other members of the group. As animal studies have shown, sound operates in a communal framework. But animal cries can never achieve the sophistication of talking because talking is more than simply signalling. Indeed, it is more than just speaking. Talking implies the ability to use our knowledge of speech to some purpose. Remembering our discussion in Chapter 2 we could say that whereas speaking requires grammatical competence, talking also requires communicative competence. Talking is the quintessential communal activity and, as such, is different from writing, which is more solitary. In order to write this I have had to find a quiet spot away from people so as to avoid interruption, and although I have a dim sense of you, my audience, as people I am communicating with, my principal relationship is with the screen in front of me. It's not reasonable, of course, for me to expect those around me to stay quiet all the time. You have only to see the difficulty with which people remain quiet at a concert, or theatrical performance, to realise how unnatural total silence is. And, as the little anecdote I quoted in Chapter 2 from Samuel Johnson illustrates, it can be very unnerving in an enclosed environment, such as that of a stagecoach. Sound is a reciprocal sense; that is, we expect people around us to respond in a direct way to the noises we make. It carries an impression of physical immediacy, even urgency. If I write to someone and don't get a reply for ages I might feel a bit put out, but if I talk to them and they don't reply within a few seconds I would feel something was wrong.

What I have been trying to impress on you is the importance of recognising, as students of language, not only that spoken and written language are very different, but that a vital element in those differences is the sensory medium which each employs. As we have seen, because of its dependence on sound, speech is ephemeral. We might preserve it on tape but we can't do so in quite the same way as we can visual images. At the same time, however, we have also seen that although it may be transient, vanishing the moment it is uttered, the time when it exists is contextually rich. We experience things in sound as events; they are actions in time. As Austin (1962) and Searle (1969), who I referred you to in Chapter 2, have argued, when we speak we perform acts. In other words, we can consider speaking as a form of 'doing'. When we come to Chapter 5, 'Studying Meaning', we shall see that a significant part of deciding what an utterance means lies in deciding what activity is being performed. And because speech is nested in sound we experience words as events, as dramatic actions, in a way in which we don't with written language. To recover the dramatic effect of something written we have to imagine it being spoken: we have to give it a 'voice'. This is often the problem many people have with appreciating poetry, and why it is so important to practise reading it aloud: they find it difficult to give the inert words on the page a 'voice'.

3.2   Approaching speech sounds

I have already used a musical analogy in connection with speaking and listening, comparing the human voice to an instrument, and comparing speaking to following a score. This is a useful route into thinking about the way in which we utilise sound in speech. The principle of harmony, or to be more precise, **euphony**, is fundamental to the production and reception of speech sounds, for not only do we have to harmonise a number of activities in order to produce sounds, but listening also involves putting together sounds from a number of different sources, even behind us, and experiencing them as a whole. Writing and reading also involve synthesising activities, but the faculty of sight on which they rely prioritises clarity as its principal ideal. We are likely to object to someone's handwriting on grounds of tidiness, but their accent on grounds of euphony, that is, they don't sound pleasant. Everyone idealises their own pronunciation just as they do their own appearance. We speak beautifully to ourselves and, as a consequence, hearing a recording is always an enormous shock. Naturally, just as with physical form, the standard of beauty, or, in this case, euphony, is socially and culturally derived. There is nothing objectively more attractive about received pronunciation (r.p.) than any other accent of English, but it has become a cultural icon of proportion and harmony.

Speaking, then, is in some ways akin to singing. The sounds we produce are notes. And – as with music – rhythm, tempo, and pitch are all important in speech production. The first noises a baby hears in the womb are the rhythmic sounds of its mother's body – the coursing of the blood, the steady inhaling and exhaling of air, and the regular beating of the heart, the bass note of the body. Intuitions about rhythm are deep-seated and automatic. If we want to know how many syllables there are in a word the easiest way is to beat a hand in time to it, saying it slowly. The syllable in fact is at the centre of spoken English. In itself it is essentially meaningless. There are two syllables in *rather*, but neither *rath* nor *er* have any meaning. Syllables are pure units of sound, which is why they don't always correlate with the written word. In the word <bather>, for example, it is impossible from the spelling to say where the first syllable ends and the second begins. Is it <bath> + <er> or <bathe> + <r>? As

I pointed out in Chapter 2, the syllable is the smallest rhythmic unit in English, rather like the individual step in dance. Speech is organised syllabically, and at the centre of the syllable is that most musical of sounds, the vowel. Consonant sounds surround the vowel, but they can never themselves, apart from a few special cases, be the centre, or peak, of the syllable.

We tend to take the existence of the syllable for granted. But in some respects it is similar to the cell in nuclear physics. It is a system of interlocking elements, in this case, sounds, which have a specific order in relation to each other. Various different sequences are permitted but there are limits to what is allowable. Have a look at the following words, for example,

clan; blame; bulb; drip; hard; swan; snow

These are all monosyllabic words. In those words which have two sounds before the vowel, the combinations are *cl, bl, dr, sw, sn*. There are no words in English which begin with the reverse combinations, that is, *lc, lb, rd, ws, ns*. This isn't to say these combinations don't occur at all in English. Clearly they do, but we find them at the ends of syllables, not the beginnings, for example *talc, bulb, hard, news, runs*. Correspondingly, there are no words which end with the initial combinations, *cl, bl, dr, sw, sn*. So although there are in theory a great many possible combinations of sounds, the number which actually occur together are relatively few, and their distribution within individual words is strictly controlled. The particular branch of phonology which studies these permissible sound combinations is called **phonotactics**.

In this particular case, the governing principle behind the phenomenon we have been observing is not hard to find. Some sounds produce more vibration in the echo chamber of the mouth and nasal cavities than others. These are said to be more sonorous, or resonant. The most sonorous sounds of all are the vowels – if you make any of these sounds in isolation you sound as though you are singing – and after them come the sonorous consonants: *r, l, n, m, w*. So the peak of the syllable is the most sonorant sound. If there is an **onset**, or initial stage, of two or more consonant sounds then the most sonorant is closest to the vowel. And if there is a **coda**, or final stage, of two or more consonant sounds, then again the most sonorant sound will be nearest the vowel. The order of the sounds, in other words, is dictated by the degree of sonority. This will automatically produce different combinations in the onset from the coda. We can say, then, that the structure of the syllable is governed by the principle of sonority. The consonant sounds which surround the vowel harmonise with it. As we noted in Chapter 2, English is a musical language.

The fact that the production of speech sounds is governed by principles and processes which are essentially musical is important in our valuation, and apprehension, of speech. Equally important is the physiology of speech, that is, the way in which we physically produce speech sounds. The organs used in speech – the lips, teeth, tongue, larynx, and lungs – are all vital in the maintenance of life. We use them both for breathing and eating. If we consider that on those occasions when we are eating and talking at the same time many of the organs are performing three different functions simultaneously, it is a wonder we don't choke more often. Arguably the most important organ in speech production is the tongue. The word 'language' comes from the Latin *lingua* meaning 'tongue', and indeed common idioms such as a *smooth/sharp tongue*, or *hold your tongue*, equate the tongue with speaking. It is the position of the tongue in the mouth, for instance, which distinguishes one vowel from another. As I mentioned earlier, vowels, unlike consonants, are produced without any restriction in the mouth. If you just open your mouth and make a sound it will be some kind of vowel. Not surprisingly, vowel sounds are the first speech sounds which babies make. The differences between the vowels largely depend on small movements we make with our tongues, and as a consequence, they are the most mobile of all speech sounds, and the most frequent indicators of differences in pronunciation and accent.

But the tongue is also centrally important in the registering of taste. Sensors, on the underside of the tongue, convey information about the food we are eating to the brain. Apart perhaps from smell, taste is the most intimate of the bodily senses. When babies explore an object their first impulse is to put it in their mouths, only in that way can they gain direct knowledge of it. There is in fact a deep symbolic link between food and language: we talk, for example, of someone 'eating his own words'. It is not surprising then that the production of speech is experienced by us as a profoundly intimate and interior process. We are situated at the centre of a world of sound, in which we receive, and produce, impulses that are tactile and gustatory (relating to the sense of taste), as well as aural. Whereas with vision, as we have already noted, the world seems to be laid out before us, with sound it appears to be inside us. We possess it more completely. There is no equivalent in the sight faculty to an attack on someone's pronunciation or accent. Even making fun of their handwriting doesn't have the same possibility of wounding. It seems like an assault on their nationality, class, education, and even intelligence. Or, to put it another way, it is perceived as an attack on taste. It is no accident that the sense of taste is symbolic of discrimination in the arts. To be without taste is the ultimate disgrace, equivalent perhaps to being without language.

Because sound is an intimate bodily experience it makes possible sensations which are linguistically synaesthesic. **Synaesthesia** is a common occurrence in the life of the senses. It involves a mixing of the senses in ways which are mutually reinforcing. Referring to a colour like blue as 'cool', or red as 'hot', for example, is combining touch and sight. Similarly with sound. Because speech is a tactile process, involving organs used in the consumption of food, it is natural, given the appropriate context, for certain sounds to evoke sensations linked with touch and taste. Poets are able to exploit this possibility to create effects of sound symbolism, usually referred to as **alliteration** and **assonance**. What happens is that the sound becomes mimetic of the sensation it is describing: that is, it seems to imitate, or mimic, the sensation. In the following line from *Ode to a Nightingale*, for example, Keats is trying to create an impression of the texture of the flowers and leaves carpeting the floor of the forest. He does so by using sounds which feel to the reader particularly tactile: 'Fast fading violets covered up in leaves'. The *f*, *v*, and *s* sounds here are all fricatives. Try saying them on their own and you will see why. They are all produced with friction, and in combination with each other can suggest the roughened feel of foliage. They provide a verbal equivalent of the tactile sense. But not autonomously. These sounds on their own have no natural or inevitable link with the texture of plants. We need the meaning of the words to trigger the possibility of synaesthesia.

Given all that I have been saying about sound, its physical immediacy, interiority, and capacity for synaesthesia, it is not surprising that we should feel speech to be a deeply personal inheritance. People's voices are distinctive. So, of course, is their handwriting, but we recognise their voice to be them in a way we do not with writing. This is not because handwriting lacks individuality; as I suggested in Chapter 2 this is one of the things we value about it, but because, by comparison with the human voice, it lacks intimacy. People's accents are part of this personal inheritance. Many tend to hold on to their accents all their lives. Change, where it does occur, happens very slowly. We can attempt to alter our accent by deliberate effort, but it is hard work and not always successful. Long exposure to different speech communities will usually produce some change, as we may notice from friends who have moved to America or Australia. But we have to be careful here in what we attribute the change to. It is not simply the fact of exposure itself. We could watch endless

American movies on television and still not speak American English. It is not simply listening to other accents which affects our own, but having to speak back. This is because of the phenomenon referred to in Chapter 2 as 'convergence'. Communicating is a cooperative process, and as such we unconsciously attempt to narrow the gap between ourselves and the person we are speaking to. This means speaking more like them, particularly if they belong to a more dominant speech community, which is the case when we are living abroad. But not only living abroad of course. Even in England with its diversity of accents, r.p. has emerged as a model of pronunciation which a majority of people aspire towards. As I have already suggested, its attractiveness has more to do with cultural, social, and political factors, than with any inherent linguistic quality. Success is the ultimate aphrodisiac in linguistic, as in other matters. As a consequence, even people who have quite marked regional accents will hear themselves to be speaking r.p., but in reality, however, their voices will always give them away. Our voices tell the ultimate truth about us. Before we learnt to write, we learnt to speak, and that will always remain the deepest and most inalienable part of our linguistic make-up.

3.3 Sounds and the alphabet

Most people are quite unaware of the sounds they are actually making when they speak. We can see this from the way they will often 'correct' the pronunciation of others whilst doing many of the same things themselves. How many parents, for example, tell their children off for not pronouncing the ends of words, and yet do not themselves say the final g in <going>, or the t at the end of <left> in <left turn>? We tend to be bamboozled by the alphabet into thinking we pronounce as we spell. But, of course, the notion that a letter has to be pronounced because it's there is nonsense, otherwise how would we say <dumb> or <subtle>? If you came across the line <wot e sez iz> in a novel you would immediately assume that the character was speaking with some kind of regional accent. But in fact it is the normal pronunciation of most people. Try saying it and you will see what I mean. The standard pronunciation of <what> is *wot* and *sez* of <says>. And as for the *h*, dropping this is something we do all the time in running speech without noticing it. The conventional spelling system does not really represent the way in which we speak, because the relationship between it and pronunciation is not systematic enough. Indeed, even if we were to alter the spelling of common words, as I have done above, in an attempt to match pronunciation, we should still be unable to represent speech properly because the alphabet itself is inadequate for this purpose.

In order to study speech sounds more closely we need, as linguists, to develop a more precise alphabet than the conventional model. But before considering how we might go about this, we need to think a little more closely about some of the limitations of the alphabet and the difficulty of representing sound in written form. One of the ways of doing this is to take a range of words and attempt to isolate and identify the sounds we are making, using their alphabetic form. You might try this with the words below. Say them over to yourself carefully and then circle round any letter, or combination of letters, which you think makes a separate sound within each word:

    (i)   <that>
    (ii)   <tube>
   (iii)   <which>
   (iv)   <ache>
    (v)   <borough>
   (vi)   <charming>

Commentary
(i) <that> has three distinct sounds: (th) (a) (t). The <th> represents a sound for which there is no corresponding letter of the alphabet. As a consequence, the alphabet improvises by joining two other letters together, to form a **digraph** (a combination of two letters representing a single sound). Other digraphs include <sh> and <ch>, where again there is no corresponding letter of the alphabet to represent the sound. One significant limitation of the alphabet is that there are more speech sounds than there are individual letters to represent them. Indeed <th> represents more than one sound. As well as realising the sound in *that* it's also used for the first sound in *thigh*. In fact, it's only the difference between these two sounds which separates *thy* from *thigh*. There is an added complication, however, in that many people do not have these sounds in their particular variety of English at all. They involve putting your tongue against your top teeth and blowing, not an easy manoeuvre. Many Londoners will perform the relatively easier manoeuvre of putting their bottom lip against their teeth and pronouncing this letter combination as *f* and *v* as in *fief* <thief> and *bruvver* <brother>. And if you are Caribbean you will probably put your tongue behind your teeth and pronounce it as *t* and *d* as in *teef* and *brudder*. The *th* sound is one of a group which are

sometimes described as 'vulnerable' because they may be in the process of disappearing from the language.

(ii) <tube> has either three or four distinct sounds depending on how you pronounce it: Ⓣ ⊖ ⓤ ⓑ. The critical question to ask here is whether there is a sound between the first consonant, *t*, and the first vowel, *u*. For many people there is – native British speakers do not normally pronounce it *toob* – but the problem is that it isn't represented in the spelling, or orthography. It's the same sound which occurs between the initial consonant and following vowel in *beauty, news, few,* and *queue*. In other words, between the first sound and the *oo* vowel. The alphabetic letter which is often used to represent it is <y> as in <yours> and <yes> but it's absent, alphabetically, in the words above. Some English speakers, notably those in Norfolk, do of course pronounce these words without the *y*, so *toob, booty, nooz, foo,* and *coo*. The sociolinguist John Wells refers to this as **yod dropping**. Many Americans also drop their yods although not in such a systematic manner as the East Anglians. They will say *dook* and *toon* for <duke> and <tune> but not *booty* for <beauty> or *foo* for <few>.

But very probably you don't sound the 'yod' in <tube> either. And yet at the same time you don't say *toob*. Many people in England, particularly the young, pronounce the word *choob*. It's easy to see why. Saying one sound is simpler than saying two, and *ch* is a form of compromise between *t* and *y*. Even those who make most fuss about 'correct' pronunciation will probably pronounce <tune> as *choon*. So the 'yod' is under threat from more than one direction – possibly another vulnerable sound. But there is little point in complaining about its disappearance in words like <tube> and <tune>. There can be no 'correct' way of pronouncing them. The spelling doesn't support the presence of the 'yod'. It's little more than a conventionalised way of representing the word. And to argue from history or tradition brings in extra-linguistic issues which effectively give the game away.

And what of the <e> we might ask? Clearly it isn't sounded whatever our accent may be, so couldn't we simply leave it off? Obviously not since we should then pronounce the word *tub*. Despite the fact that we don't speak as we spell, the spelling system does give us some information about pronunciation. The function of the <e> is to give the reader a clue to the length of the preceding vowel. Many words have this silent <e> on the end. In a sense they are fossils from the past, relics of a time when spelling more closely matched pronunciation. Nowadays, it exists to tell us that the letter <u> represents a long vowel. Letters which perform this function are called **diacritics**.

(iii) <which> has three distinct sounds: (wh) (i) (ch). Here again we have two digraphs, the last one – <ch> – representing a sound for which, as we have already commented, there is no separate letter of the alphabet. The first one is particularly interesting in that it represents a sound normally represented simply by <w>. The question then is what function does the presence of <h> serve? For most people the answer is simply 'none'. Others, however, pronounce the initial consonant here differently from that in <witch>. Say the words <whales/Wales>, and <what/watt>. Do you distinguish between the words in each pair? The <wh> digraph is an echo of a sound which has disappeared from many varieties of English, although it can still be heard in Scottish and Irish accents. It's a more breathy, or aspirated, sound than *w*. If you put your hand in front of your mouth and say it as if it was *hw* then you should be able to feel the difference. Indeed, in Old English, words like <what> had the initial consonants in reverse order. The loss of the sound has had a number of effects. Firstly, although the letter <h> has been retained, the order of the letters has changed. Secondly, in some words the sound has been replaced simply by *w*, as in *which*, whilst in others it's the aspirated bit that's been retained and the sound is an *h*, for example, who/whom. So the spelling of these words no longer represents how most people say them. To argue, as some do, that we should distinguish between <what> and <watt>, in pronunciation, because of a historic distinction, is again to fall victim to the delusion that we speak as we spell. We could call this delusion the **orthographical fallacy**.

(iv) <ache> appears to have two distinct sounds: (a) (ch), and the <e> is silent. However, the first sound, represented by <a> doesn't seem to be a single sound. If you say it slowly you should be able to feel it starting in one part of the mouth and finishing in another. It moves from one vowel position to another in a kind of glide. It is often represented orthographically by the digraph <ai> as in <laid>. Vowels which glide in this way are called **diphthongs**, as opposed to single vowels which are called **monophthongs**. Vowels are constantly being lengthened, or shortened, in the mouth, with the consequence that individual letters can frequently represent more than a single vowel. And, as with <tube>, the function of <e> is to give the reader a clue to the length of the preceding vowel. Without it we should pronounce the word as *ak*. It is another example of a diacritic.

(v) <borough> has four distinct sounds: (b) (o) (r) (ough). The last sound has changed considerably from its Old English origins. <borough> is one of many words in which an earlier fricative sound has been lost. It still survives in some Scottish words – we can hear it in the Scottish pronunciation of <loch> – but it has vanished from other varieties of English. In this case the vowel sound which has replaced it is one of the shortest and most common vowels in English. The *uh* sound is found in many English words but it has no particular letter of the alphabet to represent it. Linguists call it **schwa**, a German word used to describe a Hebrew vowel of similar quality. It hardly seems a vowel at all and only occurs in unstressed syllables. We find it in the first and last syllables of *banana*, the first syllable of *about*, and the final syllable of *brother*. It's a very colourless vowel. It can be heard all the time in running speech, particularly in small grammatical words which are lightly stressed like *and*, *for*, *of*, and *to*. It is a distinct vowel, however, and serves to distinguish *borough* from *burrow*.

(vi) <charming> has five distinct sounds: (ch) (ar) (m) (i) (ng). You may have come up with a different division so I'll go through mine in some detail. The first bit is unproblematic: <ch> is a digraph representing a sound for which, as I said above, there is no corresponding single letter of the alphabet. And for most English people <ar> is also a digraph representing a single vowel sound (the one conventionally called 'long *a*'). This may be a surprise to you in that you may feel you pronounce the <r> here, but say it slowly and consider whether it is simply a vowel sound. The majority of British English speakers only pronounce <r> when there is a vowel following, as in *borough*. This has not always been the case, however. Up until the eighteenth century *r*s were heard everywhere. But it is quite a muscular sound. It involves curling the tongue behind the ridge which is at the back of the top teeth; try saying the first sound in *rat* and you'll see. The tongue is really a dead weight in the mouth and we are constantly finding ways to minimise moving it around. Not surprisingly, the sound has got weaker over the years until it has been lost entirely in those places where it is not followed by a vowel. And even though it remains before a vowel, it is still fairly weak in many accents of English. The loss of this sound from many English words has had a profound effect on the phonology, or sound structure, of English. Just think of how we say <here>, <there>, and <cure>. In all of these cases the *r* has disappeared and we have diphthongs instead. None the less, the <r> remains in the spelling as a fossil from the past, a reminder of a time when the pronunciation was different. But perhaps fossil is not quite the right term here. It is better described as a dormant sound, for it is always possible for it to become active again. We have only to say the phrase <here and now> for the *r* to creep back (*here rand now*; see Chapter 1), because of course, it is now followed by a vowel. Not all accents have lost *r* when not followed by a vowel, however. In the Scottish pronunciation of <here> you can hear the *r* very clearly, It can also be heard in most American accents, although still a weaker sound than the Scottish. The preservation of this *r* is one of the distinctive differences between American and British English. In British accents it is largely associated with rustic speech, whereas in America it is a standard feature of what linguists call **General American**.

And what of the digraph <ng>? Again, you may think you say the <g>, but are you sure about this? For many people the last sound is produced by raising the back of the tongue towards the roof of the mouth. It's a sort of *n* sound produced from the back of the mouth rather than the front. Try saying *sin* and then *sing*. The *n* sound of the first is quite different from that of the second. This second *n* is another of these sounds for which there is no separate letter of the alphabet. We conventionally use the same letter but the sounds are quite distinct and serve to separate different words. Say *sinner* and then *singer* and you should see what I mean. If you are from London, however, you may find that, although you have this second *n* in your accent, you may not always use it in those areas where an r.p. speaker would. So, for example, <charming> might, for you, be pronounced as *charmin* (as in *huntin*, *shootin* and *fishin*). And just to complicate matters, there are some accents (notably in the Midlands) which may pronounce the *g* here. For such speakers the *ng* sounds in <charming> would have to be represented as ⓝ ⓖ.

Summary

There are a number of important points about the sound system and the way in which it is represented by the alphabet that should have emerged from this exercise. Firstly, it's not a straightforward matter to work out exactly what sounds we are making in pronunciation simply by examining words in their alphabetic form. If you have never had to think about this before you may well have found it difficult to establish just how many sounds there are in a particular word. It's easy to convince yourself you are making a sound you are not, and vice versa. Try doing the exercise above with a friend, who can listen to you and tell you how you sound to them. You may well find their opinion differs from yours about your pronunciation. Secondly, it should have become apparent that our spelling system, and indeed the alphabet itself, is simply not sensitive enough to represent accurately the way in which we pronounce words. There are variations in accent, and variations due to changes over time which our spelling system, or orthography, just ignores. But apart from this, even considering it as a system, the alphabet suffers from considerable overload. There are some sounds which have no corresponding letter of the alphabet, and for which the system has to improvise, by utilising an existing letter, or by producing combinations of letters, in order to represent them. As we saw earlier, <th> has to do for two quite different sounds, whilst for the *n* sound in <charming> there is no separate letter available. And this is only the consonants. The inadequacy of the alphabet is even more apparent when we come to vowels. There are only five vowel letters but they have to do service for 20 vowel sounds. Consider, for example, how many sounds are represented by <o>: *got, core, woman, women, dole, brother*. In fact, if we were to have individual letters for each of the distinctive sounds the alphabet has to represent we should need many more than the 26 available to us.

But would even this be enough? Even if we could establish a reasonably accurate inventory of speech sounds which took account of the information we have already come across, there is still the additional problem that we articulate sounds differently according to their distribution, that is, where they occur in a word. The way we pronounce the letter <p>, for example, is slightly different in *pin* from the way in which we pronounce it in *spin*. In the case of *pin*, the sound is aspirated, in other words, it's accompanied by a small puff of air. You will see this if you put your hand in front of your mouth and say it carefully. If you do the same for *spin*, however, you should feel hardly any aspiration at all. In fact, the *p* in this word sounds more like *b*, and it could just as easily be spelt with a <b>. Similarly, the *l* in *lake* is different from the *l* in *film*, where it's a weaker sound. If you try and say the word using the stronger *l* you end up with something like *fillum*, which is how many Irish people, who don't have the weaker *l* in their accent, pronounce the word. A great many sounds have distributional variants of a similar kind; the *a* in *bad* is different from the *a* in *bat* – the first one is slightly longer. And on top of distributional variants there are differences of pitch and voice setting which are completely individual. It is these which make it possible for us to recognise someone straightaway over the 'phone. By this time you are probably wondering how on earth it's possible to construct what we might consider a definitive alphabet.

3.4   Developing a phonemic alphabet

The general point we need to bear in mind is that any alphabet has to decide not only how to represent sound, but also how much of it to represent. And this will depend on the use for which it is intended. How much of speech is it important for us to be aware of in the transmission of meaning? No alphabet, however refined, could discriminate the language use of every individual, and it is worth asking ourselves what would be its use were it possible. As we have seen, the conventional alphabet can only serve as an approximate means of representing the actual sounds of speech. Arguably, it makes the best of a bad job, but there's no way it can cope with the shifting, manifestly variable world of sound. As linguists, however, we need a far more sensitive and extensive alphabet, one capable of representing the individual sound shape of each word with a greater degree of accuracy.

Let's imagine how we might set about developing such an alphabet. To begin with, we could decide that each speech sound would have a separate symbol. So, for example, all those different *os* in *got*, *woman*, *women*, *core*, *dole*, and *brother*, would each be separately represented as would the different *ths* in *thy* and *thigh*. And, as we would know the sound value of each symbol, we would be able to predict the pronunciation of any word from the way it was spelt. We could call these speech sounds **phones**. Each **graph**, or written symbol, would thus represent a separate phone. One initial problem we should have in compiling this alphabet, however, would be to determine what constituted an individual speech sound, or phone. That's not as simple a task as it may seem. Consider the following words:

<cool>
<cat>

There is no problem in isolating the individual sounds in each word: ⓒ ⓞⓞ ⓛ; ⓒ ⓐ ⓣ. Clearly there are six separate sound units here. The real issue is how many different kinds of sounds there are. Our intuition of course is to say 'five', since the initial sounds of both words seem the same. But this is not strictly true. These sounds are, in fact, subtly different. You can see this if you start to say *cat* and then change your mind and say *cool*. It's almost impossible; you really have to start all over again. This is because the lips are in a totally different position for the *c* of *cat* than for the *c* of *cool*. In the first case, the sound is coming from the front of the mouth, and in the second, from the back. What is happening is that when we say the initial sound we are already preparing to say the next. Sounds will always tend to move in the direction of the one following. It's a process known as **assimilation**. So perhaps there are two phones here, not just one. And whilst we are in this extra fussy mood we might also notice that an acquaintance of ours from the south of England pronounces the <oo> of <cool> so that it sounds more like a diphthong (*coouhl*). Once we begin to unravel the differences in pronunciation there seems to be no end to the number of phones we could identify, some because of different accents, and some because of the position of a sound within individual words. As we have already noticed, there are different kinds of *l* and also of *p*. Indeed, if we pursued the principle of differentiation throughout the language we should find the number of phones to be very large since all the sounds of English have pronunciation variants.

Clearly we should have to limit the descriptive capability of our alphabet in some way. It would be impossible to use an alphabet, for any practical purposes, which worked on totally phonetic principles. We need, therefore, to find some way of identifying those sounds which seem to us to be the important ones. The only way in which we can do this is by taking into account the meanings of words. In other words, our alphabet would have to be based on semantic as well as phonetic principles. Taking this as our cue we can look back at the initial sounds of *cat* and *cool* and decide that the difference between these two phones is not important enough for us to need to recognise them in our new alphabet. How do we know that? Well, if you did manage to say *cat* with the *c* of *cool* you would not end up with a different word. At best you could only be thought to be saying *cat* strangely and at worst, you would be incomprehensible. In other words, the difference between these sounds is not contrastive, swopping them round would not produce a new word. It is similarly the case with the different *p*s and *l*s. Pronouncing <spin> as *sbin* doesn't matter since we don't have a word *sbin* with which it could be confused. So there's a sense in which although these are different sounds they are also the same sound. Perhaps an analogy might help here. Let's pretend I catch the 9.45 a.m. to London every day. Now as far as I'm concerned I catch the same train each day. This would be the case even if the train itself, that is, the engine and carriages were entirely different. As long as they were taking me to London at the prescribed time I would regard them as the same. In a sense the train has a concrete and an abstract existence. It exists as a physical entity which can be changed every day, and it exists for me as a mental reality which is unchanging. And similarly with sounds. Phonetics is concerned with the physical substance of sound, that is, with phones. But there's also an abstract level to sounds, a level on which they are mental, semantic realities. It's this level which our new alphabet has to capture. On this level we need a new term to describe the initial sound of *cool* and *cat* which we are saying is the same and of which the two phones we identified above are variants. We can call this sound a **phoneme**. The best definition of this unit is Jean Aitchison's in *Teach Yourself Linguistics*: 'A phoneme is the smallest segment of sound which can distinguish two words' (1992, p. 39).

We have established an important principle of our new alphabet then which is that the symbols will only represent contrastive speech sounds. Phones are only important to us in so far as they also represent phonemes. The difference between the two phones at the beginning of *cat* and *cool* is phonetic but not phonemic. If we use the symbol /k/ to represent the phoneme we can say that it is realised, that is, represented, in sound by two phones, [kʰ+] and [kʰ–]. The plus symbol indicates that the phone is towards the front of the mouth and the minus symbol indicates its towards the back, whilst the little 'h' tells us that both phones are aspirated (try the test mentioned earlier in connection with *p*). But again, another term would be useful here to express the relationship between phones and phonemes: it would enable us to short-circuit descriptions like 'realised', or 'represented' in sound. We can say that these phones are **allophones**, that is, variants, of the phoneme /k/. To sum up the discussion so far then, we are saying that a phoneme is the sound as concept, a phone is the sound as substance, and an allophone is the phone in its capacity as physical token of a phoneme.

There is an important distinction here between phonetics and phonology. Phonetics is concerned with the acoustic properties of language; it examines sounds, or phones, without any direct reference to their capacity to act as bearers of meaning. Its primary concern is with sounds as substance. Phonology, on the other hand, relates speech sounds to their linguistic function within the semantic structure, that is, the 'meaning' structure, of the language. As such, it's concerned with phonemes, or sounds as concepts. Because, as users of the language, we are only interested in phonemes, the phonetic differences (those between phones) that we have been talking about are usually invisible to us. It's only when the differences signal a difference in meaning that we become aware of them. This is why foreign users of English are sometimes conscious of sound differences of which we are oblivious, because in their own language they are contrastive. We can see this if we return yet again to /k/. In addition to the two allophones mentioned above, both of which are aspirated, there is an unaspirated form [k] which occurs at the end of words. Try the aspiration for the final sound of *lack* and you will see that there is no puff of air. None the less, we perceive the sounds to be the same because they never contrast with each other in English. As Graddol, Cheshire, and Swan, point out, however, in *Describing Language* (1991, p. 46), they are not the same to speakers of Hindi. In Hindi, *kana*, pronounced with an aspirated initial sound, means 'to eat' but without aspiration it means 'one eyed'. The difference between these two sounds is not allophonic, as it is in English, but phonemic.

What we have constructed so far is a hierarchy of description which takes us from the physical level of the actual sound, the phone, up to the more abstract, or conceptual level of the phoneme – the sound in its capacity to affect meaning. And to indicate this we have used a particular form of notation: phonemes are always enclosed in slant brackets, phones and allophones in square brackets. To illustrate this from our discussion, we can say that the phoneme /k/ is realised in English by three phones: [kʰ+], [kʰ–], [k]. In other words, these phones are allophones of the phoneme /k/. I have spent some time on elaborating these distinctions because you will find it helpful in learning and using phonemes, allophones, and phones if you can understand the relationship between them. As we have seen, from the example in the previous paragraph, the relationship is not absolute, but relative to the particular language in question: a phoneme in one language may operate as an allophone in another, and vice versa. A final way of securing the distinctions in your mind is to think of a similar hierarchical relationship which exists within conventional orthography, that is, the way in which we represent the letters of the alphabet. The letter <s>, for example, can be written in a variety of ways: as a capital <S>, in lower case <s>, and, if we look at manuscripts from 200 years ago, as <ʃ>. In writing the word <ship>, it wouldn't matter which one we used, whether <Ship>, <ship>, or <ʃhip>, the word would be exactly the same. You should be able to see now why the term 'letter' is too inexact to be of much use: like the term 'sound', it cannot capture the distinctions we need to make accurately enough. For this we require a companion set to the phoneme/allophone/phone relationship. We can call the individual, physical shape of the letter, whether it's <S>, <s>, or <ʃ>, a **graph**. Because these graphs all represent the same letter they are also **allographs**, and instead of the term 'letter', the highest rung in the ladder, we can use the term **grapheme**, to indicate the letter as a concept, or mental reality. As a concept, it could quite easily be represented in other than written form, in morse code, for example. Just as with the sound structure of the language, then, we have a hierarchy of relationships linking physical form with more abstract realities.

Written Form

grapheme	=	individual letter as concept
allograph	=	physical representation of letter/concept
graph	=	physical substance

Sound Structure

phoneme   =   individual sound as concept
allophone   =   physical representation of sound/concept
phone   =   physical substance

3.4.1   Minimal pairs

Now that the principles on which our new 'phonemic' alphabet are in place we can move on and consider how they can be used to establish a full inventory of speech sounds. Remember that we are concerned with contrastive sounds, that is, where the presence or absence of a sound produces a new word. The simplest way to see this in action is to take a single syllable – or 'monosyllabic' – word and see how many different words can be made by altering one of the sounds. Try this with *pin*, and remember that, although for the moment you are using graphemes (letters), you are none the less thinking of phonemes (contrastive sounds):

k		*p*
d	*u*	*ss*
t	*a*	*ll*
b	*e*	*t*
p i n	*p i n*	*p i n*
f	*ai*	*th*
th		*ck*
s		*tch*
sh		
ch		

This is not an exhaustive list, and you may well have thought of other possible words. Certain limitations are imposed on us because we are using graphemes. For example, *pin* and *pine* contrast simply by one phoneme – by a monophthong (single vowel) as opposed to a diphthong (glide) – but there's no way of indicating this here since there is no separate symbol for the diphthong. Similarly, <tch>, although consisting of three graphs (thus a trigraph), is really a single sound. But using this method it's possible to begin building up an inventory of phonemes within English; where there's no convenient grapheme to symbolise a particular phoneme we can simply invent one. Each phoneme would then be represented by a separate symbol, some from the conventional alphabet, and the rest, made up. This is one of the principal ways in which linguists set about mapping the phonemes of different languages. It's based on the process of minimal pairing, that is, finding words which are differentiated from each other by a single sound.

But a note of caution here. Although we can say that words which are distinguished by a single sound are different words with different meanings, the reverse is not the case. I mean that it's perfectly possible, and indeed, quite common, for different words, or, more properly, lexemes (see Chapter 1), to have exactly the same sound structure. <pupil> meaning 'eye', and <pupil> meaning 'student' are different lexemes, but phonologically they are identical. It's partly because of this that the language is capable of generating so much ambiguity. You might imagine what it would be like if every lexeme in the English language had a different sound structure, for example, that <round> the **noun** (a round of golf), <round> the **adjective** (a round table), and <round> the **verb** (to round the corner), were all pronounced differently. This is the case for a few lexemes, for example, <conduct> – compare *your conduct* [noun] *is terrible* with *I shall conduct* [verb] *the orchestra*. As you can see, the noun is pronounced differently from the verb because the stress falls on the first, instead of the second, syllable. If all lexemes were differentiated in some phonological way we should have a more exact match between pronunciation and word meaning than exists in English. At the same time, however, it would make the language very difficult to learn, and complicated to use. Fortunately, there are other clues to meaning apart from sound, and because of these the language can afford to economise on phonological contrasts. In the case of <round>, for example, its position in each phrase alerts us to the fact that it is being used differently, and with a separate meaning – even though we may not know the terms 'noun', 'adjective', and 'verb'. The contrast here is syntactic, that is, it has to do with the ordering of the words and their relationship to each other.

An important point has emerged here concerning the contrastive principle which we have been employing, and which is worth bearing in mind. Not only is it an essential element in the sound structure, or phonology, of English, it is also very important in the syntactic and semantic structure of the language as well. It is because there are other ways of contrasting words than by sound difference, for example, position in a phrase, situational context, that phonemic contrasts can be kept to a minimum. We shall be returning to this principle in future chapters.

3.5 The phonemic alphabet

Now that we have established the principles on which our new alphabet is based, and the method by which it can be developed, we can jump ahead and consider what a complete inventory of phonemes for English might look like. You will notice, if you look at the literature on phonology, that alphabets differ slightly in some of the symbols which are used. This doesn't matter. There is nothing sacred about a particular symbol. The main thing, as far as we are concerned, is to be consistent in our use of an alphabet and avoid swapping from symbol to symbol.

Consonant Phonemes

/p/	**p**in	/ʃ/	**sh**ow
/b/	**b**in	/ʒ/	mea**s**ure
/t/	**t**ype	/h/	**h**oax
/d/	**d**ive	/tʃ/	**ch**ain
/k/	**k**iss	/dʒ/	**j**u**dg**e
/g/	**g**ale	/m/	**m**ule
/f/	**f**ield	/n/	**n**ear
/v/	**v**iew	/ŋ/	pi**nk**
/θ/	**th**igh	/l/	**l**ight
/ð/	**th**y	/r/	**r**ound
/s/	**s**ign	/j/	**y**ours
/z/	**z**oo	/w/	**w**ander

Vowel Phonemes

Monophthongs:

/iː/	kn**ee**	/ɔː/	s**aw**
/ɪ/	l**i**p	/ʊ/	g**oo**d
/ɛ/	b**e**d	/uː/	b**oo**t
/æ/	h**a**t	/ʌ/	c**u**p
/ɑː/	**ar**m	/ɜː/	f**ir**m
/ɒ/	b**o**x	/ə/	**a**bout

ː is a diacritic indicating that the vowel is long

Diphthongs:

/eɪ/	f**a**ce	/aʊ/	m**ou**th
/aɪ/	kn**i**fe	/ɪə/	d**ear**
/ɔɪ/	b**oy**	/ɛə/	h**air**
/əʊ/	n**o**se	/ʊə/	c**ure**

The best way of learning phonemes is to attach a key word to each symbol, as I have here – that way the sounds will be more firmly anchored in your memory. When you come to transcribe words from the conventional alphabet into your new one you can then compare the sound of any word you are not sure of with that of your key word. You will probably find that the consonant phonemes are not too difficult to learn since many of them use symbols from the conventional alphabetic system. The vowel phonemes, however, can be tricky. As you will see, there are 20 of these, as opposed to only five graphemes. Moreover, you may well find that some of them are not represented in your own pronunciation. For example, if you are from a region which pronounces *r* after a vowel (see pp. 58–9), you will probably not have the diphthongs in *here* and *there* in your accent, but a combination of the monophthongs /ɪ/ and /ɛ/ with /r/. And if you are from the north of England you might not have /ʌ/, a vowel phoneme which is only present in southern varieties of English.

Remember, then, that everyone will have their own personal inventory of phonemes. This is inevitable, given the variety of accents and the fact that there can be no 'correct' form of pronunciation. This doesn't mean that we are free to pronounce words how we like. In Chapter 1 we distinguished the terms 'correct/incorrect' from 'well-formed/ill-formed' and 'acceptable/unacceptable'. These distinctions are useful here. Let's say my accent is a variety of London English and that I do not have the phonemes /θ/ and /ð/ in my inventory so that <three> is pronounced /friː/ and <other> as /ʌvə/. The pronunciation of these words is thoroughly well-formed because it follows a rule of a particular speech variety in which /θ/ and /ð/ are consistently replaced by /f/ and /v/. Their acceptability, however, will depend on the context in which they are used. They may well be acceptable with my friends and peers but not if I am reading the news on the BBC. Acceptability involves a social judgement, well-formedness a linguistic one, and we need to be clear in our minds about the difference between the two. It is not our concern as linguists to act as censors. However, there is no linguistic rule which would allow me, individually, to pronounce <three> as /griː/ and <other> as /ʌlə/. This would not only be unacceptable but ill-formed since it follows no known rule except that of personal whim. A pronunciation needs to be sanctioned by some speech community in order to be considered a variety of English.

So, the point is not to worry if your transcription of a particular word does not entirely match that of someone else's. Transcriptions will have varying levels of acceptability. Many introductions to linguistics, and also dictionaries, use received pronunciation as their model, partly because this is the most culturally accepted variety, and also because it would be too confusing to attempt to represent all the possible variants. Indeed it is the model I have adopted here. But there is nothing sacred about r.p. and you may well find that some contemporary books on linguistics have a different inventory from mine. This is not something you should worry about. And of course, we are, for the moment, only thinking of the pronunciation of words singly, that is, in citational form. All sorts of strange things start happening to them in running speech. But we shall come to that in due course. And a final point, this is a list of phonemes, or contrastive units; the individual allophones by which they are realised in the language are not represented here. As we have already said, each phoneme will have a variable pronunciation depending on distribution – where it occurs in a word – and accent. In other words, this is a 'phonemic' alphabet not a 'phonetic' one. A phonetic alphabet would provide, in addition to the phonemes, a complete inventory of all the phones, or phonetic variants, of the language. For the purposes of understanding the structural principles of English we do not need to know all these variants, but, as I've already said, it's important to know what the difference between a 'phonetic' and 'phonemic' description of English is. The distinction is particularly important to sociolinguists, concerned with studying accents, since using the phonetic alphabet enables them to give a more precise description of an accent than relying purely on a phonemic one would do.

3.5.1   Describing phonemes

Unlike graphemes, phonemes do not have names. If you see the letter <c> you can choose to refer to it either by its name /siː/, or by the sound it represents, /k/. But it's safer to use the name because the letter sometimes represents /s/. Names, then, serve the useful function of distinguishing the graphemes from each other, and this is necessary because, as we have just seen, they do not always consistently represent the same sound. Phonemes, however, do – this is part of their *raison d'être* – and consequently don't require names to distinguish them. None the less, it's important for us to know in what ways they are distinct from each other. If, as we have been arguing, the contrastive principle is the cornerstone of the phoneme's existence, the question still remains as to how, or in what ways they contrast. It's all very well to say that *pin* and *bin* contrast, as a minimal pair, in terms of one sound, but what is the difference between these two sounds in physical terms? In order to answer this we need to know something about the physiology of speech production, that is, the way in which sounds are articulated in the mouth. As a way into this it's a good idea to think about some of the differences yourself. Let's start with consonant phonemes.

(a) *Describing consonants*

Have a look at the minimal pairs below and consider what is the nature of the differences between the initial sounds. You will need to transcribe the words first:

    (i) *sue/zoo*
    (ii) *sue/shoo*
    (iii) *sue/too*

Commentary

(i) *sue* /suː/ *zoo* /zuː/. The initial sounds here, /s/ and /z/, are formed in exactly the same part of the mouth. If you say them slowly you should be able to feel the sides of the front part of your tongue making contact with the ridge just behind your top teeth and air coming down the middle of the tongue in a hissing manner. In fact so similar are the sounds that you can begin to say *sue* and then change to *zoo* with no change in the speech organs. The only difference here is that one sound, /z/, is **voiced**, whilst the other, /s/, is **voiceless**. Voicing is a vital physiological process in speech production. To understand what it is you will need to refer to Figure 3.1. It's caused by air coming through the gap, or glottis, in the

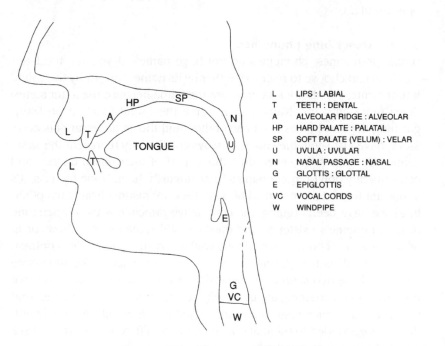

L	LIPS : LABIAL
T	TEETH : DENTAL
A	ALVEOLAR RIDGE : ALVEOLAR
HP	HARD PALATE : PALATAL
SP	SOFT PALATE (VELUM) : VELAR
U	UVULA : UVULAR
N	NASAL PASSAGE : NASAL
G	GLOTTIS : GLOTTAL
E	EPIGLOTTIS
VC	VOCAL CORDS
W	WINDPIPE

FIGURE 3.1 The organs of speech

vocal cords, situated in the larynx, or Adam's apple, and causing them to vibrate. Voiceless sounds are produced when the cords are far apart and so not vibrating; and voiced, when they are rubbing together. The best way to experience the phenomenon is to put your fingers in your ears whilst saying the sounds. Or, alternatively, put your fingers either side of your larynx.You should be able to feel a buzzing sensation when you say /z/, but not when you say /s/.

All the phonemes are divided into those which are produced with voicing, thus voiced, and those which are not, thus voiceless, or unvoiced. All the vowel phonemes are voiced. Say them aloud using the test above and you should be able to feel this without too much difficulty. You may find that consonant phonemes are a little more difficult to classify; this is because we are accustomed to saying them with an accompanying vowel sound, so they can all seem voiced. But go through them all carefully, trying to say them on their own, and you should be able to determine into which category each falls. The answers are in Figure 3.2, if you wish to check your findings.

(ii) *sue* /suː/ *shoo* /ʃuː/. The initial sounds here /s/ and /ʃ/ are both voiceless sounds and they also involve the same hissing sound, with air coming down the middle of the tongue. The difference between them, then, must rest on something else. If you say them one after the other you should feel, unlike /s/ and /z/, a difference occurring in the position of your tongue. Instead of the front part making contact with the hard, or alveolar, ridge, the middle part is rising towards the roof, or hard palate (see Figure 3.1). It's as if the sound is moving backwards. So although these two sounds do not contrast in terms of voicing, they do as far as where they are formed in the mouth is concerned. In other words, they contrast in terms of their **place of articulation**. After voicing, place of articulation is the second major way in which phonemes are distinguished from each other. All consonant phonemes are described firstly, as voiced, or voiceless, and then according to their place of articulation. Here is a summary of the main place classifications. Try sounding each phoneme so that you can feel where it is formed; the classification moves from the front of the mouth to the back. Figure 3.1 will help you check the description.

Bilabial phonemes (bottom lip against top lip) /b/ /p/ /m/ /w/
Labio-dental phonemes (bottom lip against top teeth) /f/ /v/
Dental phonemes (tongue against top teeth) /θ/ /ð/
Alveolar phonemes (tongue against alveolar ridge) /t/ /d/ /s/ /z/ /l/ /n/

Post-alveolar phonemes (tongue just behind alveolar ridge) /r/
Palato-alveolar phonemes (tongue against hard palate and alveolar ridge) / dʒ/ /tʃ/
Palatal phonemes (middle of tongue against hard palate) /ʃ/ /ʒ/ /j/
Velar phonemes (back of tongue against soft palate/velum) /k/ /g/ /ŋ/
Glottal phonemes (sound produced from the glottis only, with no other restriction in the air flow) /h/

You may have noticed, in making these sounds, that even when a phoneme is formed in the same part of the mouth as another phoneme, that is, has the same place of articulation, and shares the same voicing, there is still something which makes it different. It is this which we can notice in our remaining pair of words.

(iii) *sue* /suː/ *too* /tuː/. The initial phonemes here, /s/ and /t/, are both alveolar sounds (formed with the front of the tongue against the alveolar ridge, see Figure 3.1), and so have the same place of articulation, and they are also both voiceless. Nonetheless, they are clearly contrastive, since *sue* and *too* are minimal pairs. So the question is how do they differ? In this case the difference has to do with the kind of sound which is produced. Saying /t/ involves stopping the air in your mouth by means of your tongue in contact with the alveolar ridge, and then releasing it suddenly, like a mini explosion. Phonemes produced like this are called **stops**, or **plosives**. Saying /s/, however, involves releasing air. The resulting hissing sound is the consequence of friction caused by the air between the tongue and the alveolar ridge. Not surprisingly, phonemes produced like this are termed **fricatives**. These two phonemes, then, differ in terms of their **manner of articulation**, that is, the kind of sound produced.

In addition to being classified according to place of articulation, and voicing, then, consonant phonemes are also classified according to their manner of articulation. Below are the main classifications. Say the sounds over carefully so that you can feel how they differ:

Plosives (total closure of speech organs and air released suddenly) /p/ /b/ /t/ /d/ /k/ /g/
Fricatives (near closure of speech organs and released with friction) /f/ /v/ /θ/ /ð/ /s/ /z/ /ʃ/ /ʒ/ /h/
Affricates (total closure of speech organs and air released with friction) /tʃ/ / dʒ/
*****Nasals** (air released through the nasal passage) /m/ /n/ /ŋ/

Liquids
  (i)   (partial closure of speech organs and air flows over sides of tongue) /l/
  (ii) (near closure of speech organs and air flows down middle of tongue) /r/
**Glides: (speech organs almost close and then glide away from each other) /w/ /j/

* These are the only nasal phonemes, the remainder are all oral. They are the result of the soft palate, or velum, dropping and releasing air through the nose. If you say the word *sudden* very slowly you should feel the soft palate lowering for the final syllable. Alternatively, try saying the nasal phonemes whilst holding your nose – it's impossible.

** These phonemes are sometimes referred to as semi-vowels since they involve hardly any restriction. If you say them you will see that they resemble the vowels /uː/ and /iː/ respectively. **Glides** and **liquids** are sometimes collectively called **approximants**.

Summary/consonant phonemes
It should have become clear by now that, as we commented earlier, all consonants are produced by restricting the air flow in some way, either partially or totally. The precise manner in which this is done results in different kinds of sounds. You may think that /h/ is an exception to this since there is no restriction in the mouth, but this is because the restriction occurs at the vocal cords. Making this sound is rather like panting. We have distinguished three ways of describing consonant phonemes: **voicing**, **place of articulation**, and **manner of articulation**. These constitute the principal **distinctive features** of consonants. There are others but, for the moment, these are the important ones to get familiar with. Together, they enable us to differentiate the phonemes from each other and establish in what ways they contrast. Some may do so in terms of only one feature, for example, voicing, whilst others may contrast in two, or even three. Figure 3.2 sets out the distinctive features we have established so far.

As you can see, no phoneme occupies exactly the same space. Also, whilst a number exist in pairs, a voiced and a voiceless, others do not. There is no voiced counterpart to /h/, for example, and no voiceless counterpart to any of the glides, liquids, or nasals. This is not the case for all languages, however. It's important to remember that the phoneme inventory for other languages will be different. Welsh, for example, does have a voiceless /l/ – it's the first and middle sound of *Llanelli*. English people tend to pronounce it as *thl* but this is an Anglicised version. If you

	bilabial	lab-dental	dental	alveolar	post-alv	pal/alv	palatal	velar	glottal
plosive	p			t				k	
(voiced)	b			d				g	
fricative		f	θ	s		ʃ			h
(voiced)		v	ð	z		3			
affricate							tʃ		
(voiced)							dʒ		
nasal									
(voiced)	m			n				ŋ	
liquid									
(voiced)				l	r				
glide									
(voiced)	w					j			

FIGURE 3.2   Consonant phoneme table

put your tongue in the position for /l/ and blow instead of hum you will get the voiceless sound. The number of potential speech sounds, and, therefore phonemes, is quite large. English simply makes a selection from the many which are available. This is useful to bear in mind because it explains why, in words borrowed from foreign languages, our pronunciation is often very different from the spelling. For example, we have many words borrowed from Greek which begin with the letters <ph> (<philosophy>, for example). We pronounce this as /f/ because we do not have a fricative /p/ in our system, only a plosive. Greek, however, does because its phonology is different from that of English.

(b)   Describing vowel phonemes
(i) *Monophthongs (pure vowels)*
Unlike consonant phonemes, vowel phonemes do not involve any restriction in the air flow. Instead, air is manipulated in the oral cavity by the position of the tongue, and the shape of the vocal tract. As a consequence, manner of articulation is the same for all vowels: there is no equivalent with vowels to the fricatives and plosives of consonantal articulation. Similarly, voicing is the same for all vowels, because, as we have said, all vowels are voiced. Because of this, describing vowel phonemes is a less exact process. Differences between vowels

depend on very small movements of the tongue and mouth and you may find it a little difficult at first to tell exactly where a sound is coming from. Can you tell, for example, whether the vowel sound in *hat*, that is /æ/, comes from the front, middle, or back of your mouth? Probably not.

The only way in which you can get any sense of where a vowel is being produced in the mouth is to say the vowel phonemes in sequence. Try saying the vowel in *knee* (/iː/) and then the vowel in *boot* (/uː/). You should be able to feel the first sound coming from the front part of your mouth, and the second from the back. There is a difference also in the position of the tongue. See if you can work out what it is. Now try saying the vowels in *hat* (/æ/) and *arm* (/ɑː/). Again, you should be able to feel the second sound coming from further back in the mouth. What these exercises should demonstrate is that /iː/ and /æ/ are front vowels, whilst /uː/ and /ɑː/ are back ones. However, there are further distinctions which we can make, for although /iː/ and /æ/ are from the front of the mouth, they differ according to the height of the tongue. In the case of /iː/ the tongue is close to the roof of the mouth, whilst with /æ/ the tongue drops and the mouth opens.

So there are two parameters here which are important in distinguishing one vowel from another. The first has to do with the area of the mouth where the sound comes from, and the second concerns the height of the tongue: if it's near the roof of the mouth the sound is described as **close**, and if it's near the bottom it's **open**. Using these two parameters we can describe /iː/ as a 'close front vowel' and /æ/ as an 'open front vowel'. Similarly with /uː/ and /ɑː/. In the case of /uː/ the back of the tongue is close to the roof of the mouth, whilst with /ɑː/ it drops and the mouth opens. So /uː/ is a 'close back vowel', and /ɑː/ an 'open back vowel'. Say them all in sequence, first the front vowels, and then the back, until you are happy with these descriptions:

/iː/	close front vowel	kn**ee**
/æ/	open front vowel	h**a**t
/uː/	close back vowel	b**oo**t
/ɑː/	open back vowel	**ar**m

The rest of the vowels are distributed between these points in the mouth, some are closer than others and some more open, whilst some are more to the front and some more to the back. In other words, their positions are relative to each other. You will find this important when you come to study accents because a change in the position of one vowel affects the positions of those around it. Everyone's vowel positions differ slightly. The position of /uː/ in Cockney, for example, is different from that in conservative r.p. This doesn't matter to us at the moment, however, since we are thinking of phonemes rather than phones. The following vowels are all front ones:

/iː/   kn**ee**
/ɪ/   l**i**p
/ɛ/   b**e**d
/æ/   h**a**t

Their positions are shown in Figure 3.3. This is a diagrammatic representation of the inside of your mouth. You're probably thinking that it doesn't look much like your mouth, but it's not meant to be a realistic picture. It's a diagram of the vocal area and shows the single vowels of received pronunciation in relation to each other. As you can see, it resembles a grid pattern with horizontal lines intersecting the vertical ones with some phonemes nearer to these intersections than others. The best way of thinking about these intersections is as a way of mapping vowel sounds. We need such a map because of the difficulty of giving a precise description of their location. The intersections serve as reference points within the mouth from which vowel sounds could come. Using this diagram try saying the front vowels slowly, in sequence. You should feel your tongue dropping and the sounds moving back slightly.

Now try saying the following vowels, which are all back ones, in sequence:

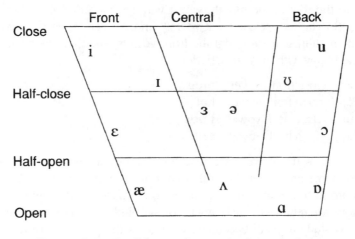

FIGURE 3.3   English vowels – received pronunciation

/ɑː/   **ar**m
/ɒ/   b**o**x
/ɔː/   s**aw**
/ʊ/   g**oo**d
/uː/   b**oo**t

As you say them you should feel each successive sound coming from slightly higher as your mouth closes and the back of your tongue rises. Follow them in the diagram (Figure 3.3).

The remaining monophthongs, /ʌ/, /ɜː/, and /ə/, are all central ones. This is a rather grey area in speech production and it takes some practice to sense accurately where these vowels are coming from. This is partly because it's a feature of colloquial English to centralise vowels, thus the frequency of schwa in ordinary speech. So it may initially seem as though all vowels are coming from this 'Bermuda triangle'. However, if you say a front vowel – /æ/ in *hat* – followed by the central vowel /ʌ/ in *cup* followed by a back vowel – /uː/ in *boot* – it is possible to sense small movements backwards. And repeating the sequence /ʌ/ – /ɜː/ should demonstrate the small difference in height which distinguishes these two phonemes:

/ʌ/   c**u**p
/ɜː/   f**ir**m
/ə/   **a**bout

There is a third parameter which is important with vowel phonemes, apart from the area of the mouth and the height of the tongue, and that is the shape of the lips. Say the back vowels over again and observe what happens to your lips. You should feel them gradually rounding, until with /uː/ they are completely round. If you say the front vowels over, however, you will notice that the lips are spread rather than rounded. All vowel phonemes are described in terms of this shape: they are either **spread** or **rounded**. You should also notice that some are more spread than others, and that there are degrees of rounding, but despite these individual variations, they are conventionally put into one category or another.

Summary/monophthongs
Putting together the information we have gathered from place of articulation, and taking it as understood that all vowel phonemes are voiced, we could describe the monophthongs of English in the following way. Check the descriptions with the diagram (Figure 3.3).

/iː/	close front spread	knee
/ɪ/	lowered and centralised close front spread	lip
/ɛ/	mid-front spread	bed
/æ/	open front spread	hat
/uː/	close back rounded	boot
/ʊ/	lowered and centralised close back rounded	good
/ɔː/	mid-back rounded	saw
/ɒ/	open back rounded	box
/ɑː/	open back spread	arm
/ʌ/	open central spread	cup
/ɜː/	mid-central spread (stressed vowel)	firm
/ə/	mid-central spread (unstressed)	about

(ii) *Diphthongs*

So far we have been considering what are called the 'pure' vowels of English, that is, those vowels in which the mouth takes up a single position. In the case of diphthongs, however, the configuration of the mouth changes in the course of articulation. Fortunately we do not need to worry too much about describing them because their phonemic quality, that is, their contrastiveness, lies in the direction of the glide which takes place, rather than in the creation of new positions or kinds of articulation. In other words, they move from one pure vowel to another. There are three diphthongs which glide towards /ɪ/. They are:

/eɪ/	face
/aɪ/	knife
/ɔɪ/	boy

There are two which glide towards /ʊ/. They are:

/əʊ/	nose
/aʊ/	mouth

The remaining three glide towards /ə/. They are:

/ɪə/	dear
/ɛə/	hair
/ʊə/	cure

Say them individually one after another and their diphthongal nature should be evident. As I said earlier, you may not have all of these diphthongs in your accent. Or it maybe that the direction of the glide is a little different in some instances. Diphthongs do have a tendency to shift round in the mouth. Where this is so it is usually the starting point of the diphthong rather than its destination which is different. If you watch Australian soaps you may have noticed that young speakers have a distinctive way of saying the diphthong in *no*. Anthony Burgess (1993, p. 68) suggests that it is probably /ʌʊ/ rather than /əʊ/. Occasionally, diphthongs may get even longer and develop into triphthongs, which are glides between three vowel positions. An example of this is the vowel sound in *fire*.

3.6   Sounds in connected speech

Up to now we have been looking at words in isolation from each other and I have been encouraging you to test for phonemes by pronouncing words in their citational form. But of course this is not really how we encounter words in normal speech. All sorts of things happen to phonemes in connected speech because we are accustomed to taking short-cuts. The nature and degree of short-cutting depend on how well we know the other person, how good their own English is, and the context in which we are speaking to them. We are sometimes told that people who leave out sounds or run them together are speaking sloppily, but in fact only advanced speakers can do this confidently. They can do so and still be understood because there is considerable redundancy in speech. The art is in knowing just how far to short-cut, and in being able to adjust the manner of our speech accordingly. All of us exist within speech communities which are very diverse in the demands they make on our communicative abilities. There is very little point in establishing one mode of articulation as the 'correct' one and then trying to enforce it by social and educational pressure. It's a bit like teaching everyone to drive at the same speed, or follow the same route. Language is a way of expressing our individuality and this means we must be free to make linguistic choices. More important than learning one mode of pronunciation is acquiring the ability to **style-shift**. Style-shifting is the ability to alter the **register** of our speech, that is the level of formality and informality, according to the social and situational demands of the speech context. Clearly, we do a lot of this quite naturally without having to think about it. If, for example, we are speaking to someone whose knowledge of English is limited, we automatically slow down our delivery and enunciate each phoneme carefully and distinctly. Speaking to a close friend, however, we can economise on this effort, knowing that we shall still be understood.

One of the useful exercises you can undertake is to listen to the way in which people around you talk, paying attention not to the content, but to their speech delivery. Most people belong to at least three speech communities: home and family; friends and peers; strangers and outsiders. You will find considerable variation in the articulation of an individual across these communities. In addition to these social contexts, however, there are also situational constraints on speech. We are constantly altering the pace at which we speak, depending on whether we are having a heated argument or chatting amiably over the garden fence. A wider consideration of all these factors would involve us in **discourse analysis** (see Chapter 6), since not only are we making pronunciation choices, but also lexical (vocabulary) and syntactic choices, but for the present we'll confine ourselves to pronunciation.

Most of the economising which takes place in connected speech occurs at word boundaries. As I commented in Chapter 2, the boundaries between words are more mental, than physical, realities. People unacquainted with English, for example, would not detect from our speech any boundary between words at all. Because of this, native speakers are quite happy to smooth the passage from one word to the next, knowing that we will hear with our grammatical ears. This is one of the reasons why we often think we are hearing and pronouncing words in their citational form when in fact we are not. Here are some of the principal ways in which we characteristically economise in pronunciation. [Note that in order to transcribe these processes we need to use phonetic script.]

Elision: this involves the omission of a phoneme. If you say the following phrases fairly quickly (imagining that you are saying them as part of a sentence), you will find that /t/ disappears at the end of the first word:

> *West Germany* [wɛs dʒɜːməniː]
> *last year*   [lɑːs jɪə]
> 'I went to West Germany last year.'

Try also: *bend back*: *changed colour*: *hold tight*.

Assimilation: this involves a phoneme moving to the place of articulation of the following phoneme. This happens because when we are preparing to articulate a phoneme, we are already thinking of the one which will follow it. Try the following phrases and observe what happens at the word boundaries when you say them rapidly:

> *that cup*   [ðæk kʰʌp] velar assimilation
> *black pen* [blæp pʰɛn] labial assimilation
> *this year* [ðɪʃ jɪə] palatal assimilation

Try also: *ten pence*: *ten girls*.

Sometimes elision and assimilation both occur. In the phrase *last year*, for example, once the /t/ has been elided, /s/ can move to the place of articulation of /j/, that is, the hard palate, and become /ʃ/ – [lɑːʃ jɪə]. And in the case of *won't go* we first of all have assimilation, which produces [wəʊŋk ɡəʊ], and then elision [wəʊŋ ɡəʊ].

Reduction: this involves the substitution of a weaker vowel, usually schwa, /ə/, but sometimes /ɪ/ or /ʊ/, for a stronger one. Many mono-syllabic words in connected speech lose the stress which they have in citational form, and the vowel is consequently reduced to a colourless *uh*. This frequently happens with what are sometimes referred to as the small 'function' words of English, for example, *to, the, and, for* and so on. The following sentence, *I went for a walk*, with the words pronounced in their citational form would be /aɪ wɛnt fɔː æ wɔːk/. But its form in running speech would probably be [aɪ wɛn fər ə wɔːk]. Vowel reduction is a com-mon occurrence in polysyllabic words also. All such words have one pri-mary stressed syllable in which the vowel phoneme is usually strong. But the other syllables, because they are more weakly stressed, are com-monly subject to vowel reduction. In *banana*, for instance, there are three syllables, *ba-na-na*, but only the middle, stressed one, has a strong vowel, the other two both have schwa. When we abbreviate words in very casual speech it's usually the unstressed bits which are left off – *brill* (brilliant), *cos* (because), *mum* (mummy). And indeed, when young children are learning words it's the stressed bits they latch on to – *nana*, not *banana*.

Liaison: this involves the insertion of a sound in connected speech which is normally absent in citational form. Say the following phrases and see if you can determine what is happening at the word boundaries:

	it
see	*Una*
	at
	over
	it
do	*Una*
	at
	over

You may have noticed that there is a tendency in the first set to insert /j/ between /iː/ and a following vowel ([siːj uːnə]), and in the second set, /w/ between /uː/ and a following vowel ([duːw uːn ə]). As we noted earlier, these consonants are sometimes referred to as semi-vowels, and they are clearly related in terms of both place and manner of articulation to the vowels /iː/ and /uː/. Indeed, <w> is called 'double u'. They serve as glides to smooth the passage from one vowel to another at word boundaries.

The other sound which is often inserted at word boundaries is /r/. Words like <father>, <here>, <far> have an <r> in their orthography, but not in their pronunciation. This is the result of the loss of this sound following a vowel – a phenomenon discussed earlier. However, when they form part of a phrase in which the succeeding word begins with a vowel, /r/ reappears, for example:

father and son	[fɑːðər ən sʌn]
here and now	[hɪər ən nɑʊ]
far and away	[fɑːr ən əweɪ]

Sometimes /r/ even appears where it is not present in the orthography, for example, <India and Pakistan> – [ɪndɪər ən pʰækɪstɑːn]. Perhaps you can see why; the clue is in the diphthong at the end of *India*.

3.7   Final summary

We have been concerned in this chapter to look at the way in which a linguistic description of speech could be arrived at. Beginning with the nature of sound, and the special relationship it has to us, we have explored its use in the medium of speech. We have seen that in order to understand the structure of spoken language we have had to develop a deeper understanding of the relationship between sound and meaning than is possible simply by reference to the alphabet. This has entailed developing a new alphabet founded on the principal of contrastiveness and the establishing of minimal pairs. Such an alphabet would allow for the fine distinctions which have to be made between sounds as concepts (phonemes) and as substance (phones/allophones). We have seen that the features on which the contrastiveness of phonemes rely are the product of the physiology of speech production. And finally, this chapter has looked at some of the changes in the pronunciation of words which occur in connected speech.

Having laid the basis of the sound structure of language we have only just begun to unlock the mysteries of spoken language. We have a tool now which will allow us to explore the nature and diversity of accents and how changes occur in pronunciation. This will take us in the direction of sociolinguistics. And we can also look more closely at intonation and speech patterns. This will take us towards discourse analysis and stylistics. We shall touch on these areas in Chapter 6, and you can if you wish, jump ahead and look at the relevant sections there, otherwise it's time to move from phonology to the next linguistic level, syntax.

Further reading

Ashby, P. (1995) *Speech Sounds* (London: Routledge).
Carr, P. (1993) *Phonology* (Basingstoke: Palgrave Macmillan).
Geigerich, H. (1992) *English Phonology: An Introduction* (Cambridge: Cambridge University Press).
Hawkins, P. (1992) *Introducing Phonology* (London: Routledge).
Katamba, F. (1988) *An Introduction to Phonology* (London: Longman).
Kreidler, C. W. (1989) *The Pronunciation of English: A Coursebook in Phonology* (Oxford: Blackwell).
Lass, R. (1984) *Phonology: An Introduction to Basic Concepts* (Cambridge: Cambridge University Press).
Ong, W. (1982) *Orality and Literacy* (London: Methuen).
Trask, R. L. (1995) *Dictionary of Phonetics and Phonology* (London: Routledge).

Notes

1. I am indebted to the second chapter of Walter Ong's *Orality and Literacy* for some of the following argument.
2. Throughout this chapter I have used angle brackets when specifically referring to the written form of a word, and italics when referring to its pronunciation form.

4 Studying Syntax

4.1   Introduction: beginning syntax

Syntax is one of those words which can usually be relied on to send a shudder down the spine of many a prospective student. The word itself conjures up images of Latin grammars with their fearful talk of parsing, conjugations, and declensions; all very technical and rather dry. And even though modern linguistics has left much of that behind, it's still the case, as the linguist Steven Pinker points out, that a fair amount of scholarly writing is impenetrable to the ordinary reader, as this extract illustrates:

> To summarise, we have been led to the following conclusions, on the assumption that the trace of a zero-level category must be properly governed. 1. VP is α-marked by I. 2. Only lexical categories are L-markers, so that VP is not L-marked by I. 3. α-government is restricted to sisterhood without the qualification (35). 4. Only the terminus of an X°-chain can αmark or Case mark. 5. Head-to-head movement forms an A-chain. 6. SPEC-head agreement and chains involve the same indexing. 7. Chain coindexing holds of the links of an extended chain. 8.. There is no accidental coindexing of I. 9. I–V coindexing is a form of head-to-head agreement; if it is restricted to aspectual verbs, then base-generated structures of the form (174) count as adjunction structures. 10. Possibly, a verb does not properly govern its α–marked complement.   (Pinker, 1995, p. 104)

This looks like the stuff of nightmares. Surely it has to be easier than this? Well, yes and no. Syntax is an area of extraordinary richness and complexity. If you stop to think of the enormous quantity of new language which we are producing every day, the new sentences or utterances which have never before been written or spoken, it's not surprising that trying to map this territory and establish some ground rules is a large undertaking. And, like most territories, it has its mountainous regions for intrepid explorers and its more accessible slopes for novices or day trippers. The extract above is taken from Noam Chomsky, arguably the boldest linguistic explorer of modern times, and it would be nothing short of a miracle if we could keep up with him without some pretty serious linguistic press-ups.

But we don't need to try, because, as I suggested in Chapter 1, more important than attempting to digest whole wedges of information or critical theory, is developing the right mental attitude to the subject. We need to become explorers ourselves, and in doing so it's worth bearing in mind that even the humblest investigator can spot things which more refined approaches sometimes overlook. No book on language, however comprehensive, will provide you with an infallible account of syntax. They will all differ to some extent, both in what they choose to talk about, and the way they choose to say it. In some cases the differences will be purely local ones, with writers taking a different view about individual aspects of syntax, whilst in others, they will be methodological and result in quite distinct descriptive and explanatory frameworks. So the first point to be clear about is that the final authority for all matters syntactical is us. There is no manual of syntax. Which isn't to say, however, that there isn't a broad measure of agreement among linguists about how language is structured at this level. Indeed, one of the ways in which linguistics has matured as a subject has been in the emergence of just such a consensus. None the less, to borrow a cliché from party politics, linguistics is a 'broad church', and nowhere broader than in the domain of syntax. A useful question to ask yourself when confronted with some syntactic account is 'Does this make sense of the way I use language?' If the answer is 'no', then the next question is 'What would make it so?' The answer to that might be fairly difficult, and not immediately forthcoming, but in pursuing it you will be thinking linguistically.

But before we go any further, let's establish what syntax is. When we looked at phonology in the last chapter, we saw that it was concerned with the way in which we structure sound into meaningful sequences to make words. Syntax is concerned with a similar kind of structuring, but at a different level, or layer, of language. Here, we are examining the way words are arranged in speech or writing to make well-formed **strings**: a 'string' is the term which linguists use for sequences of words such as phrases, clauses, and sentences. You may find that some books use the terms 'syntax' and 'grammar' interchangeably, and indeed older approaches to language did not distinguish between the two. Nowadays, however, it's more usual, particularly in American texbooks, for grammar to have a wider application. For linguists like Chomsky, 'grammar' refers not only to the rules of syntax, but also to those underlying the sound structure and semantics of the language. It is in this wider sense that I shall use the term.

The second thing to get clear is that studying syntax does not mean learning it. And here it's possible for me to give a positive answer to the question I posed earlier: 'Surely it has to be easier than this?' Because the plain fact is that you know all you need to know about syntax already without realising it. The classical philosopher Socrates taught that before we were born we knew everything, but that the process of birth involved forgetting it all. As a consequence, knowledge, for Socrates, is simply recollection: learning is remembering. I've always found this a very heartening view of knowledge, partly because it puts it within the reach of everyone, and partly because it accounts for the pleasure which comes from genuine learning as opposed to the indifference which accompanies the mere acquisition of facts. Learning is rediscovering ourselves. Now I've no wish to urge a supernatural view of language on you, but, stripped of its otherworldly cloak, Socrates' view is not so daft. A great deal of our knowledge about language is unconscious. There is a good deal of evidence now to suggest that we are programmed in some way from birth to learn language. In other words, that part of our human inheritance includes some linguistic knowledge. Just how much, and of what kind, is still very much at the cutting edge of linguistic debate. Linguists refer to it as **universal grammar**, the exploration and mapping of which arouses the same heady enthusiasm as nineteenth-century explorers felt in tracing the source of the Nile. It has become the Holy Grail of linguistic enquiry, the philosopher's stone which can transmute base metal to gold, or in our case, the world into language.

But what this means, from our perspective, is that the starting point for our enquiries is ourselves as native speakers of English. I urged you in Chapter 1 to regard yourselves as a linguistic resource, and nowhere is this more important than in the study of syntax. People beginning linguistics commonly underestimate or undervalue what they know. They may say they can't tell whether a word is an adverb or an adjective, or that they don't know what a determiner is, but in fact all they're unsure about is the classificatory label. It's the terminology which is the problem. When it comes to constructing sentences, however, native speakers of English invariably judge word classes correctly. Take a look at the sentences below, which each need a single word to complete them, and you will see what I mean. Have a go at listing the words which could appear in the gaps:

Give me_____book
I love your_____
She_____the ball
He played very_____
She seemed_____

Commentary

If you did this small task you probably found it fairly straightforward, which is just as it should be. Here are just a few possible answers:

the	money	kissed
Give me *a* book	I love your **smile**	She **threw** the ball
my	**attitude**	**kicked**
well		*clever*
He playcd very **badly**	She seemed *nice*	
correctly		*sad*

Performing this task correctly involved using your knowledge of word classes. Only a certain type of word can be put into the slot *Give me____book*. The fact that linguists call it the **determiner** class isn't important. Similarly with the other sentences: only a word functioning as a noun can occur in *I love your____*; as a verb in *She____the ball*; as an adverb in *He played very____*; and as an adjective in *She seemed____*. In other words, whilst you may not feel secure about applying the *terminology* of word classes, you understand the concept effortlessly. In fact without such knowledge, constructing a well-formed sentence would be an enormous labour. We should have to learn each individual permutation of words off by heart. Knowing the principle of word classes, however, allows us to economise on all this effort, and also to produce entirely new sentences. Language operates its own filing system so that when we get to the blank slot in *I love your____*, instead of having to search through every word in its memory bank, the brain can simply access the appropriate file and all the nouns will become instantly available. And like most filing systems, language allows for cross-indexing, so that some words, like *round*, for instance, as we saw in the previous chapter, can pop up in more than one file. Language also allows some degree of flexibility and innovation in word filing. Some varieties of English, for example, cross-index adjectives like *clever* and *bad* as adverbs, allowing us to say *he played very bad/clever* (as opposed to *badly* or *cleverly*). Cross-indexing also explains the colloquial use of *well* in southern English, as in *it's well good*. In this case, *well*, in addition to being filed with words such as *nicely* and *cleverly*, has also been filed with words like *very*, *quite*, and *almost*:

cleverly	**cleverly*
nicely	**nicely*
He played **well**	He was **well** good
*quite	*quite*
*very	*very*
*almost	*almost*

* = ill-formed

Examples like *well good* are inevitably considered acceptable, or unacceptable, according to the prevailing social taste, and the context in which they are used, but they are perfectly well-formed. And finally, there is the mischievous cross-indexing of creative writers, as in the e. e. cummings example in Chapter 1 – 'anyone lived in a pretty how town' – where the word *how* initially seems to have been misfiled, but then seems to be very appropriate. Changing the file status of a word, or **conversion**, is one of the frequent ways in which language allows us to exercise our creativity.

We have discovered a number of things from this exercise: firstly, that our ability to generate well-formed word strings, that is, our syntactic understanding, rests, in part, on our knowledge of word types, or classes; and secondly, that this knowledge is largely unconscious of, and separate from, any ability we may or may not have to articulate it. It's as if we knew the rules of playing chess without being able to say what they were. So the first thing I suggest you do, if you are beginning with syntax, is to review how much you already know. It's a good idea to make a list of some of the things you are able to perform, no matter how simple or straightforward they may seem. Just as we did in Chapters 2 and 3, we need to defamiliarise the material we are considering. Some of the most basic structures in the language involve considerable syntactic under-standing. We tend to take this knowledge for granted simply because the syntactic operations have become so automatic. Here are just a few of the things we can do without thinking:

   (i)   form statements: *he is bathing the baby*
  (ii)   form questions: *is he bathing the baby?*
 (iii)   form negatives of statements: *he isn't bathing the baby*
 (iv)   form negatives of questions: *isn't he bathing the baby?*
  (v)   form the past tense: *he was bathing the baby*
 (vi)   form the passive voice: *the baby was bathed by him*

(plus the negative and question forms of the past tense and passive)

I suggest that in making your list you concentrate on one sentence, as I have done, and just see how many ways you can manipulate it. Again, the fact that you may not have the terminology at this stage to label the process doesn't matter. What you are doing is bringing some of your knowledge to the surface, so that it can be examined more closely. Having done this, you can then select a particular operation for closer examination, and ask yourself what exactly is going on. For example, how do we form questions? Let's spend a few minutes on this and see what we can observe. In the example I have given – *is he bathing the baby*? – the question is made by inverting the first two words of the statement form. Is this always so we ask ourselves? Clearly not, because if we change the form of the statement slightly, to *he baths the baby*, the question form is not *baths he the baby*? but either *is he bathing the baby*? or *does he bath the baby*? We know, intuitively, that to form a question of this type (they are called 'yes/no' questions) we need a certain sort of word present in the structure to invert with *he*. If it's not there, we have to put one in. You can test this out by making up other sentences and putting them into the interrogative (question) form. It's at this point, having observed a phenomenon, that you need a descriptive vocabulary to capture it. To acquire this it's necessary to have a good reference guide, such as David Crystal's *Rediscover Grammar* (1988), by your side. Or, if you feel more ambitious, Quirk and Greenbaum's *A Student's Grammar of the English Language* (1990). Both of these are descriptive grammars, and will help fill in any gaps you discover in your grammatical knowledge, which is the best way I suggest you use books of this sort rather than attempt to read them from cover to cover. In this instance they will tell you that words which perform the function we have been discussing, like *is* and *does* in the examples above, are called **auxiliary** verbs (colloquially known as 'helping' verbs), as opposed to main, or **lexical**, verbs (the main verb in the sentences above is *to bath*). So we have established a rule for ourselves that 'yes/no' questions require the presence of an auxiliary verb. And then we can go on to ask if it's always the item immediately in front of the auxiliary verb which undergoes inversion. As before, the answer is clearly 'no', because even if we insert a few words in between, the process still picks out the salient one:

> *he I think I am right in saying is bathing the baby*
> **is saying bathing the baby*?
> *is he bathing the baby*?

Again, we intuitively know which word to invert with the auxiliary verb. The fact that it's called the **subject** need not worry us at this stage. The only way to explain this phenomenon is to suppose the existence of a hidden structure of relationships within each sentence. It's not overtly manifest in the words. That is, you couldn't look at any of these sentences on the page and mechanically predict how to form a question from any of them. Only by knowing the code which is being obeyed could you determine that.

This is only the beginning of what we can learn about auxiliary verbs. If you look again at the sentences, you will see that they are necessary to form negatives. The negative particle *n't* attaches to them, not the main verb. If we have any statement which we want to negate with the simple word *not*, we must ensure there is an auxiliary verb there for it to hook on to. Try it out and you'll see. And you might also notice that when sentences like *he is bathing the baby* are put into the past tense, it is the auxiliary verb which changes form to indicate this – *he was bathing the baby*. They are obviously enormously powerful, syntactically. In fact, modern linguistics sees them as at the heart of sentence structure precisely because they are vital to so many operations which we perform. Ironically, despite their importance syntactically, they are the sort of words which we leave out if we're sending a telegram: *George not having good time*, we would say, rather than *George is not having a good time*. Auxiliary verbs belong to what are termed 'function' words. These include words like *and*, *but*, *to*, *the*, *of*, and many more. To use Steven Pinker's description, they are 'bits of crystallized grammar' (1995, p. 118). They are there to provide the scaffolding for the sentence. When we send telegrams we assume that sufficient scaffolding is in the mind of the receiver to allow him/her to reconstruct the full text. But I won't go on any more about auxiliary verbs. The general point I want to impress on you, is that if you pursue any of these items of knowledge, or perhaps we should now say, grammatical competence, even a little way, you will find yourself on the first step of linguistic enquiry. As I pointed out in Chapter 1, modern linguistics embodies Chomsky's practice of 'observation', 'description', and 'explanation'. Linguists observe a pattern of behaviour in language, describe it, and then seek to find an explanatory rule. The assumption is that the various units of syntax – phrases, clauses, and sentences – are produced from a blueprint in the brain. The passage quoted at the beginning of this chapter, for all its daunting mathematical appearance, is attempting to establish some of the parameters of that blueprint.

'Alright,' you may say, 'I have some idea of what syntax is about, but I still don't know what the purpose of studying it is. Why should I bother, particularly if I know it already?' This is the question most frequently asked by students and, unfortunately, the answer which most teachers give is the equivalent of saying 'because it's there'. It's a serious question, however, and deserves fuller consideration. Life, after all, is not so very long that we can feel comfortable about spending large amounts of time wondering how questions are formed and what the nature of word classes is. There are those who enjoy puzzles for their own sake and who, if asked the question 'How can we explain the behaviour of auxiliary verbs?' might worry away at it happily for hours. And indeed, there is a problem-solving element in linguistics which it's important to keep sight of. But most of us expect something more, and we are right to do so. Some may be seeking greater security in their own use of language, perhaps wishing to speak and write in a more socially approved manner in order to get a better job, or enter a different social circle. And although this is not really a linguistic concern, nevertheless, there is a social reality which we have to take account of. Whether we like it or not, 'bettering' oneself through language is likely to be a continuing human endeavour. But, for reasons which we have already encountered, people studying syntax with this in mind will be largely dissatisfied with the approach of modern linguistics. There are plenty of 'prescriptive' accounts of syntax available which aim to lay down the rules for a socially acceptable grammar, but, as proper linguistic explorers we cannot settle for mere 'acceptability'. Our sights are set on 'well-formedness', on grammatical competence, the very summit itself, of which syntax is, arguably, the central peak. What is it then that we expect to learn by avoiding the lower slopes and going for the top? In answer to this I want to suggest that there are, broadly, two kinds of knowledge which syntacticians pursue, and which in turn are responsible for two different but related accounts of syntax. I term these 'formalist' and 'functional'.

4.2 Formalist approaches to syntax

You will notice, in your study of linguistics, that many writers on the subject use imagery drawn from computing, indeed I have myself. Talk of networks, information modules, processing, accessing, filing, data retrieval, and storage, is not uncommon. The brain is visualised as an enormously complex computer with language as one of its system folders. Viewed within this context, the study of language is concerned with trying to understand the program which runs the system. Linguists working in this tradition are ultimately pursuing the cognitive, or thought, processes of the human mind as they are present in language. Their final destination is the mind, and the nature of knowledge itself. The principal figure here is Noam Chomsky. 'Chomskyan' has become an epithet attached to a plethora of linguistic approaches which see language as a mental phenomenon. For Chomsky himself, the prospect that language might hold the key to how the mind works is an attractive lure. Not all linguists are similarly inspired, however, and by referring to it as a tradition I do not mean that all think alike, but, none the less, it is true to say that a common way of analysing language has arisen which has achieved considerable currency throughout the world. And whether one is concerned simply with observing and describing linguistic phenomena, or with scaling the heights of theoretical explanation, the formal structures of analysis which have evolved from viewing language in this way are enormously powerful.

One of the principal problems, however, which linguists like Chomsky have in trying to explain linguistic knowledge is that it is not open to direct inspection: it is locked within our heads. All we have is the evidence of it in particular acts of communication by speakers. Inevitably, then, linguistics has to work backwards from individual word strings to the hidden operational code. It's this code which enshrines the competence of native speakers of a language. In essence it's an abstraction. And here we encounter a second problem. For the actual performance of a language, the way in which it is realised in spoken or written form, may involve all kinds of things which the Chomskyan linguist is not concerned with, such as slips of the tongue, false starts, hesitations, and sentences broken off. So the first thing the linguist has to do is clean up, or sanitise, the language. S/he uses idealised examples of language use in which the competence of the speakers is not obscured by issues of performance. **Idealisation** involves three things: **regularisation, decontextualisation**, and **standardisation**. Let's go through them briefly. Regularisation is fairly straightforward, and involves disregarding all of the non-fluency features, such as slips of the tongue and so on, listed above. They are not part of the system and only muddy the waters. Decontextualisation entails studying word strings which exhibit complete grammatical structures and which can be understood on their own, rather than fragments and abbreviations. As I pointed out in Chapter 2, a great deal of communication is carried on by means of mutually understood short-cuts, for example:

A: *The team are playing tonight.*
B: *Where?*

B's question is context dependent in that it needs the previous sentence to make any sense. Moreover, it presupposes the existence of a full sentence, *Where are the team playing tonight?* of which it is an abbreviation. There is obviously a skill in abbreviating in this way, but for many linguists it is part of communicative, rather than grammatical, competence, and as such, something to be studied as an aspect of discourse analysis. Lastly, standardisation: this entails ignoring ways in which language can vary either through stylistic or dialectal (that is, regional) differences. In the following examples, the word *drinking* is replaced firstly by a slang term *boozing* and then by a dialect word from East Anglia, *codswobbling*, but as you can see, the structure of the string remains the same:

> *He spent the night* **drinking**
> *He spent the night* **boozing**   (stylistic variant)
> *He spent the night* **codswobbling**   (dialectal variant)

Tidying up language in this way has advantages and disadvantages for us as linguists. On the debit side it ignores a lot of evidence about language use which is, arguably, very interesting. Most of us do not communicate in this idealised way all the time. Real speech is rather messy: we abbreviate our utterances, repeat ourselves, hestitate, and slip from formal language to slang without noticing it. Interestingly, syntacticians are not the only people to tidy speech up; dramatists also do it, although with different priorities in mind. Speech in a play is rarely the same as in real life – you only have to compare a tape recording of actual speech with representations in play form to see that. For both linguists and dramatists, however, there is a purpose to this sanitising of the language. In the case of drama it's to elicit the dramatic patterns of language, sometimes obscured by the realities of speech, whereas in the case of linguistics, it's to uncover the underlying structure, or grammar, of language, equally obscured by the realities of speech.

You may have noticed that we are back to a distinction which I have been anxious to press on you from the beginning of this book as crucial to linguistics, that is, between **language as concept** and **language as substance**. We considered this in our study of sound, where we differentiated between phonemes and phones, and here it is, surfacing again, at the level of syntax. Linguists try to accommodate this distinction in various ways. For Chomsky, it's crucial to the divide between competence and performance, which I talked about in Chapter 2. As we noted there, the distinction isn't without its problems, since unravelling the two is not always straightforward, but in making it, however, Chomsky is following in a well-worn track first laid down by Ferdinand de Saussure, a Swiss linguist, at the turn of the century. Saussure distinguished between *langue* and *parole*: *langue* indicating the language system, the program, which we all have in our heads, and *parole*, the individual use of that system. You will find that linguists refer quite frequently to this pairing and interpret the distinction in different ways. Saussure isn't entirely clear himself about them in his book *Cours de linguistique générale* (1913 reprinted 1966), but we can't really blame him for that since the book was compiled posthumously from lecture notes taken by his students. With that in mind we have to be grateful that anything survived. *Langue* and *parole* are similar terms to competence and performance but wider in application. *Parole*, for example, covers more than the actual production of language, which is the usual limit of performance. It also has implications for the meaning of utterances. But it is time to ask ourselves how a formal account of syntactic features might help us understand the nature of language.

4.2.1 Developing a constituent grammar

Formal accounts of syntax are based on establishing the basic constituents, that is, categories, from which word strings are formed. Sentences, the highest units of syntactic analysis, are seen as hierarchies of interlocking smaller units, or constituents. At the bottom of the hierarchical ladder are words, the smallest constituents of all, so let's start there.

(i) *Word rank*

We'll take a fairly uncomplicated sentence, of the idealised kind, which linguists often use:

> *The cat devoured the tiny mouse*

At the simplest level, or rank, of analysis we can say that it consists of words arranged in a certain order. We are not free to put the words in any order we like; we can't, for example, say *cat the devoured tiny the mouse*. This would not be well-formed. However, we could change the individual words themselves for others and still have a grammatically well-formed string. Instead of *tiny* we could have a whole array of adjectives, for example, *small*, *large*, *tired*; instead of *devoured* an array of verbs, *ate*, *licked*, *swallowed*; and similarly for the other words. Remembering our earlier discussion, you will recall that it is here that the concept of word classes is important. From a formal point of view, the class of a word is determined not by its meaning, but by how it behaves in the language, for example, if a word can act as a noun, then it is a noun. As a consequence, we can form a large number of sentences simply by inserting words which can behave similarly into the slots of the string. In other words, the string is a frame for the generation of a host of other sentences. Could it be, then, that language is some vast engine for producing endless strings or combinations of words according to a pre-set pattern? There is some evidence to support this. Saussure argued that we could look at any string of words as having two axes: a horizontal one, along which words combine with other words, and a vertical one, along which they interchange with others. The first he called **syntagmatic**, and the second, **paradigmatic**.

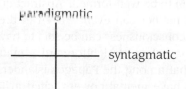

Using this diagram we can see that any word in a string is at the point of intersection of these two axes. This means that we can represent the underlying structure of the string above as follows:

determiner + noun + verb + determiner + adjective + noun

However, there are difficulties here. Clearly, this structure will fit a great number of sentences, from *the lion ate the beautiful antelope* to *my son kissed his kind grandmother*, but can we put any verb, noun, adjective, or determiner into their appropriate slots and still have well-formed sentences? Consider, for a moment, the following permutations and ask yourselves whether you would consider them well-formed. And if not, on what grounds:

(1) *The rabbit devoured the tiny mouse*
(2) *An orange devoured a tiny mouse*
(3) *My house liked the tiny mouse*
(4) *My sincerity liked the tiny mouse*
(5) *My birth liked the tiny mouse*
(6) *The cat lied the tiny mouse*

Commentary

These sentences all follow the structure of our original one, but some of them are demonstrably odd. Most people would probably accept the first one as alright since, although rabbits are herbivores, and don't eat mice, it's none the less possible to imagine a deviant rabbit which might. The second one, however, seems to violate all rules of common sense. Oranges can't eat, and therefore, how can this be well-formed? But wait a minute: just imagine someone saying to you '*in my dream last night an orange devoured a tiny mouse*'. Not very likely, perhaps, but in dreams all sorts of weird things happen, as they often do in children's stories, from which this sentence could equally come. And as for (3), it may seem daft, but there is nothing to stop me, if I wish, from endowing my house with feelings. People do this all the time with objects, such as cars and boats, and they are never locked up. No one, however, would surely consider (4) or (5) to be well-formed? Abstract qualities cannot be said to like things, and neither can events, even in dreams. Only objects with some degree of consciousness can be said to have the capacity for liking. But again, this is not so straightforward a matter. The linguist George Lakoff reports that among the Papagos islanders, events and properties are assumed to have mental powers (cited in Radford, 1988, p. 11). In other words, the concept of 'sincerity' or 'birth' being endowed with the power to like would not be inconceivable. These sentences might thus be perfectly normal to the Papagos islanders. There is an important point we should take notice of here: a sentence can be semantically odd and yet syntactically well-formed. But what of (6)? Unlike the previous sentences, the oddness of (6) has nothing to do with its meaning. It's true that most people would not accept the concept of cats lying, but it's always possible that there exists a society which does, and certainly in medieval England the concept would not have seemed so strange. No, the real oddness lies elsewhere. Alone of all these examples there is something wrong in its construction. We need the preposition *to* or *about* after *lied* since in English we don't simply *lie* someone. This is a syntactic, rather than a semantic, obligation and it relates individually to this verb.

Let's pause here for a while and consider what conclusions we can draw about the freedom we have to compose well-formed sentences. It seems as though we have, on the one hand, syntactic frames which allow us to combine and order words on the basis of their class. So there are syntactic rules here. On the other hand, however, the issue of which particular words can appear together depends on a variety of constraints. In the case of (2) and (3) there are considerations of individual disposition and imaginative context to be taken into account, whereas in (4) and (5) it is the social and cultural context which is important. But none of these sentences is syntactically ill-formed, however odd they may seem. Even in (4) and (5), we have nouns and verbs where they're supposed to be and the sequences are syntactically regular. In the case of (6), however, we have a sequence which is not permitted by the individual character of the verb *lied*, and as a consequence this sequence is ill-formed. All of this suggests that in composing well-formed strings we draw on at least two components. First, a syntactic component which informs us about the sequencing of items. This tells us for instance that a determiner is followed by a noun or that in a sentence consisting of two noun strings the verb will come between them. Second, a lexical component which lists all the words that we know together with details of their classifications and special restrictions about their use. It's here that we learn about the special requirements of *lie* or that *music* is a particular kind of noun which cannot occur with the determiner *a*, that is, we cannot say *a music*. To be well-formed a string has to match the appropriate words with the slots syntactically available. But, in addition, the lexical component informs us about the meanings of words and about which sequences make sense and are consequently acceptable. This semantic ingredient has access to the real world but is mediated by our culture. So, we carry in our heads syntactic rules of a very general and accommodating kind, and a dictionary, or **lexicon**, as linguists call it, which provides us with grammatical and semantic information about our personal vocabulary. This lexicon draws its information not only from the language itself, but also from the world about us. In other words, it's not a watertight compartment. Changes are taking place in individual entries all the time, allowing us to say things which were previously unsayable. It is here that a great deal of the creativity within language takes place. Using Saussure's distinction between *langue* and *parole*, we could say that this leakage of the system to the real world, in which meanings are generated, is that part of linguistic activity covered by *parole* – language at the level of individual use – as opposed to *langue*, the abstract system of relationships within which items fit.

(ii)   *Phrase rank*

So far we have been thinking of syntax as a process of combining words together drawn from various classes. But there is something missing from this account. In the discussion above, I referred more than once to the 'syntactic frame' within which words are placed in sentence strings, but you may have noticed that I glossed over saying very much about it. It is now time to examine it more closely. The first point to make is that it consists of more than words drawn from different classes. We don't form sentences by thinking of a determiner, then selecting a word which can syntactically follow it – an adjective, then perhaps a noun, followed by a verb – and so on. That would be rather like dressing ourselves by starting with our socks, then selecting shoes to match, and working our way up our bodies to the hat. No doubt some people do dress like that, but it's hardly guaranteed to produce the desired effect. Most of us select the central items we want to wear and then choose the other bits and pieces to fit in. Similarly with language – only here the central items are phrases. They are the next rung up the constituent ladder.

What evidence have we from our sample sentence of the existence of these central blocks?

The cat devoured the tiny mouse

We said above that although we are free to change individual words by substituting others of a similar class, we are not free to put them in any order we like, for example:

*Cat the the devoured mouse tiny

If we move *the* in the string *the cat*, we have to move both words not just one. In other words, they form a unit. And in the case of *the tiny mouse* we have to move all three words, making sure that we keep them in the same order. So, for example:

The tiny mouse devoured the cat

is perfectly well-formed whereas

*Tiny mouse the devoured cat the

isn't. In any sentence, certain words seem to be glued together, that is, they form units, or constituents, above the rank of word. If this is so, then we need to revise our account of how sentences are formed. Sentences are created not by putting words together, but phrases. Phrases are intermediate between the raw rank of vocabulary and the sophisticated rank of sentence. I suggested to you in the Introduction that the grammar of English was organic, in other words, similar to a living thing, in that fresh items of structure were being generated all the time. I'm reminding you of that now because I want you to think of a sentence, not as a mechanical assembly of words, but as a tree, the branches of which are phrases, and the leaves, words.

Branches, of course, come in different shapes and sizes; some are large straggling things, almost the size of a tree, and some extremely small and more like twigs. Similarly with phrases. In the case of the cat and the tiny mouse, the branches are fairly small, but they could be made bigger, and indeed, smaller. If, for example, we followed our sample sentence with another, we probably wouldn't repeat the phrases in exactly the same form, but we might have something like

The cat devoured the tiny mouse. **She** *ate* **it** *quickly*

In this case **She** substitutes not simply for *cat* but *the cat*, and similarly **it** replaces the entire phrase *the tiny mouse*, not just a part of it. There is an important point here which you might find a little strange at first: a phrase can consist of only one word. This is because, whilst it may only be a single word in the sentence you are using, it nevertheless has the potential to grow. We can see something of that potential if we return to our original phrase *the cat* and think of how it could be expanded, instead of contracted:

(1)   **The very large black cat** *devoured the tiny mouse*
(2)   **The cat which I bought yesterday** *devoured the tiny mouse*
(3)   **The cat owned by next door** *devoured the tiny mouse*
(4)   **The cat purring like mad** *devoured the tiny mouse*

In each case, if we rearranged the sentence, as below, the words in bold could all be moved as a single unit:

the very large black cat
the cat which I bought yesterday

The tiny mouse was devoured by   _____

the cat owned by next door
the cat purring like mad

And not only that, but if we continued any of (1)–(4), with the follow-on sentence:

   She *ate it quickly*

She would be substituting for all of the words in bold. So these are all phrases. They all pass the two basic tests for the existence of phrases, which we have been applying, and which we can now formally state:

(i) if a sequence of words can be moved as a group, they may form a phrase (the movement test); (ii) if a sequence of words can be replaced by a single word, they may form a phrase (the replacement test).   (Fabb, 1994, pp. 3–4)

To be considered a phrase a string needs to satisfy at least one of these requirements.

But 'wait a minute', you say, 'some of these phrases look more like sentences to me'. Indeed, but here we come to another important point: phrases can contain larger units within them, even sentences. It's a process which linguists call **embedding**. This is crucial to the way in which language works. It allows us to enrich what we are saying whilst still keeping the grammatical relationships clear. No native speaker of English, for example, would be in any doubt from the above sentences as to what did the devouring, and all of these phrases can be shortened to *the cat*. Using our tree metaphor, this is the main part of the branch from which the other bits are sprouting. It's not uncommon in nature to see branches with larger, subsidiary, ones growing out of them, and neither is it in language. And if you think about these phrases from an experiential perspective, all of the words apart from *cat*, which we can regard as the key word, are telling us something about it. The words which come before *cat* are said to **pre-modify** it. They tell us about its permanent features, that is, the fact that it's very large and black. Those which come after **post-modify** it. They tell us about its more temporary characteristics: the fact that someone owns it (at the moment), that I bought it yesterday, and that it is currently purring. If this isn't sufficiently clear, perhaps changing the metaphor might help. We could say that *cat* is at the centre of a constellation of words held in place by its gravitational pull. The words which pre-modify are more strongly bound to the head word than those which post-modify, and even in the case of the former there is a fixed order of precedence: we are not free to change it to *the black very large cat*, for example. Certain words seem more important in describing the cat than others and the language shows that importance by the degree of closeness it allows (see section 6.4.1 for further discussion). You might consider what would happen if we inserted the word *persian* into the phrase. In this case it would surely have to go closest of all – *the very large black persian cat* – since it serves to classify what kind of cat we are talking about. What I have called the 'gravitational pull' of this constellation of words, the force which holds them together, resides in the word *cat*, or more precisely, in its 'noun-ness'. All of these examples are in fact noun phrases, and as such they derive their particular structure from the character of the word which forms their centre.

I have spent some time on this, because grasping the principle of the phrase is crucial to understanding modern approaches to syntax, many of which adopt what is called a **phrase structure grammar**. But let's return to our original sentence and see what its structure looks like now. One way of doing this is to set it out in the form of a tree diagram, with branches and leaves (Figure 4.1). This diagram tells us that the sentence is made up of a noun phrase, plus a verb, plus a noun phrase. So far so good, but can we refine this structure any more? Remember that one of our tests for the existence of phrases was the replacement rule ('if a sequence of words can be replaced by a single word they may form a phrase'), and consider the following:

*The cat devoured the tiny mouse, and the dog **did** too*

What does the word **did** replace here? Clearly it's the whole sequence *devoured the tiny mouse*, since if we spelt out the fully idealised form of the text, it would read:

The cat devoured the tiny mouse and the dog devoured the tiny mouse too

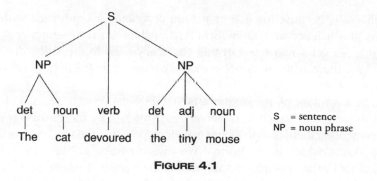

FIGURE 4.1

We have already said that *the tiny mouse* is a noun phrase, but it now looks as though this is embedded in a larger phrase of which the verb *devoured* is the key word. Based on this analysis we could revise our tree diagram to look like Figure 4.2.

This diagram tells us that the root of this sentence (S) has produced two large, forking branches, a noun phrase and a verb phrase, which have each produced in turn two more branches, leading, in the case of the noun phrase, to a determiner and a noun, and in the case of the verb phrase to another noun phrase and a verb. This second noun phrase has produced a determiner and an adjective plus a noun. Finally, each of the word level categories have taken words from the lexicon to fill their respective places. Notice that in describing the process in this way, I have begun from the root and have ended up with the words, or individual leaves, rather than the other way round, and that, in keeping with the organic imagery, I have used the language of generation. This is

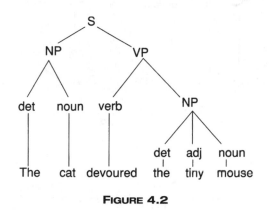

FIGURE 4.2

deliberate, because the grammar I am describing is concerned with the way in which certain grammatical relationships generate sentence structures.[1] To get a real sense of this you really need to invert the diagram and see the way the sentence grows like a tree from the bottom upwards (Figure 4.3).

The advantage of tree diagrams is that they enable us to see at a glance the hierarchical structure of sentences. This is why the normal way of representing them is as in Figure 4.2. Here, power is seen to flow from the top down, which is the normal way we envisage it. The tree is held together by the principle of **dominance**. Each point of intersection in it is called a **node**, and each node dominates those below it. S, for example, dominates all the items below it. But, because it is closer to the nodes NP and VP, it is said to 'immediately' dominate them. Similarly, VP dominates everything below it, but immediately dominates verb and NP, and so on. This enables us to give a formal description of relationships without relying on general categories like **subject** and **object**. In the sentence above, for example, *the cat* is conventionally referred to as the subject of the sentence, and *the tiny mouse* as the object. But, using our new system, we can say that, in English, the subject of a sentence is that NP immediately dominated by S, whilst the object is the NP immediately dominated by VP. Let's just recap for a moment before carrying on. I have been trying to impress on you, for the last few pages, the centrality of the 'phrase' within English sentence structure. All phrases have as their kernel a word drawn from one of the major classifications of English. The items which come before the kernel word pre-modify it, and those which come afterwards, post-modify it. So far we have only mentioned noun and verb

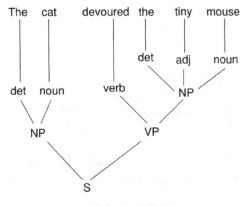

FIGURE 4.3

phrases, but there are also adjective, adverb, and preposition phrases, and we'll consider these next. The first general point to make, then, is that phrases are extensions, or projections, of what we can call the main lexical, or word, categories. And secondly, any sentence can be broken down into its phrasal components. The simplest sentence, such as the one above, consists of a noun phrase plus a verb phrase. More complex sentences can be created because of the principle of embedding which allows us to include phrases, and indeed sentences, within other phrases. And where we do have sentences which are so embedded, as in *the cat which I bought yesterday*, they also can be broken down into phrases.

It's time now to look at a few more phrases. Remembering our criteria for identifying them, consider the words in bold, below, and see if they qualify as phrases:

(5)   *The cat sniffed the tiny mouse* **very quickly**
(6)   *The cat sniffed the tiny mouse* **in the kitchen**
(7)   *The cat seemed* **angry with the tiny mouse**

Commentary

(5)   **very quickly**. This clearly conforms to the rules for phrase membership. It can be moved as a unit – **very quickly** *the cat sniffed the tiny mouse*; and it can also be replaced by a single word. If we say *The cat sniffed the tiny mouse very quickly and the dog sniffed the tiny mouse* **similarly**, then **similarly** substitutes for the complete phrase. Since the core word here is an adverb this qualifies as an adverb phrase. And together with *the tiny mouse* it also forms part of the verb phrase. We can test this by using the replacement test again in the following way: *The cat sniffed the tiny mouse very quickly, and the dog* **did** *too* where **did** substitutes for the entire string *sniffed the tiny mouse very quickly*. The structure of this sentence, then, is as in Figure 4.4.

(6)   **in the kitchen**. Here again, this also qualifies as a phrase. First, we can move it around as a unit – **In the kitchen** *the cat sniffed the tiny mouse*; and second, we can replace the whole string with the word **there** – *The cat sniffed the tiny mouse in the kitchen. She found it* **there**. Since *in* is a preposition this qualifies as a prepositional phrase. But we can break this phrase down even further. The string **the kitchen** also fulfils the criteria for phrase membership. It can be replaced by **there** – *The cat sniffed the tiny mouse in the kitchen. She found it in* **there**. And it can be separated as a unit from the preposition *in*. Consider the following exchange:

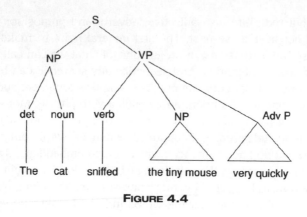

FIGURE 4.4

Q: *Which kitchen was cleaned?*
A: **The kitchen** *which the cat sniffed the tiny mouse in.*
(or: **The kitchen** *in which the cat sniffed the tiny mouse*)

Admittedly, neither are particularly elegant replies, but both are possible. The point is that in the case of (6) we have a noun phrase embedded within a prepositional phrase. This is a peculiarity of all prepositional phrases. Alone of all the phrase types their structure is invariably composite, as we can see in Figure 4.5. Like the adverb phrase, considered above, *in the kitchen* is also part of the larger verb phrase. We can see this if again we try the test used earlier – *the cat sniffed the tiny mouse in the kitchen, and the dog did too* – where *did* replaces everything from *sniffed* onwards.

But there's still something about (6) which we haven't quite captured. If you think about its meaning there are two possible interpretations. It could be saying that the sniffing was done in the kitchen (and that's the most normal interpretation) or it could be saying that the mouse which was sniffed

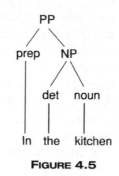

FIGURE 4.5

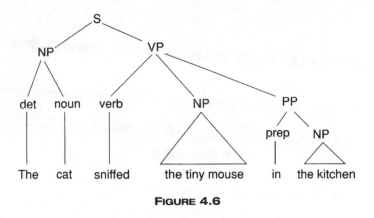

FIGURE 4.6

lived in the kitchen. In other words, there are two possible structures here. One of the advantages of tree diagrams is that they allow us to see at a glance what these differences are. Compare Figures 4.6 and 4.7.

We can see straightaway from these two diagrams where the source of the ambiguity lies. In Figure 4.6, where the sniffing is done in the kitchen, the prepositional phrase is immediately dominated by VP, whereas in Figure 4.7, where the mouse lives in the kitchen, it's immediately dominated by NP. The hierarchical arrangement of the phrases is different in each case and correlates with a distinct difference in meaning.

(7) *angry with the tiny mouse*. Like the other phrases this string also fulfils our basic criteria. It can be moved around as a unit – *angry with the tiny mouse was how the cat seemed*; and it can be replaced by a single word. If we say *the cat seemed angry with the tiny mouse and the dog*

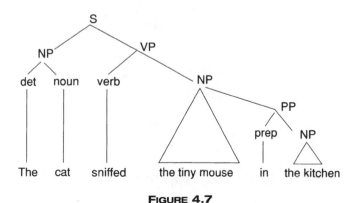

FIGURE 4.7

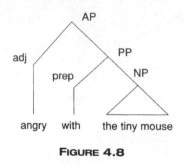

FIGURE 4.8

*seemed **so** too*, then *so* substitutes for the complete phrase. Here, however, the key word is an adjective, angry, the rest of the phrase is simply post-modifying it, that is, expanding on the cat's anger. So this is an adjectival phrase. But notice that it has embedded within it a prepositional phrase – **with the tiny mouse**. And prepositional phrases, as we know, contain a noun phrase. The structure of the phrase, then, is as shown in Figure 4.8.

But, as with the previous sentences, the process of embedding goes even further than this, because the adjectival phrase is also part of the larger verb phrase. This is evident if we use the substitution test: *The cat seemed angry with the tiny mouse and the dog **did** too* – where **did** stands for the entire string from *seemed* onwards. The structure of the sentence, then, would look like Figure 4.9.

You should by now have some idea of the nature of phrases as constituents of sentences, and of the value of representing the rela-

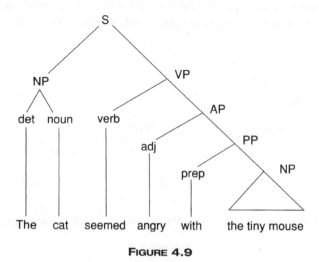

FIGURE 4.9

tionships between them in diagrammatic form. Symbolising structure helps us to observe regularities in the way in which word categories behave: that only nouns can occur with a determiner, for instance, and that prepositions characteristically link a noun phrase with another constituent. As we have already seen, these regularities are important indicators of word classifications. It can also help us to distinguish between sentences which have an identical form but different structures – as in sentence (6). All the phrase constituents of sentences have their own characteristics, acquired from the particular class of word which forms their head, and they can all be studied in terms of the items which can pre-modify or post-modify them. I don't propose that we should attempt that here, but one important principle which you will find it useful to bear in mind is that heads select the items which modify them. For example, if, in sentence (7), we changed the adjective *angry* to *interested*, we should have to alter the preposition following to *in* or *by*, since interested doesn't allow us to say *with*. And if we changed *seemed* to *sniffed* we should have to change the adjective phrase to some other kind of phrase since *sniffed* can't be followed by an adjective phrase. These restrictions are known as selection restrictions and, as we saw earlier, every native speaker of the language has information about them in his/her internal lexicon. They are of major significance in the case of verbs because of their degree of dom-inance within the sentence. To a large extent it is the selection restrictions of particular verbs which determine the character of sentences. I hope I have said enough for the moment to give you at least a flavour of phrase structure analysis. We shall in fact be returning to phrases in Chapter 6 ('Studying Linguistics Further') because this is not the end of the story as far as formal analysis is concerned. In recent years linguists have dissected the 'phrase' even further and considerably refined our understanding of the structure of this constituent. The development is known as **X bar theory**. If you wish to pursue it now, then turn to Chapter 6, otherwise we shall pass on to the next rank.

(iii) *Sentence/clause rank*

Sentences are the highest rung of syntactic analysis. It is perhaps surprising, then, that no one is completely sure what the definition of a sentence really is. You probably remember various definitions such as 'the utterance of a complete thought' or a 'grammatically complete sequence'. But there are numerous examples of sentences which are in no way complete. Like this one. The most useful description, in practical terms, would seem to be 'any sequence of words which is capable of standing alone'. By this criterion anything is capable of being a sentence given the appropriate context. Sentences are units of written, rather than spoken, English, and as such are really a stylistic convenience. But, as we have seen, there is clearly a level of organisation in English above the rank of phrase. How are we to approach this? It's here that we need to bear in mind the distinction made earlier between grammatical and communicative competence. Communicatively, we do all sorts of things to sentences: abbreviate them, leave bits out, and so on. But we couldn't do this unless we knew what was being shortened or elided. It is our grammatical competence which allows us to take such liberties. Formal syntacticians, then, are not concerned with 'real' sentences, that is, what occurs between full stops, because these could consist of anything we wish, but with what we have been calling 'idealised' sentences. These are considered to be the bedrock of our grammatical competence and it is from these that the rules of sentence construction can be elaborated.

You will find that some linguists use the term **clause** to describe the level of organisation above 'phrase' and reserve 'sentence' for the overarching construction. 'Clause' thus becomes the syntactic term to describe the grammatical arrangement of phrases, and 'sentence' the stylistic unit which we find between full stops. Sentences which consist of an incomplete clause – *Help!* – can be termed minor, as opposed to major ones – *Please can you help me?* – consisting of a complete clause. And sentences in which there is more than one clause because of embedding, or subordination of some kind, can be described as complex – *Please can you help me find my kitten?* Whilst those in which two clauses are coordinated can be described as compound – *Please can you help me and then I can go home?* This is very much the British way of doing things. Americans, on the other hand, find this messy and prefer not to use the term 'clause' at all. They find it easier to use 'sentence' for everything, and provided we continue to distinguish between different types of sentences, this serves reasonably well. When it comes to embedded clauses, for example, American linguists opt to call these S2 and S3 and so on (that is, 'sentence two' and 'sentence three'), reserving S1 for the overarching construction.

But whether we wish to use the term 'clause' or stick to 'sentence' the important point to remember is that we are concerned here with idealised, that is, complete sentences/clauses. And not only that, but we are also, for the moment, restricting ourselves to **kernel** sentences/clauses. The reason for this will become clear shortly. Kernel, here, refers to constructions which have not been altered in any way, for example, by being turned into questions, being made negative, or turned into the passive. In other words, with simple statements. Bearing this in mind, let's consider the idealised sentence we started out with and see what rules we can deduce.

The cat devoured the tiny mouse

As we have seen, this can be said to consist of a noun phrase plus a verb phrase. We could express that using a tree diagram, but we could also employ what are termed **rewrite rules**:

S → NP + VP

The arrow here indicates that whatever is on the left can be replaced by, or rewritten as, whatever is on the right. We can continue by giving rewrite rules for NP and VP:

NP → DET + N
VP → V + NP
NP → DET + ADJ + N

The final stage would be to indicate the words which could fill these respective word slots. However, we could economise on this sentence formula. As you see, there are two entries for NP. With a little bit of ingenuity we can amalgamate them in the following way:

NP → DET + (ADJ) + N

The brackets round ADJ indicate that it is optional. This gives us then:

S → NP + VP
NP → DET + (ADJ) + N
VP → V + NP

When we get to NP at the end of the rules we are recycled back to the entry above. Using these rules we could generate many sentences, but we could make them even more powerful with a few refinements. There are some noun phrases, for example, in which there is no determiner (*cats devoured the tiny mouse*). If we put brackets round the determiner we can indicate that it's optional as well as the adjective. And it's also possible, as we have seen, for the noun phrase to be replaced by a pronoun. Optionality can be indicated by using curly brackets – these show alternatives. NP now looks like this:

$$NP \rightarrow \begin{Bmatrix} (DET) + (ADJ) + N \\ PRO \end{Bmatrix}$$

What this tells us is that a NP can consist of just a noun, or a noun plus either a determiner or an adjective, or both; or, finally, simply a pronoun.

We have manipulated NP to make it more powerful but what about VP? Not all verb phrases consist of a verb plus a NP. Some just consist of a verb, for example, *the cat died*. Well, given our new bracketing tools we can easily extend the range of the VP rule by putting brackets around NP:

VP → V + (NP)

These rules are still not powerful enough, however, to allow us to generate sentences (5)–(7). For that we should need to add a bit more to the VP rule. But I think by now you have probably got the idea. You can see how it would be possible, by continually refining the rules – using the symbols at our disposal – to arrive at a complete set of rewrite rules for the generation of kernel sentences of English. This is all very well and good, you may say, for simple sentences (that is, those which consist of just a NP plus a VP – in British terminology, a single clause) but many sentences which we encounter contain other sentences/clauses within them. How can we incorporate them within our rules? Well, it's surprisingly easy. In the following sentence, for example, we have two sentences combined (the notation here follows the American principle):

(*I know* [*he is a rogue*])
S1   S2

In this instance the second sentence *he is a rogue* is embedded within the overarching one *I know he is a rogue*. How can we describe this? The best way is to see S2 as part of the verb phrase of S1. And if we try the replacement test which we have been employing to test for verb phrases we can see that it passes:

*I know he is a rogue – and you **do** too* [i.e. *know he is a rogue*]

All we have to do then is make an adjustment to our rewrite rule to allow for this possibility within VP. Thus:

VP → V + (NP) + (S)

This now tells us that in addition to the other possibilities within VP the opportunity exists for us to embed another sentence. And the rules for the construction of that sentence are covered by our first entry: S → NP + VP. In a similar way the rules can be added to so as to accommodate other forms of sentence embedding. We haven't the space to embark on a complete breakdown of English sentences but the aim of rewrite rules is to provide a notation sufficient to describe the basic mental syntactic frame that allows us to generate well-formed strings. Perhaps you can see why, given the potential complexity of these rules, that the quotation from

Pinker at the beginning of the chapter is in the form it is. For what is being described here is the operational code underlying our basic competence. And I think you will agree from what we have managed to describe of it so far that it possesses more than a passing resemblance to a computer program.

Summary so far

We have seen that formal syntactic approaches are concerned with linguistic units as constituents, that is, words are constituents of phrases, and phrases are constituents of clauses/sentences. They attempt to trace the hierarchical nature of sentence organisation and describe the rules which enable us to form idealised, kernel sentences. These rules are founded on the basic character of English phrases, which in turn are extensions of the major word classes. In addition to this syntactic component, which exists in the mind of all native speakers of the language, we also possess a lexicon which contains all the words at our disposal together with information about their individual characteristics as well as the range of meanings of which they are capable. Well-formed strings are created by matching words with the positions available to them in the syntax. However, information in the lexicon, particularly semantic, varies according to our cultural and social background. It is the variable nature of this information which results in strings being considered acceptable or not acceptable in particular circumstances.

This, however, only takes us so far. For we produce many sentences which are not of the kernel kind. Up to now we have only been concerned with statements, but what about questions, or commands, or passive constructions, all of which involve some rearrangement of items. We might, for example, want to say *did the cat devour the tiny mouse?* or *was the tiny mouse devoured by the cat?* Neither of these sentences can really be described as NP + VP. Apart from anything else they start with a verb, not a noun, and in both cases the auxiliary verb is separated from the main, or lexical, verb. In other words, we need another set of rules in addition to the ones we have already elaborated, to account for the way in which we transform kernel sentences into the great variety of utterances that we are capable of producing. 'Transform' is the key word here because the rules which describe this ability are collectively known as **transformational grammar**. Phrase structure grammars characteristically have two sets of rules: one of the kind we have looked at in this chapter, and the other which we shall look at in Chapter 6 ('Studying Linguistics Further'). If you wish to, you can jump ahead and read that section now, otherwise it is time to turn to a different kind of syntactic grammar.

4.3 Functional approaches to syntax

So far we have been looking at approaches to syntax which have not really been concerned with the meaning and use of utterances. Language is viewed as a mental phenomenon rather than something we employ every day to make ourselves understood, or to signal some intention to someone. I have tried to suggest that there is a considerable linguistic advantage in exposing the skeletal structure of language. But it is achieved at a certain price. Functional approaches allow us to put some flesh on the skeleton, to see language as a social and human phenomenon rather than simply a mental reality. Functional syntacticians see language as a sophisticated tool which enables us to understand ourselves and our environment, and to communicate with others more effectively. The purpose of studying language, from this perspective, is not to understand the human mind, but to understand ourselves in relation to the world, in other words, as social beings.

You will find that most syntactic accounts of language, even those which are principally formal, will acknowledge some degree of functionalism, and may well use functional categories. The most basic involve using terms such as **subject**, **predicator**, **object**, **complement**, **adjunct/adverbial**, sometimes referred to as SPOCA, for short. We can think of these as grammatical functions or roles which constituents fulfil in sentences. From this approach a simple sentence is said to consist of a **subject** and a **predicate**. Defining these terms precisely is not entirely without its problems, but in broad terms the subject is what the sentence is about, or its topic, and the predicate (a word which comes from a Latin verb meaning 'to claim or declare') is the claim being made about the subject. So in the sentence

The man died

The man is the subject, or topic, and *died* the predicate, or claim being made. If we added on *with his hands behind his back* that would all become part of the predicate since it is all part of the claim being made about *the man*. In other words, subject and predicate are a functional way of saying NP + VP. The vital bit of the predicate is the verb since this is the word which enshrines some sort of process, and this is called the predicator. The other functions – object, complement, adjunct/adverbial – all come within the predicate, and their presence or absence help to characterise individual verbs. Do you remember what we said earlier about selection restrictions and the lexicon? Well, functional categories help us to describe these restrictions fairly precisely. Some verbs, or predicators, are normally followed by an object – the thing or person which is directly acted on by the verb. As we have seen already, *die* isn't one of these, so it doesn't select an object: it's intransitive, that is, the meaning doesn't carry across to an object, except in very exceptional instances such as *he died a good death*. It's not impossible that at some time it could develop a broader transitive meaning, in which case it would be reclassified.

If we continue with these grammatical functions a little further we can say that there are some verbs/predicators which require two objects, an indirect and a direct, for example, *give* as in

> *She gave me a book*

She gave me is clearly incomplete – something has to have been given. We can reword this as *She gave a book to me*, which tells us that *me* is the indirect object and *a book* the direct. And there are verbs which don't take objects, like *seem*, but which none the less are incomplete without something following – *She seems nice* – for example, where *nice* is not the object of the predicator but its complement. Such verbs are thought of as *intensive* because their complements share the same area of reference as the subject. That leaves us with the adjunct, or adverbial, function. I give both terms because you will find that linguists differ over which term they consider most appropriate. Adjuncts/adverbials are normally optional in a sentence. They give circumstantial information about time, place, and manner. So, in the following sentence, for example, the phrases in bold are all fulfilling this function:

> *She gave me a book **yesterday/with a smile/in the garden***

If we were to describe these phrases formally, the first one is an adverb phrase, and the last two are prepositional phrases. It's because the term 'adverb' is used in formal descriptions that some linguists prefer to use 'adjunct' when talking about this function. It helps to make the point that other phrases can be adjuncts and also makes us aware of their optional inclusion in sentences. As a consequence of their optional character, they don't form part of the selection restrictions of verbs. That is, there are no verbs which must be followed by an adjunct.

I have given a brief sketch of these grammatical functions because they are the ones most commonly talked about in grammars. However, functional approaches go well beyond this. And it's easy to see why. If we take the sentence

(1)   *The ball was thrown by the hairy man*

and ask what is the subject here, the answer is not immediately obvious. In grammatical terms we would say that *The ball* is the subject. We can test this by putting it into the plural and noticing what happens to the verb:

(2)   *The balls were thrown by the hairy man*

Subject and predicator (verb) are in what is called **agreement** with one another – both go into the plural (in Standard English) – whereas changing *hairy man* to *hairy* men would have no effect whatsoever on the predicator. But, on the other hand, the person who is doing the throwing – the one responsible for the activity of the verb – is *the hairy man*. This would appear most clearly if we put the sentence into its active form

(3)   *The hairy man threw the ball*

So it looks as though in (1) we have two subjects not just one. One way of resolving this would be to call *The ball* the grammatical subject, and *the hairy man* the logical subject. And if we were to refine this even further and ask what kind of logical subject is *the hairy man*, we could do as the British linguist Michael Halliday would, and refer to it as the **actor**, in other words the person who has performed the action.

Once we look more closely into the functional categories of SPOCA we discover that not only are there different types of subjects but also objects and predicators as well. Halliday's approach is to see the sentence, or clause, as he prefers to call it, in terms of the following functional categories: **participant**, **process**, and **circumstance**. The participant function incorporates subjects, objects, and complements; process incorporates predicators; and circumstance incorporates adjuncts. So, in the sentence we had earlier, *She gave me a book yesterday/with a smile/in the garden*, there are three participants, *she, me, a book*; one process, *gave*; and a variety of circumstances. Using this kind of division it is possible to provide a functional framework to complement the formal one we have just been considering. Let's look more closely at how Halliday attempts to link function to form. You might find it helpful at this point to refer back to the discussion of Halliday's macro functions in Chapter 2.

4.3.1   Developing a functional grammar
(i)   *Ideational function*
You may remember that the ideational function is concerned with the way in which we represent our experiential world in language, in other

words, with how we use language to make the world intelligible to ourselves and others. The first way in which we can think about the clause, or simple sentence, then, is as a representation of experience. Consider for a moment the following sentences in terms of the processes indicated by the verbs, and the participants involved in them.

(1) The boy kicked the post
(2) The man liked the new house
(3) The child is homeless
(4) The girl laughed
(5) The visitor said 'hello'
(6) There is a woman over there

Commentary

(1) *The boy kicked the post.*   We can describe the process here, *kicked*, as a **material** one. Material processes are characteristically 'doing' verbs, *running, dressing, climbing* and so on. An indication of this can be seen in the fact that we rarely use them in the simple present tense (that is, *I run*) but tend instead to employ the present continuous, or 'ing' form (*I am running*). We associate them with continuous activity of some kind. The participants in (1) are *The boy* and *the post*. In functional terms we could, following Halliday, describe the boy as the **actor**, that is, the person responsible for the action. Categorising *the post* is not so easy, but Halliday suggests the term **goal**, meaning the thing which is acted upon. You will find that other functionalists use slightly different terms; some prefer **affected**, **patient**, or **medium** instead of goal, and you may also come across **agent** instead of actor. One of the operations we can characteristically perform with material process verbs is to change the clause/sentence from active to passive. This involves swapping over the grammatical subject and object whilst maintaining the functional relations of actor and goal:

The post was kicked by the boy

Even though *The post* is now in the subject position it is still functioning as goal, and correspondingly, *the boy*, although in the object position, remains the actor. Rearranging the clause in this way allows us, if we wish, to leave out the actor:

The post was kicked

Many notices employ the passive with actor/agent deletion because it makes the participant responsible for the action anonymous, and the notice more authoritative, for example:

> *Trespassers will be prosecuted*
> *Shoes must be worn in the gym*

(2) *The man liked the new house.* The predicator here is characteristic of a range of processes to do with feeling and thinking. They are not material – no concrete action is performed. Any action is internal rather than external. Verbs such as *hate, love, know, think, understand*, fall into this group. All of them encapsulate processes which we could describe as **mental**. The participants in mental processes are different from those in material ones. We can't really describe *The man* as an 'actor' since he doesn't perform the process of liking. He's the one who experiences the sensation of liking. Halliday refers to this subject as the **sensor**, and the thing sensed as the **phenomenon**. Mental verbs are different from material ones semantically and this is reflected in their grammatical capabilities. They do not form the present continuous, the 'ing' form, so easily: **The man is liking the house, *I am understanding your point.* They are sometimes referred to as **stative** verbs in that they describe a state or condition as opposed to material verbs which are **dynamic**. There are quite a number of verbs, however, which have a material and a mental meaning. The verb to *see*, for example, can be used in this way:

> *The man can see a tree*
> *The man can see your argument*

In the second of these two sentences *see* has the meaning of 'understand', a mental process. This is quite different from the material process of seeing in the first, although related to it by the figurative process of metaphor. I shall have more to say about metaphor in the next chapter, but for now perhaps we can just note that many metaphors are formed out of material processes in just such a way as we can witness here, that is, a physical action comes to represent a non-physical one. We can also note that one of the subtleties of the material/mental distinction is that it allows us to see how the grammatical capabilities of verbs depend on their semantic meaning. Not only are mental verbs more difficult to put into the present continuous, but they do not so easily form the passive as material ones. *The tree was seen by the man* is unproblematic, whereas *your argument was seen by the man* sounds rather odd.

(3) *The child is homeless.* The process here is different again from (1) and (2). The process encapsulated in the verb here is neither material nor mental. It's best described as **relational** in that its main purpose is to relate the two participants together. This is a characteristic feature of verbs which are intensive. If we were using the terminology used earlier we would call *homeless* a complement in that it shares the same area of reference as *The child*, that is, it relates to the child. With relational verbs, like *be, become, appear*, there are a greater number of possible participant roles because of a broader range of possible relationships. We'll just confine ourselves to one pairing, that of **carrier** and **attribute**. In (3) *homeless* is the attribute – the condition being attributed – and *The child* is the carrier, or the person who is in that condition. The relational process does not allow its verbs to form the passive – **homeless was being the boy*.

(4) *The girl laughed.* The predicator here falls into a category of verbs such as *cough, yawn, smile* which Halliday classes as **behavioural**. They have some similarity to material verbs in that they describe physical actions of some kind but they are different in that the action is not performed on any-thing – **a girl laughed a boy* is meaningless, whereas *a girl kicked a boy* isn't. Moreover, behavioural verbs need a subject which is animate, or living. People and animals smile, yawn, and cough, but not trees or rocks (except figuratively). Material verbs, on the other hand, can have trees or rocks as subjects, for example *the tree swayed in the wind*. In this respect, behav-ioural verbs are like mental ones, which also require animate subjects. So they are a distinct group, semantically and syntactically. We can see this again in the fact that they only require one participant – the person doing the laughing, coughing, or yawning. Halliday terms this participant **the behaver**. Verbs of this category are, like relational verbs, characteristically intransitive, in that they do not take an object – we can't *laugh* something – and consequently don't form the passive. *The girl laughed loudly* cannot be turned into **loudly was laughed the girl*.

(5) *The visitor said 'hello'.* The process here belongs to a large category called **verbal**. This includes verbs such as *say, report, claim, question*, and *explain*. Here again there is some similarity with material processes but also significant differences. As with mental and behavioural processes, the participant performing the activity has to be animate. But one special feature of verbs in this category is that the participants can be swapped round without any change in meaning: *'hello', said the visitor* has the same propositional meaning as *The visitor said 'hello'* (although it differs in force). And they can also usually form the passive – *'hello' was said by the visitor*. Halliday terms the first participant – *The visitor* – the **sayer**, and the second – *'hello'* – the **verbiage**. In the case of verbal processes there may also be a person to whom the words are said. Halliday terms this participant the **target**.

(6) *There is a woman over there.* The last category of processes is a fairly small one. It consists of clauses in which *there* acts as grammatical subject, for example *there was a little cat, there seemed to be a problem*, and so on. In these cases what we essentially appear to be doing is affirming the existence of something or someone, that is, 'a cat/problem existed'. Halliday terms this process **existential**. When we look at the participants, however, we can see that *there* doesn't really represent anything except the need for a subject. In functional terms therefore it has no importance outside its grammatical role. The only significant participant here is the thing or person being affirmed as existing, in this case *a woman*, and this Halliday refers to as the **existent**. You might notice that these clauses are very inflexible in that they cannot be manipulated as some of the others can either to form the passive, or the present continuous.

(ii)   *The textual function*
Not only does the structure of the clause reflect the way we represent the world, but it also reflects the importance we attach to those representations in our communications with other people. When we speak or write, we construct our clauses so as to present the information in a certain way. In other words, the clause functions as a **message**. Because of this, we have to decide how to order the parts of the message so as (a) to make it clear to our audience, and (b) to emphasise, or make prominent, the essential elements of it. These tasks are not handled by the syntax alone. Intonation also plays an important part in fulfilling the message function of texts, and we shall be considering this in Chapter 6. But for the moment, we'll confine our attention to the part played by the structural arrangement of the clause.

Any text/utterance is necessarily delivered in a linear manner and, as a consequence, we are forced, as listeners/readers, to process it in a similar fashion. Because of this, it is easier for us to process a lexical string in which the burden of new information comes towards the end of the clause. We expect the starting point of the clause, the subject, to present us with information which is largely *given*, that is, assumed to be known; this gives us time to prepare ourselves for the *new* to come later. If, for example, you were looking out of your window and noticed a bird on the lawn, you would be far more likely to say *there's a bird on the lawn*, than *a bird is on the lawn*. In this case the existential sentence, with *there* as an empty subject, prepares us for the receipt of the information. Another way of putting this is to say that in an English clause the usual **focus** of information is towards the end. I say 'usual' because this is not always the case. There may be some very good reason why we might want to start with the focus. Warnings and orders, for example, usually leave out the subject – *look out*, or *get out of the way*. The new information is promoted to the front of the clause; the subject *you* is taken as given and therefore not strictly necessary. The way linguistics handles these constructions is to distinguish between **marked** and **unmarked** uses. The concept of marked/unmarked is a useful one to get hold of. Anything that's unmarked linguistically is normative, or unremarkable, in its structure, whereas an element which is marked is significantly different, deviant, or anomalous. Marking a constituent by moving it syntactically is one way of increasing its prominence. We could say, then, that orders and warnings are marked utterances, in that they manipulate what we called earlier 'kernel' clauses, in order to grab our attention.

The information constraints acting on the clause also help to explain why English, characteristically, has a subject/predicate structure. If you look back at the sentences we considered when discussing formal approaches, you will see that, in tree diagram terms, they are predominantly right branching – the heaviest branches are to the right of S. We instinctively try and reserve the weightiest bits of new information for the predicate. As a consequence, the verb phrase is usually the heaviest branch of the tree. We could say, then, that in an unmarked English clause, the basic structure, in addition to NP + VP and subject + predicate, could also be described as given + new. Information approaches to the clause are also very rich in explaining a variety of syntactic operations which we characteristically perform. Processes involving ellipsis, for example, in which we leave out constituents of the clause, enable us to abbreviate and simplify our utterances whilst maintaining the recoverability of the message: *James enjoys tennis more than John*, is clearly less cumbersome than *James enjoys tennis more than John enjoys tennis*. Similarly, the requirement to make our messages clear means that we normally, that is, in unmarked clauses, try to ensure that items which are semantically adjacent (those which are dependent on each other in meaning) are syntactically adjacent. Thus *the day came at last when we were due to leave* is more marked in structure than *the day when we were due to leave came at last*, because of the separation, in the first version, of the clause *when we were due to leave* from the noun phrase, *the day*, which it post-modifies.

What we have really been considering here are what are sometimes referred to as the **thematic relations** of the clause. The concept of theme is an important one in functional approaches to syntax. We have said that the focus of an unmarked clause is on the new information at the end. By contrast, the theme is the first constituent. It's important to be careful here because linguists do not use the term 'theme' in the same way as literary critics. That is, it does not denote a running or leading idea, but rather, the starting point of the clause – what it is going to be about. Consider for a moment the differences between the following pairs:

1 (a) *Gas explosion kills thousands* (b) *Thousands killed by gas explosion*
2 (a) *The rain came down*   (b) *Down came the rain*

You will have noticed, I'm sure, that in each case sentence (b) rearranges sentence (a) by swapping over the first and last elements – in 1(b) this involves putting the verb, or predicator, into the passive. Despite the changes, however, there is no alteration in the essential, or propositional, meaning of the initial sentences. The same information is given to us, it is simply presented in a different order. The differences are thematic. What comes first in an English sentence is of crucial importance in telling us what the sentence is going to be about. In 1(a), for example, *Gas explosion* occupies the place of theme, and in information terms the sentence is saying 'I'm going to tell you about a gas explosion'. In (b), however, *Thousands* is the theme, and the sentence is saying 'I'm going to tell you something about thousands of people'. The information in both, as is the way with newspaper headlines (of which these are typical examples), is all new, there is nothing given, so the whole of the text is in focus. That in itself makes these marked clauses. They differ, however, in what they choose to make prominent, or thematise, as the topic of the clause. In the case of 2(a), the thematic sequence is unmarked: *The rain* occupies the place of theme. It is also the given part of the clause – the determiner *The* identifies it as something already existing – whilst the remainder is new information. In 2(b), however, part of that new information is put at the front of the clause and given prominence by being not only the focus, but also the theme of the clause. *Down* is thus a marked theme, and its unusual location at the beginning of a sentence such as this would no doubt alert us to the probability that its source was literary.

There are several types of themes in sentences, from those which express mood (*frankly, I don't give a damn*), to those which are more content laden (*your idea is nonsense*), but all I have attempted to do here is give you a flavour of what is a very rich field. Not surprisingly, functional approaches concentrating on textual aspects feature quite highly in discourse analysis and we shall be returning to them in Chapter 6. You might notice, incidentally, that the thematic principle helps to provide a semantic explanation for the inversion process which takes place in 'yes/no' questions, which we remarked on earlier. If you remember, we said that in a sentence like *he is coming*, the question, or interrogative, form is created by inverting the auxiliary verb *is* with the subject *he*. In other words, using our new terminology, the auxiliary verb is 'thematised'. Why should this be so? Well, very simply, because it is this part of the verb phrase which expresses polarity. What I mean is that if we wish to negate the sentence we attach the negative particle to the auxiliary verb – *he isn't coming*. It's appropriate, then, in a sentence which is querying whether or not he's coming, that the bit which carries the affirmative/non-affirmative load should be thematised.

(iii)   *Interpersonal function*

We have seen that, for Halliday, the clause functions as a **representation** and as a **message** and that in each case this has implications for its syntactic structure. But in addition to these, the clause also functions as an **exchange**. Communicating linguistically involves an interactive event between two or more people in which we take on certain roles – the most fundamental being speaker/writer *v.* listener/reader or, put more simply, addresser *v.* addressee – and attempt to influence, or understand, others. Traditionally, sentences are classified as **declarative**, **interrogative**, or **imperative** – you will find the **subjunctive** also talked about, but this form is in decline in present-day English. These forms correspond to some of the fundamental speech acts (see Chapters 2 and 5) which we use language to accomplish. Declaratives are used to give information, and perform the function of statements; interrogatives are used to request something, and perform the function of questions; imperatives are used to give instructions and perform the function of commands. Having said that, however, it's important to bear in mind that exact correlation between form and function only occurs in idealised sentences. We frequently use declaratives to ask questions and, on occasions, to issue instructions. The declarative utterance *you're going out*, could function as a question or an order depending on the intonation pattern.

What we are essentially talking about here is the subject of **mood** in language structure. This is a complex area of linguistic study and we can only touch on it here, but you may well find it one of the more fascinating aspects of linguistics because of the direct link with interpersonal meanings. As with thematic meaning, mood is not solely the responsibility of the syntax. As we have just seen, intonation also plays an important part, but we shall confine ourselves to syntactic issues here. One obvious way in which mood is characteristically signalled in English is by the inclusion of specific words such as *please, possibly, kindly, frankly*. Linguists refer to this as lexicalising mood. But mood is also signalled through the syntax of sentences. Halliday identifies two sorts of exchanges which he argues all utterances can be divided into. The first consists of demands for, and offers of, goods and services of some kind, for example *give me a biscuit* and *would you like a biscuit?* In these cases what is at issue is a literal, or actual, exchange. The second consists of demands for, and offers of, linguistic information, for example, *what is he giving her?* and *he's giving her a biscuit*, where the issue is a verbal, rather than a literal, exchange.

Halliday argues that when children first learn to speak it is exchanges of the goods and services variety which predominate. In other words, they use language primarily – though not exclusively – as a way of indicating their needs and getting what they want. The use of language for the exchange of information comes later. To begin with, then, language, in its interpersonal function, is principally a means to an end. The speech acts which are performed are direct, and language serves what we can think of as essentially extra-linguistic purposes. Language, of course, never loses this connection with an extra-linguistic reality, but it also acquires a new purpose, in the giving and receiving of information, which we can think of as linguistic. As well as being a means to an end language is now an end in itself since the precise way in which a question or statement is encoded is part of its meaning. In our brief look at indirect speech acts in Chapter 2, we used the example of a boss wishing to see an employee and couching the demand as a request: *could I see you for a minute?* We can see now that although this has the form of an interrogative it is only apparently functioning as a question. Most employees would interpret it as a demand of the goods and services type, since what is expected is their attendance in the boss's office. None the less, it is expressed as an interrogative, requesting information, with the expectation of a verbal reply, *yes, of course*, or something of that nature. This overlaying of one kind of intention, namely of the goods and services type, with one of the verbal information variety results in the generation of an indirect speech act. Correctly interpreting indirect speech acts involves being able to relate the syntactic form of an utterance to its interpersonal function. This becomes evident if we change the tense of the boss's request to the present, that is, *can I see you for a minute?* As we noted in Chapter 2, the move into the present tense signals a small, but significant, shift in mood. There is no change in propositional meaning, both sentences have the same basic sense, but there is less deference and more urgency about the present tense. Indeed, we would expect a boss to use it whilst expecting an employee to use the past. Tense is being used modally here, that is, as a marker of mood.

Examining the interpersonal dimension of syntax means looking closely at the relation between the form and function of utterances. As we have seen, sentences might have the form of declaratives, interrogatives, or imperatives, but function quite differently. There is a much discussed example in linguistic literature concerning the range of ways in which the demand for salt can be encoded, which illustrates this:

    (i)   *Pass the salt*
   (ii)   *Please pass the salt*
  (iii)   *Can you pass the salt?*
  (iv)   *Could you possibly pass the salt?*
   (v)   *You couldn't possibly pass the salt, could you?*

What you can observe here is the element of politeness and deference increasing with each permutation of *pass the salt*. (i) has the form and function of an imperative/command of the goods and services variety; (ii) lexicalises a degree of politeness by adding *please*, while (iii) grammaticalises it by turning it into an interrogative, seeking information; (iv) increases the politeness by changing the tense to the past, and by including *possibly* – a lexical marker of tentativeness; and finally, (v) uses a declarative/statement followed by a tag question. As I commented in Chapter 2, we can say, as a general rule, that the more indirect the demand, the more polite it is felt to be.

(iv)   *The poetic function*

If you look back to Chapter 2 you will see that, in addition to the other functions of language which we described there, we also observed that of providing intrinsic pleasure in the medium itself. This is language as play, the central concern of which is uniqueness of utterance. Functional approaches, including that of Halliday, often have very little to say about this because of their preoccupation with language as a tool. Roman Jakobson, however, the grandfather of functionalists, clearly saw it as important in enabling us to include within linguistics considerations of language novelty which had previously been the preserve of literary criticism. The processes by which the poetic function affects language are generally referred to as **figurative**, and involve imaginative activities such as **metaphor**, **metonymy**, and **simile**. These are best discussed in the context of the semantic level of language, and we shall be considering the poetic function more substantially in the next chapter. None the less, there is every indication that the inherent pleasure which we take in language is important in the generation of new syntactic possibilities.

We observed earlier that the material process verb *to see – I see the man –* is also capable of expressing a mental process – *I see your point –* because of metaphorical extension. This is part of a well-known phenomenon by which physical activities come to represent mental realities. The verb *depress*, for example, clearly a mental process verb, originates from a material one meaning 'to push down', a sense which survives in instructions such as *depress the plunger*. We can see how the metaphorical meaning might arise by a process of analogy between the act of pushing something down and the condition of feeling down. The presence of metaphor in language has traditionally been regarded as anomalous, an oddity to be found in poetry and literary language generally, but this is to underestimate its importance in generating new bits of grammar. As the linguists Lakoff and Johnson have shown in *Metaphors We Live By* (1980) and Lakoff and Turner in *More than Cool Reason* (1989), much of our everyday language is dependent on metaphor. And apart from any cognitive function which may be fulfilled here, there is the delight in creating new and unique combinations of words. Once *depress* and *see* become mental process verbs it becomes possible to use them with a different range of subjects and objects, and as a consequence, the entries for them in our internal lexicon have to be updated.

These, of course, are examples of words which have long ago lost their metaphorical impact. However, the same impulse towards invention and novelty is continually at work. Part of the *raison d'être* for a metaphor lies in its capacity for originality – why talk about *skimming the Net* [computer network], a fair enough metaphor but rather dull, when we can *surf* it. The same principle operates at the level of word classes. The process of conversion by which nouns such as *author* change to verbs *to author*, which we touched on earlier, is driven by the need to find ever bolder and more arresting ways of expressing ourselves. I suggested earlier that language is organic and nowhere is this more evident than in the ever-changing capacities of individual lexical items. Old usages wither away, but in their place come new ones, bringing into being fresh combinations and altering the lexical component of our mental dictionaries. In many ways, then, we could argue that the powerhouse of syntactic innovation is a consequence of the poetic function's drive to achieve uniqueness of expression.

4.4 Conclusion and final summary

I have been suggesting that there are, broadly, two different traditions of syntactic enquiry which are responsible, in turn, for quite distinct methodologies. In doing so I have, necessarily, simplified what is a very diverse field. It is rare to find linguists who do not take some account of both formal and functional approaches, and many straddle both in some form or other. The differences are largely those of emphasis. I am suggesting that you see them as complementary rather than opposed accounts. Formal approaches tend to be more austere, diagrammatic, and rule conscious. Functional approaches, by contrast, are concerned more with communicative aspects of language and with the principles which govern syntactic behaviour. And whereas formalists (such as Chomsky) occupy themselves with idealised examples of English, functionalists (like Halliday) will also consider unidealised sentences exhibiting ellipsis, abbreviation, and thematic rearrangement. Both, however, recognise the difference between what we have called idealised, kernel, sentences and their non-idealised, non-kernel, counterparts, although they account for it in separate ways. Halliday uses the concept of marked/unmarked and relates it to various communicative meanings. Chomsky, on the other hand, accounts for it as a distinct grammatical process called 'transformation', the rules for which are part of what is known as transformational grammar (see Chapter 6). Formalists tend to see syntax as an almost autonomous mental activity to be mapped by tree diagrams and rewrite rules, whereas functional approaches give greater consideration to the meaning of utterances, and as a consequence see syntax more as a way of encoding meaning.

One day, perhaps, we shall have a complete explanatory model of English syntax. Until then, we have to be content with partial accounts. But it is perhaps not surprising that we should have different emphases in this field. I have been trying to impress on you all along the two dimensions of language, that is, language as 'concept', and language as 'substance'. This is variously described by linguists. Chomsky refers to 'competence' and 'performance', Saussure to *langue* and *parole*. We could see the distinction between 'form' and 'function' as yet another indication of this divide. Considering form leads us to the abstract operational code, whereas considering function leads us in the opposite direction, to the world which we inhabit and to which we strive endlessly to give expression. It is to this world, the world of meaning, that we must now turn.

Further reading

Baker, C. L. (1989) *English Syntax* (Cambridge, Mass.: MIT Press).
Brown, K. and Miller, J. (1991) *Syntax* (London: Routledge).
Burton-Roberts, N. (1986) *Analysing Sentences* (London: Longman).

Fabb, N. (1994) *Sentence Structure* (London: Routledge).

Freeborn, D. (1995) *A Course Book in English Grammar*, 2nd edn (Basingstoke: Palgrave Macmillan).

Greenbaum, S. (1991) *An Introduction to English Grammar* (London: Longman).

Hurford, J. R. (1987) *Grammar: A Student's Guide* (Cambridge: Cambridge University Press).

Leech, G. (1994) *A Communicative Grammar of English* (London: Longman).

Leech, G., Deuchar, M. and Hoogenraad, R. (1982) *English Grammar for Today* (London: Longman).

Newby, M. (1987) *The Structure of English: A Handbook of English Grammar* (Cambridge: Cambridge University Press).

Radford, A., Atkinson, M., Britain, D., Clahsen, H. and Spencer, A. (1999) *Linguistics: An Introduction* (Cambridge: Cambridge University Press).

Thomas, L. (1993) *Beginning Syntax* (Oxford: Blackwell).

Wekker, H. and Haegman, L. (1985) *A Modern Course in English Syntax* (London: Routledge).

Young, D. J. (1984) *Introducing English Grammar* (London: Routledge).

Note

1. I am using the concept of generation with a slightly different sense from the way it is used in the term **generative grammar**. See the Glossary.

5 Studying Meaning

5.1 Introduction: the problem of 'meaning'

Introductions to linguistics will usually have a section on some of the ways in which we can assign a meaning to word strings, and for the majority of us it is this ability of words to 'mean' which constitutes their most important function. Much of our linguistic life is spent trying either to understand others or to ensure they understand us. But here we encounter a recurring difficulty because although language is designed to enable communication, it frequently seems to obstruct it. As we observed in Chapter 2, we can never seem to find the right words when we need them. Provokingly, it is just at those moments when we need language most – when we are in love or angry – that it seems to fail us. But this is not really the fault of language itself. The difficulty has more to do with our expectations than with the system. Most of the time, language performs the necessary functions we require of it without any effort, and we assume this will always be so. But we have only to think how complex and subtle is our inner world of thoughts and feelings, to realise that the demands we make of language can only partially be realised. In Chapter 2 I quoted a few lines from the poem *Four Quartets*, in which the poet T. S. Eliot comments on the frailty of words and the impossible burden we impose on them. Let me remind you of them again:

> . . . Words strain,
> Crack and sometimes break, under the burden,
> Under the tension, slip, slide, perish,
> Decay with imprecision, will not stay in place,
> Will not stay still.

> ('Burnt Norton', ll. 149–53)

Eliot is writing as a poet, and possibly more aware than most of us of the difficulties presented by language. Nevertheless, what Eliot calls 'the intolerable wrestle with words' is at times experienced by us all, and it provides a useful starting point for us in our consideration of the relationship between language and meaning. In our previous chapters we began by 'defamiliarising' the linguistic level under consideration, and I propose that we do the same here. In other words, instead of plunging straight into semantics and tackling it head on as a linguistic discipline, let's take time to review why it is that language and meaning don't provide the perfect fit we might like them to.

To begin with, as we saw in Chapter 2, words don't always have the same meaning for everyone. Leaving aside those speakers whose knowledge of the language is imperfect, it is still the case that many words do not convey a uniform meaning because our understanding of them is not uniform. The linguist Nelson Francis has said, 'Words do not have meanings; people have meanings for words' (1967, p. 119). If this is the case it raises very real problems for successful communication. Conservative models of communication used to show an idea leaving the head of the speaker, and going via a language tube to the head of a listener. It's known colloquially as 'the conduit' view of language because it visualises language as a container of meaning. The speaker encodes the meaning and the listener decodes it. But this is an unreal view of communication. It is very rarely that we understand an idea in exactly the same way as the speaker intends us to. Words aren't sufficient to achieve that. This is an ancient problem, and one with which philosophers are familiar. As we saw earlier, there is a tendency to think that abstract nouns such as *beauty* and *love* have the same precise reference as concrete nouns like *table* or *chair*. But this is really a trick of the mind. In reality we are surrounded by mysteries, kept conveniently at bay for us by the conventional categories of language.

Yet another, related, difficulty is that many words often have private associations for us. The most obvious example is children's names. In one sense we could say that names do not have a meaning in themselves since all they do is refer to something. What does Robert mean, for example? All it does is indicate a particular individual. And yet for most people names are not neutral entities; they are laden with associations. Thus the difficulty of deciding on a name for one's own child. To say these associations are not part of meaning is to shut our eyes to much of what people value about language. Names are only an extreme example of a common phenomenon. To some people a word like *beach* might conjure up happy childhood memories of playing on the sand: the word acts as a key to unlocking an inner world. Others, however, might have very different associations, or none at all. Fortunately, many associations are fairly general, such as daffodils with spring and fog with winter. If this were not the case, communication would be severely limited. None the less there is still a sense in which we all have a private vocabulary, unique to ourselves. It is because of this that word association tests can on occasions be revealing. It is the departure from the received association which psychiatrists are really searching for.

On a more practical level, however, probably the biggest difficulty most of us have in determining meaning has to do with the influence of context on utterances. In working out the meaning of what is said to us we have to take into account not only the words themselves as individual items, but also the circumstances in which they are uttered, the medium used, and the person who is addressing us. All these factors have a bearing on how we understand the words. The same message delivered verbally can have a very different meaning for us when written down. Some years ago a North American academic, Marshall McLuhan, popularised the idea that 'the medium is the message'. In other words, that the medium, or channel of communication used, is itself a message irrespective of the words. In its extreme form the idea has gone out of fashion but, nevertheless, McLuhan performed a valuable service in drawing attention to the importance of the channel of communication in the determination of meaning. But perhaps even more important for us in determining meaning are the circumstances of the utterance and the relationship of the addresser to us. Let's take a brief example: a declaration of love – *I love you.* Clearly, the meaning we assign to this is different if the speaker is our lover as opposed to our parent or child. In other words, the person who is addressing us influences the meaning we give to what s/he says. Similarly with the situation in which the declaration is made. If it is prompted, or said to get out of the washing up, it will have a different meaning from an unprompted, non-manipulative declaration.

What we are faced with here is not simply the difficulty of meaning, but the larger problem of interpretation. It's not enough to know what words mean in isolation. We have to be able to interpret them in concrete situations. This entails more than linguistic knowledge. It involves a knowledge of the world, of human psychology, and practical realities. This is because meaning is not the sole prerogative of language. We also convey meaning through our bodies, by gesture, posture, and looks, that is, by **non-verbal communication**, and through our voices, by intonation and rhythm. All of these can have a **paralinguistic** function, in other words, they can run alongside the words contributing to the total meaning of the communication, either by reinforcing the word meaning, or sometimes, contradicting it. Interpretation is a difficult skill and one which involves more than simply decoding the language. We have only to think of the way two people can have a conversation and come away with entirely separate interpretations of what has been said, to realise this. Commentators on discourse point out that in any speech context there exists the possibility of at least four interpretations: a **surface**, or 'open', meaning – one of which all parties are aware; a **speaker's**, or 'concealed', meaning – one intended by the speaker but not consciously known to the listener; **a hearer's**, or 'blind', meaning – one perceived by the hearer but not consciously known to the speaker; and a **listener's**, or 'hidden', meaning – one which is apparent to someone overhearing the exchange but not to the participants themselves.

These are just a few of the principal reasons for what we can term the **indeterminacy** of linguistic meaning: the impossibility of determining, absolutely, what a given string of words actually means. Other reasons would include the way in which words change their meaning over time, so that we cannot always be sure, for example, when reading a text from the past, what the words meant in their original context, and the influence of fashion which is continually bringing words into prominence and giving them extra semantic 'spin', to adapt a contemporary idiom. Given all this, it might seem surprising that communication takes place at all. But, of course, it does, and for the most part very successfully. This is principally because of two things: first, whilst we may not be able to establish the total meaning of any given string, we can usually establish enough for an exchange of meaning to occur. And second, irrespective of the slipperiness of words and the unfixed nature of 'context', we know, as speakers of the language, and members of particular linguistic communities, the chief processes by which words signal meaning. This is part of what we have termed our linguistic competence, both grammatical and communicative, and it is aspects of this competence which we should now examine more closely.

One thing that should be clear from our discussion so far is that the term 'meaning', on its own, is quite inadequate to describe the various interpretative possibilities we have touched on. It will do as a convenient label in casual conversation, but it won't really pass muster for us as serious linguists. We need to develop terminology capable of capturing the more subtle distinctions between the kinds of meaning we have been observing. Let's start by reconsidering the declaration *I love you*. We said that the meaning of this depended on the context in which it was uttered. But this is not entirely true. Even out of context the sentence has a meaning of sorts. We may not know who *I* and *you* refer to, whether lovers, family, or friends, but we know *I* refers to the speaker, and *you* to the person being addressed. Similarly, whilst we don't know what the nature of the love is that is being declared, we do know, as users of the language, what range of feelings the word is capable of expressing. And this is true even if we have different views about what love is. We know, for example, that it is more than affection, and less than adoration. This general level of meaning, which is available to all of us, we can call the **sentence meaning**, or **sense**, of the string. The fuller, contextual meaning, which we get from knowing all the circumstances in which it is uttered, we can call its **utterance meaning**, or **force**. The distinction between sense and force is a crucial one in linguistics and serves to distinguish two different, but related, approaches to the study of meaning. The study of sense is the concern of **semantics**. What is at issue here is the way in which words 'mean' independently of their situational context. I have purposely prefaced 'context' with 'situational' here to distinguish it from linguistic context. Semantics then is primarily concerned with grammatical competence, with meaning as a product of the linguistic system. The study of force, on the other hand, is the concern of **pragmatics**. This is a more recent addition to the linguistic arsenal of terms than 'semantics' and refers to the contribution made by situational context to meaning. Pragmatics explores the interpretative strategies we employ for deciding on the meaning of utterances. If, for example, you ask your partner, late at night, whether s/he wishes for a cup of coffee, and the answer is *coffee keeps me awake*, the only way of determining if this means 'yes' or 'no' is by knowing the context of the reply. The sense, in other words, is not enough, we need to know the force. And that, in turn, rests on our communicative, as opposed to simply grammatical, competence. Having established some basic distinctions, let's begin our study of linguistics proper by looking more closely at semantics – with words in relation to each other.

5.2   Studying semantics

Most children at some point in their lives experiment with making up a language. They invent nonsense words in which the sounds are randomly connected to each other and take great delight in playing at talking. In a sense they are imitating their first encounter with words, before they could assign any meaning to them. Then, the language they heard around them was a form of babble. Once sounds acquire meaning, however, they become transformed; they acquire what Ferdinand de Saussure calls **value**, just as a metal coin does when stamped with the appropriate royal seal. I am beginning with this fairly obvious point because it enshrines a fundamental point in linguistics: the relationship between the sound of a word and its meaning is not a natural one. As I pointed out in Chapter 1, words are not facts of nature like rocks and trees, but cultural objects, products of the human brain. As such, the relationship between any string of sounds and the meaning they represent is completely conventional. The fact that the sounds /tri:/ ('tree') are used to indicate the object growing in the ground is simply because this is the way our language works, but there is no reason why any other string of sounds wouldn't do, providing other people could understand us. In other words, the relationship between what we can call the sound image of a word and what it represents is symbolic. The knowledge of these symbolic relationships is part of our grammatical competence as speakers of the language.

Having established this, we can probe a little further and ask what the nature of these symbolic relationships is–what is it that any sound image is actually representing? The clearest answer to this is given in *Cours de linguistique générale* (1913, rep. 1966). Saussure's book is the cornerstone of modern semantic approaches, and whilst there have been many accounts of his analysis of the sound–meaning relationship very few are as readable as the original. If you wish to get to grips with this area of linguistics I would strongly recommend you to read it. Let's briefly consider his argument. According to Saussure, a word combines two elements, a sound image, which is its physical form, and a sense, or meaning. Saussure, however, uses slightly different terminology. What we have been calling the 'sense', he refers to as the **signified**, whilst the sound image he terms the **signifier**. This is because, for Saussure, words are **signs**: their relationship to the outside world, as we have noted already, is symbolic. In the case of *tree*, what this means is that the word acts as a sign comprising a sound image, or signifier, /tri:/, and a sense, or signified, indicating 'treeness'. In other words, the signifier acts as a label, not for an object but a concept. And what about actual trees, we might ask? Where do they fit into the picture? Well, the point Saussure makes is that there is no direct relation between the sound of a word and the object(s) it refers to: it is the signifier and signified together, that is, the complete sign, which refers to the outside world. This is logical, if you think about it, because before you can identify something called /tri:/ you must already know what one is: in other words, you must possess the concept 'tree'. As for the objects themselves which one uses the sign to refer to, Saussure calls these **referents**. So words have two kinds of semantic meaning: first, they **signify** one or more senses, or signifieds, that is, they have **signification**, and second,

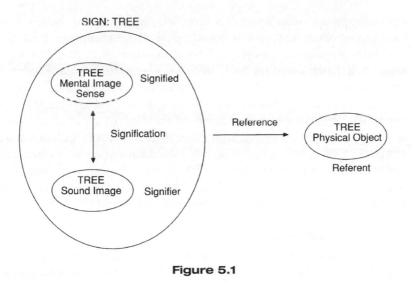

Figure 5.1

they refer to things or activities in the outside world, so they have **reference**. If this is not sufficiently clear, have a look at Figure 5.1.

'Reference' and 'signification' are semantic relationships which apply generally to items in our mental lexicon, but at the same time not all the words we use are equally rich in these two linguistic dimensions. Words like *truth, sincerity, virtue* – or abstract nouns – have a complex signification. Their sense is very full, but we would be hard pressed to say what they referred to in the exterior world: thus the title '**abstract noun**'. On the other hand, words such as *Gloria* and *London* – or **proper nouns** – which refer to unique entities, have very little conventional signification. If someone were to ask 'what's the meaning of *Gloria*?' it would be difficult to make a sensible reply (although, as we observed earlier in the case of *Robert*, the word might well be rich in personal meaning). And finally, 'function' words (as we called them in Chapter 4) – for example *of, and, if* – seem to be weak in both reference and signification when compared with either abstract or proper nouns. These are words which, as we saw earlier, provide the scaffolding for sentences and often play a crucial part in establishing logical relationships. Their signification is grammatical in nature, rather than lexical. Another way of putting this is to say they have grammatical sense, as opposed to the lexical sense of nouns and verbs.

5.2.1 Working with sense

I said a few moments ago that we needed to develop a more precise terminology to talk about semantics, and we made a start with distinguishing between sense and force. Having done that, however, it has to be admitted that sense is not a great advance on the word 'mean'. It is still a very elusive concept. Indeed, if we were asked to define it we would probably have to fall back on 'mean', with the consequence that we should have a circular definition. Because of its vagueness we need to narrow down exactly what kinds of meaning the term is capable of referring to. It's here that we become aware of the relative lack of terminology in semantics when compared with other linguistic levels. Unlike syntax and phonology, semantics tends to rely more heavily on terms which are already heavily used in everyday language. Nonetheless, if we consider 'sense' more closely we can see that it has various layers. The two most important of these are **conceptual sense** and **associative sense**.

(i) *Conceptual sense*

This is probably what most people understand by sense. In fact, a good many linguists tend to limit the term to this level of meaning. Conceptual sense denotes the stable semantic features of a word. If, for example, you had to say what the words *woman* and *man* meant, one answer would be to say that a woman was a 'human, adult, female' and, correspondingly, a man would be a 'human, adult, male'. These items of information, or semantic features, serve to categorise the terms *woman* and *man*, as well as to distinguish them from related terms. For example, *man* is distinguished from *bull* by the feature 'human', from *woman* by the feature 'male', and from *boy* by the feature 'adult'. We can set out the relationships in formal terms as below:

woman:	[+ human + adult + female]
man:	[+ human + adult + male]
girl:	[+ human − adult + female]
boy:	[+ human − adult + male]
bull:	[− human + adult + male]

Semantic feature analysis attempts to account for the conceptual sense of a word according to the presence or absence of a specific feature in the word's profile. It works very well for words with a high lexical content and allows us to map a certain level of sense onto words with some degree of accuracy. What we are identifying is a kind of core meaning which is fairly resistant to changes of time or culture. The conceptual senses of *woman* and *man* have been the same for centuries, and will probably be so for a good few more. This is not to say there might not be disagreement over which category to place particular individuals in – cultures differ over when someone is considered a man, for example – but the conceptual sense of a word is not dependent on its reference: it is what the word can be said to denote. It's important to bear in mind, however, that a word may have more than one conceptual sense. The noun *flight*, for example, can have the senses of 'a series of steps', 'a journey by air', 'a unit of the air force', 'the power of flying', and 'a digression'. All of these are related in some way, and we shall be looking at sense relations a little later on, but they are different enough to constitute distinct conceptual senses.

(ii)   *Associative sense*

Conceptual sense only gets us so far in trying to understand how words mean. They are very rarely simply carriers of neutral cognitive meaning. As well as their denotative meaning, words also acquire considerable associative meanings from the social and cultural contexts in which they are used. This extra resonance, or echo, can be employed to powerful emotive effect. Some linguists prefer to see this as an aspect of force rather than sense, using the term 'semantic' force to distinguish it from 'pragmatic' force, but I suggest we keep it within the realm of sense because it is just as much an integral part of a word as its conceptual sense. Here are the principal associative processes which affect the meanings of words.

(a)   *Connotation*

What a word 'connotes' is much less stable and more indeterminate than what it 'denotes'. We are talking here about the kinds of values and attitudes invoked by a word apart from its core meaning. Clearly these are more culturally dependent and more likely to change over time. Let's briefly consider the connotations attached to *man* and *woman*. What, for example, is the meaning of *man* in the sentence *he's a real man*? Most people would agree that more is being conveyed than simply 'human, adult, male'. The conceptual sense is only partially helpful here. We need to know what extra qualities the speaker judges a man to have; and we could probably hazard a guess at 'bravery', 'resilience', 'strength', 'lack of sentiment', and so on. There is no absolute limit to what we might infer here because connotative meaning is more open-ended than conceptual. And what about *she's a real woman*? Again, we should most likely agree that this means more than 'human, adult, female' and we might surmise 'attractive', 'shapely', 'sexually mature'. Interestingly, *man*, in Anglophone cultures, connotes positive, character-forming qualities whilst *woman* is limited to more sexual connotations. The terms are only equal in their conceptual sense, whereas their associative senses differentiate between them on the basis of mental, or moral, versus physical attributes. What a word connotes often gives a clearer insight into social and cultural attitudes than what it conceptually means. In this particular instance, the connotative differences between *man* and *woman* are a reflection of current assumptions about what constitutes maleness and femaleness. This has a direct bearing on language use since we cannot always use the term *woman* as the female counterpart of *man*. In some contexts it is still considered rude to refer to someone as a *woman*. Compare, for example, *give it to the woman*, *give it to the lady*, and *give it to the man*, as instructions to a child to return a dropped coin. The first of these is usually considered less socially acceptable than the others. And occasionally the connotations of a term are so strong that they are more dominant than its conceptual sense. This is why, despite the contradiction in conceptual sense, it is possible to refer to a man as *an old woman*. Here, the denotative meaning has been totally submerged by the connotations surrounding the phrase *old woman*.

Not surprisingly, connotative meaning is consistently exploited by writers who wish either to engage our emotions, stimulate our imaginations, or enlist our prejudices. Advertising, for example, makes extensive use of it. The name *Fairy Liquid* – used for a popular brand of washing-up liquid – counts on us activating more than the conceptual sense of fairy ('supernatural magical being'). It suggests something soft, effortless, and gentle, thus kind to the hands as well as the dishes. And poets, too, rely heavily on connotative meaning. 'Quinquireme of Nineveh' intones the poet John Masefield, at the beginning of his poem 'Cargoes', counting on the words triggering associations in the reader of the colourful world of classical antiquity. They may not be triggered, however, and this is where writers take a risk, because there is no way that connotations can be completely predicted or controlled. They spread outward through the language like ripples in water but they are dependent for their activation on readers who share the same cultural landscape. And some words create more ripples than others. If, for example, we take the words *grin, beam, smile*, and *smirk*, and ask which is the least positively or negatively marked, the answer is surely *smile*. Indeed, the other words could all be defined in terms of it, that is, they are all types of smile. This is because their conceptual senses overlap. The real differences between them lie in their associative senses, some of which are more marked than others – *beam* is a smile which connotes happiness, whereas *smirk* is a smile which connotes gloating of some kind. A similar kind of scale can be seen in the words describing bodily shape – *slender, slim, thin, skinny*. They share a similar conceptual sense based on types of thinness, but have different connotative meanings depending on the perceived relative merits of each. Many words belong to scales of this kind where terms differ according to connotative value but share a common conceptual sense which is embodied in the central, unmarked, or core term of the scale. Persuasive writing, such as tabloid journalism and advertising, makes great use of non-core vocabulary precisely because of the greater connotative impact of which such words are capable.

(b) *Collocation*

If you look up the adjective *clear* in a good dictionary of contemporary English you will probably find it will list at least ten different meanings, depending on the linguistic context in which it is used, from *clear conscience* and *clear sky* to *clear case* – as in a *clear case of theft*. In each instance the meaning of *clear* is slightly different; *clear conscience* means 'without guilt', whereas *clear* in *clear case* means 'unmistakable'. At the same time, however, we should find it hard to say that in each instance there was a separate conceptual sense. We can see enough commonality of meaning to assume an underlying sense. All the examples I have given have the meaning 'free from', whether free from complications (*a clear case*) free from guilt (*a clear conscience*) or free from clouds (*a clear sky*). The differences between them come from the words clear is put with, or, in other words, **collocates** with. 'Collocate' is a verb meaning 'to go with', and one of the ways by which we know the meaning of a word is, as the linguist John Firth says, by knowing 'the company it keeps' (Crystal, 1987, p. 105).

Consider, for example, the words *strong*, *mighty*, and *powerful*. They seem interchangeable in terms of their conceptual sense, and yet they are clearly not so when we come to think of their uses. Try putting them with *language*, *ocean*, and *tea*. You will find that some combinations are more possible than others. Only *strong* collocates with *tea*, for instance – *powerful/mighty tea* would be comical. Not only that, but there are significant differences of meaning; tea is strong in an entirely different way from which language is strong. And again, *strong language* is quite separate from *powerful language*; one implies the use of swearing, and the other, of persuasive rhetorical devices. Examples such as these proliferate through the language; cows and humans *wander* but only humans *stroll*; *deep* and *profound* go with *sympathy* but only *deep* with *hole*, and so on. You might have a go at trying out various combinations of words yourself to see what collocational possibilities exist within the language. We could say that in order to know the meaning of a word in the language we need to know its collocational range, that is, all the linguistic contexts in which it can occur. Part of the natural evolution of language is in the development of new contexts and the demise of old ones. And it is also worth noting that one of the ways in which creative writers experiment with language is by generating odd collocations. In 'Fern Hill', for example, a poem by the Welsh poet Dylan Thomas, about the world of childhood innocence, Thomas alters the phrase 'once upon a time' to 'once below a time'. The odd collocation now suggests, strikingly, the timelessness of being young.

(c)   *Stylistic variation*
One of the consequences of the way in which English has developed over the past 1500 years has been the emergence of different **registers**, or styles, of English. This has been partly due to the influx of new words from other languages such as Latin and French and partly to the variety of social needs which English has had to fulfil. If we are in a court of law, for instance, we might need to use the term *larceny*, which is of French origin, whereas talking with our friends we would probably use the term *theft*, which is of Anglo-Saxon origin. Doctors talk of *haemorrhaging* (Greek), and *lacerations* (Latin), rather than *bleeding* and *wounds* (Anglo-Saxon). In all these cases, there is no real difference in conceptual sense between the terms used. The differences have to do with levels of formality. Part of being able to use the language effectively is the ability to switch between these levels when it is socially appropriate to do so. Consider the following words for example, all of which are conceptually the same: *steed, horse, nag, gee-gee*. We can see that they belong to different contexts. *Steed* is poetic in style, and would be appropriate in a literary work about the knights of the round table; *nag* is slang and is normally used only in colloquial English; whilst *gee-gee* belongs to the nursery and is used with children. In other words, these terms are stylistically marked. The least marked is *horse* because it can be used in any context and, as a consequence, we can refer to it as the **normative** term.

As a further example, think about the following terms, all of which are used to describe living quarters, and see if you can sort them according to the particular style of communication they might belong to: *domicile, residence, abode, home, pad*. As in the case of words for *horse* there is one normative term, in this case *home*, and several marked terms, all of which can be slotted into various linguistic contexts. It's possible to take many lexical categories and sort the individual items into groups of this kind. These are sometimes referred to as **semantic fields**.

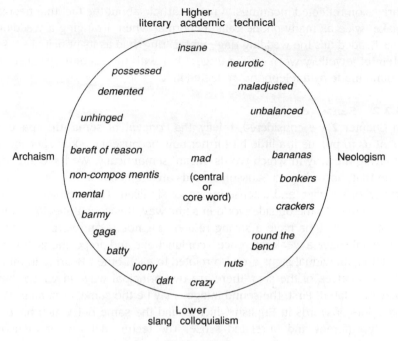

Figure 5.2

Figure 5.2 shows the semantic field for *mad* from Geoffrey Hughes's book *Words in Time* (1988, p. 19).

(d)   *Reflection*

We noted earlier that a word can have more than one conceptual sense. This is clearly true of *flight*, and it is equally the case with many other words. As a consequence, it is often difficult when using a word with a particular sense, to keep the other one(s) out of our minds. When we talk of the *nuclear family*, for instance, we mean the small tightly knit family of mother, father, and children, but it's difficult to keep the other sense of *nuclear* to do with the discovery of atomic energy, as in the *nuclear age*, completely at bay. This is not surprising, as the 'family' sense has derived at some stage from the scientific one. What we are saying then is that senses reflect each other and that this too is part of the meaning of which individual words are capable. Reflected meaning bedevils words to do with sexuality. Terms such as *gay, intercourse, queen, fairy*, are often very difficult to use precisely because of this. But the great resource of reflected meaning is the possibility it opens up for the generation of ambiguity, and more especially, of puns. Tabloid journalism thrives on reflected meanings. A recent article about the fact that people make twice as many phone calls as normal when arranging a wedding was headed 'It's the wedding ring', where 'ring' had as its principal sense 'item of jewellery worn on the finger', but with the secondary sense of 'sound made by a telephone' reflected in it.

5.2.2 Sense relations

In Chapter 2 we considered, briefly, the concept of **semantic space**. I want us to pursue it a little bit further now because it's a key concept in studying the way in which words 'mean' semantically. We have already seen that, according to Saussure, words are signs consisting of a sound image, or signifier, and a sense image, or signified. The complete sign is used to refer to the outside world in some way; this constitutes its 'reference'. Some signs have a strong reference – nouns and verbs – whilst some only have a weak reference – conjunctions and prepositions. But, in addition, individual signs are also related to each other. Bearing in mind the two halves of the sign, there are two principal ways in which they may be related. First, the sound images may be the same, or similar. We have lots of words in English which sound the same but which have a totally different and unrelated sense. The technical term for them is **homophones**, for example *vain/vein, air/heir, whether/weather*. More interesting, from our point of view, however, are those instances where words are only similar, but not identical, in sound. This particular feature of language is called **rhyme**, for example, *brick/sick, basket/casket*. There are various types of rhyme, but they all work on the same principal of similarity of sound versus difference of meaning.

The second way in which signs may be related is in terms of their senses. It's here that the concept of semantic space is so useful. Each sign, by virtue of its relationships with other signs, occupies a certain amount of territory in the linguistic system. The total extent of this territory is referred to by Saussure as the sign's 'value'. The senses of words, both conceptual and associative, are constantly adjusting to the presence of new words or the absence of old ones. We can see this most clearly if we take a brief look at the history of certain words. For example, Old English used to have a word *mete* which meant food; at some point in our history it came into competition with a rival, possibly from Old Norse, *foda*, also meaning food. Since words rarely, if ever, occupy exactly the same space, one of these had to alter in either its associative, or its conceptual, senses. In this case *mete* shrank in meaning to signify the 'flesh of animals', that is, a particular kind of food (our *meat*), leaving *foda* to have the larger meaning. We can still get a glimpse of the older meaning of *meat* in the proverb 'one man's meat is another man's poison'. In the nineteenth century both words came into competition with a word of French origin, *victuals*, from *vitaille*, but it didn't survive the contest, and is now obsolete. Similarly, Old English *steorfan*, meaning 'to die', lost ground to another Old Norse word *deyja*, and came to have the more limited meaning of 'die through lack of food' (our *starve*).

We could say then, that whilst words are not creatures of nature, they are still subject to the survival of the fittest. Their senses contract and expand to fill the space available for them within the system. Fortunately, English is such a large and generous host that words which are forced to contract in one sense are able to expand by generating another, related, one. As well as its specific sense, for example, *starve* can also have the looser meaning of 'be hungry', as in *I'm starving*. Many words which would otherwise have a very limited use have acquired a more general sense in this way, for example *horrible*, *frightful*, *ghastly*. Some people hold up their hands in dismay at the increasingly loose usage of such terms. The eighteenth-century writer Samuel Johnson referred to them as 'women's words', regarding them as a female affectation, whilst, in the nineteenth century, Oliver Wendell Holmes called the phenomenon 'verbicide'. Others have called it 'weakening', or 'distortion'. But before seeing it as an instance of language decay, it's as well to bear in mind the point I quoted earlier from Nelson Francis, 'Words do not have meanings; people have meanings for words.' If we no longer use the word *horrible* with the sense of 'full of horror', it may be that we no longer need it to carry that precise sense.

The argument which we are pursuing here is a natural consequence of the existence of words within semantic fields. A field is an area of meaning which coheres around a topic or concept, for example the topic of madness (discussed earlier); or drunkenness, with its associated terms *tipsy*, *inebriated*, *intoxicated*, *smashed*; or poverty – *indigent*, *distressed*, *financially embarrassed*, *hard up*, and so on. What we are observing here is the phenomenon of **synonymy**, or sameness of sense. But as we have already noted, the concept of semantic space prohibits two words having exactly the same meaning. And indeed, if we examine the words in any field we shall find that there are differences, however small, which serve to distinguish items from one another. When we looked at phonology in Chapter 3, we noticed that the contrastive principle was central to the concept of the phoneme. And it's a similar case here. The point I am making, then, is that synonymy can only really exist in the linguistic system as similarity not sameness of meaning. In order to make this absolutely clear, let's consider, briefly, some of the ways in which synonyms do differ. What, for example, are the chief differences between the following sets?

   (i)   *die*; *pass away*
   (ii) *chap*; *bloke*
  (iii) *hide*; *conceal*
  (iv) *stubborn*; *obstinate*
   (v) *broad*; *wide*
  (vi) *royal*; *regal*

Commentary
If you have followed the argument concerning the difference between associative and conceptual sense, you shouldn't find it too difficult to determine the differences here. The words in each set share the same conceptual sense. This is really the source of their synonymy. But they differ either stylistically, connotationally, or collocationally. The first two sets, for instance, are stylistically different: *pass away* is a polite euphemism for *die*, and *bloke* is a more colloquial and rather less polite word for *man* than *chap*. Examples (iii) and (iv) are connotationally different: *conceal* has a stronger sense of deception than *hide*, whilst *obstinate* has a stronger sense of wilful determination than *stubborn*. And the words in the last two sets differ in terms of their collocational range: both *broad* and *wide* can be used with road, but only broad with accent, and in the case of *royal* and *regal*, only *royal* can be used with *mail* and *duties*. All of these words are examples of what we might call 'close' synonymy, where their individual senses almost, but not quite, overlap. Many words, however, exhibit 'loose' synonymy. That is, they overlap in one of their conceptual senses but not in others. For example, *mature*, *adult*, and *ripe* all share the sense of 'in peak condition', but differ in other senses. Similarly, *loose*, *inexact*, *free*, *vague*, and *relaxed* overlap in some senses and not in others. Indeed, dictionaries frequently use the principle of loose synonymy to define a word. Words exist in families, and as with families, individual members share certain characteristics whilst lacking others. Thesauri are based on this principle of family resemblances.

Another way of putting the argument so far is to say that words, or more particularly, the senses of words, define themselves against each other. They do so, however, not only by being similar to each other, but also by being different. We can see this if we consider the reverse side of the coin from synonymy, namely, **antonymy**. Like synonymy, antonymy is also a natural feature of language, and just as it is rare to find two words which are completely identical in meaning, it is similarly rare to find two which are exactly opposite. What we find in fact are various kinds of oppositeness. See if you can work out in what ways the following pairs are opposites:

(i) *wide; narrow*
(ii) *old; young*
(iii) *married; single*
(iv) *alive; dead*
(v) *buy; sell*
(vi) *lend; borrow*

Commentary

The first two sets – *wide; narrow*, and *old; young* – are **gradable antonyms**. In other words, they are at opposite ends of a scale. In the case of *wide* and *narrow*, for example, there are degrees of width in-between. Something can be very narrow or very wide. As a consequence, whilst a road cannot be both wide and narrow, saying it's not wide doesn't necessarily mean it's narrow, and vice versa. The point is that we are not dealing here with an absolute scale, but a relative one. A wide stripe on a dress is narrower than a wide corridor. So wide and narrow derive their meaning from being graded against each other and with reference to the real, or extra-linguistic, world. The same is true for *old* and *young*, *big* and *small*, *hot* and *cold*, and many other such pairs. Interestingly, one term in each pair also has a broader meaning than the other. For example, if you ask how old someone is there is no presumption that they are old, they might be very young, but the same is not true if you ask how young they are. In this case it would be unusual if the answer came back *I'm eighty years young*.

Pairs (iii) and (iv) are **complementary antonyms**. The scale here is absolute not relative. This means that there are only two possibilities, rather than infinite degrees in-between. To say someone is not married means they are single, and if they are not dead they must be alive. However, such is the nature of language that it cannot allow such a neat arrangement to last. We often grade these and talk of someone being *very dead* or *half alive*. And the poet Danny Abse refers to 'the much married life in me' in his poem 'Not Adlestrop'. Pairs (v) and (vi) are different again. As with complementary antonyms they are not gradable opposites. *Buying* and *selling* are not activities which are performed by degrees. Similarly with *debtor* and *creditor* – either you fall into one of these categories or you don't. At the same time, however, they are not complementary, since to say you are not buying does not mean you are selling, and not lending does not mean borrowing. So there is no absolute scale here either. They are best understood as relational antonyms. If you sell something to me, then I buy it from you, and if I am your debtor, you are my creditor. These antonyms exhibit what is known as 'reversability'. Other examples include *husband/wife*, *above/below*, and *rent/let*.

So far we have been considering the semantic space which words occupy in terms of individual senses that they carry. But, as we have already noted, words are capable of signifying more than one sense, both conceptually and associatively. Because of this they can belong to more than one semantic field. The word *mad*, for example, which we considered earlier, as well as having the sense 'insane', can also signify 'angry', as in *please don't be mad with me*. So in addition to belonging to the semantic field of madness, it is also a member of the field of anger. As such, it has synonymous relations with *irate* and *furious*. This capacity for words to bear more than one sense is referred to as **polysemy**. The linguist David Crystal illustrates this strikingly in *The Cambridge Encyclopedia of the English Language* (1995, p. 161), by showing all the possible senses of the word *line*. There are at least 30 of them. Here are just a few of the principal ones:

(i)   occupation: *what line are you in*?
(ii) row of characters: *indent a line*.
(iii) queue: *form a line*.
(iv) telephone connection: *give someone a line*.
(v)   rope: *throw someone a line*.
(vi) policy: *adhere to a line*.

Many words acquire new senses by developing a metaphoric or transferred sense. This is a common process by which most nouns are capable of both a literal and a metaphoric meaning. Prime examples of this are the parts of the body, for example *eye*, *leg*, *hand*, and *foot*, as in *eye of the needle*, *hand on the clock*, *foot of the bed*, or a little more elaborate, *womb*, as in the *womb of time*. I shall have more to say about this a little later. Part of the power of metaphor is that it exhibits what we have called 'reflected meaning', that is, we are aware when using it of an original sense from which it has been derived. When we lose that reflected meaning the metaphor becomes dead. And as I have commented already, our language is littered with the bones of dead metaphors. Yet another common way in which some nouns develop extra senses is by acquiring an abstract, as well as a concrete, meaning. Words like *book*, *text*, *thesis* can all be used to mean something abstract in addition to their concrete senses. Consider, for instance, the difference between *his thesis is wrong* and *his thesis is on the table*. If that isn't sufficiently clear, try putting the senses together, *his thesis is on the table and is wrong*.

A note of caution about polysemy though before we move on. In the case of words like *flight* and *line* we are really looking at separate, but related, senses which have developed from a single core word, or, to be more precise, 'lexeme' (see Chapter 1). We need to distinguish these from those instances where we have words which are identical in sound and shape, but which are entirely different lexemes, that is, they bear no relation to each other: for example, *mail* (armour) and *mail* (post). The fact that these lexemes look and sound the same is a matter of coincidence: they are accidental lookalikes rather than twins. The term which describes this linguistic coincidence is *homonymy*. Having said that, however, it is sometimes very difficult to decide whether identical words are polysemic or homonymous, that is, whether they are instances of the same lexeme, or just different lexemes. There is an unresolved debate in linguistics about the criteria to be used in differentiating between them. So if you find it problematic you are not alone.

I have said quite a lot about semantic fields and the way in which words relate to other words in the same and opposing fields. But before leaving this section there are two more important field relationships which we need to consider. We have seen that words like *demented, insane, loony*, and so on, are all members of the field of madness: their sense overlaps with that of *mad*. At the same time, however, there are many different varieties of madness, each with its own technical label: *schizophrenia, psychopathy, paranoia*, for example. These are not really synonyms for being mad, but subordinate types included within the term *mad*. In other words, *mad* is a general category which has within it a subset of more specific terms. The linguistic relationship which exists between the inclusive category and this subset is termed **hyponymy**. Hyponymy is a hierarchical relationship. Someone who is schizophrenic is necessarily mad, but someone who is mad doesn't have to be schizophrenic. The way that

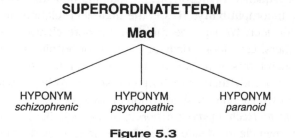

SUPERORDINATE TERM

Mad

| HYPONYM | HYPONYM | HYPONYM |
| *schizophrenic* | *psychopathic* | *paranoid* |

Figure 5.3

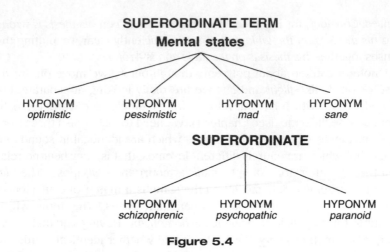

SUPERORDINATE TERM
Mental states

HYPONYM *optimistic*   HYPONYM *pessimistic*   HYPONYM *mad*   HYPONYM *sane*

SUPERORDINATE

HYPONYM *schizophrenic*   HYPONYM *psychopathic*   HYPONYM *paranoid*

Figure 5.4

linguists describe this relationship is to say that the term *mad* is the superordinate category of which the term *schizophrenic* is a hyponym. That is to say, schizophrenic is just a small part, or hyponym, of a larger, more inclusive, category. Have a look at Figure 5.3.

The interesting thing about these hyponymic relationships is that they can be extended further. *Mad*, for example, belongs within the larger field of mental states. This field includes terms like *optimistic, pessimistic, mad*, and *sane*. So *mad* is itself a hyponym hierarchically subordinate to a superordinate category. We can extend our diagram to show this (see Figure 5.4).

Hyponymy is an important hierarchical relationship within fields. Lexicographers, or dictionary makers, rely heavily on it in providing word definitions. A bicycle, for example, can be described as a 'type of vehicle', red as a 'type of colour', apple as a 'type of fruit', and so on. And each of these has its own subsets – there are types of red and types of apples. Once the central hierarchical relationship has been established, the definition usually proceeds by distinguishing the term from its co-hyponyms, so that we do not confuse a bicycle with a scooter, or an apple with an orange.

One consequence of hyponymy is that many fields exhibit what is known as **incompatibility**. This is the final field relationship which we need to consider. We can see this feature more clearly in some fields than in others. Let's look briefly at the field of hospital personnel. This includes such terms as *doctor, nurse, orderly, matron, sister*, and so on. All of these occupy their own semantic space. To begin with, they all have their own satellite of synonymous terms. In the case of *doctor* we have *physician, leech, medic, sawbones*, and *quack*. But in addition, they have their own clearly defined boundaries. Indeed, part of the meaning of *doctor* is 'not nurse, orderly, matron' and so on. As with antonymy, the senses are defined against one another, although not with the same sharpness of opposition: being a doctor is not the opposite of being a matron. Broadly speaking, we can say that words which are mutually exclusive members of the same field exhibit incompatibility. The field of musical instruments is one in which the hyponyms exhibit incompatibility very strongly. You would be thought distinctly odd if you were to say *I'm thinking of an instrument and it's a violin and a piano.* Fields based on fruit, flowers, and colours are similar in this respect. Consider the following: *I'm thinking of a fruit and it's an apple and an orange; I'm thinking of a colour and it's red and black; I'm thinking of a flower and it's a peony and a rhododendron.*

Conclusion so far

In Chapter 1 I quoted the philosopher Ludwig Wittgenstein, who said 'the meaning of a word is its use in the language'. To a large extent what we have been looking at so far has been the implications of that view. Words mean in relation to each other, as well as in relation to an external reality. The first type of meaning we called 'signification' or 'sense', and the second, 'reference'. Words signify through a complex web of relationships by means of which they establish their own individual semantic space. Fundamental to all of these relationships are the concepts of similarity and difference. These are basic to the way in which words express meaning. But it's important to remember that similarity and difference only operate within a system which is itself relational. Words define themselves against each other. Just like the members of any large family they preserve their individuality as part of a shared, corporate, identity. Much of linguistics is concerned with examining this corporateness. Its central preoccupation is with observing, describing, and explaining common patterns of behaviour, whether of sounds, phrases, or sense relations. But no word behaves in exactly the same way as another. Indeed, the more we explore language, the more the contrastive principle as we termed it earlier, or, more properly, the 'differentiation' principle, seems to be at the very heart of the system.

Summary of sense and sense relations

Types of sense:	Conceptual sense
	Associative sense [includes *connotation*, *collocation*, *stylistic variation*, and *reflection*]
Sense group:	Semantic fields

Sense (field) relations – relationships between signifieds:

synonymy

antonymy

polysemy

hyponymy

incompatibility

Non-sense relations – those between signifiers only:

homonymy

rhyme

5.2.3 Processes of semantic change

The consequence of our argument so far is that words do not have an absolute sense, that is, their signification varies across cultures and across time. As we have seen, conceptual sense is the most stable sense, but even here there are a variety of ways in which the meaning, or signification, of a word may alter with the passage of time, and changing cultural context. Studying these processes is an interesting branch of semantics, termed 'historical' or **diachronic** semantics. I'll mention the principal processes very briefly because I want to spend some time on one in particular. Words can be subject to extension, that is, they can grow larger in meaning. For example, the word *virtue* originally signified a quality which only men could possess, but now is gender free in its signification. And they can also experience the opposite process, **limitation**, which involves the loss of one or more senses – for example *miser*, which at one time had as one of its meanings 'wretch'. Other processes involve **pejoration**, whereby a term acquires a pejorative meaning, and its contrary, **amelioration**. The word *gossip*, for example, originally meant a 'god-relative', without any of the pejorative sense of a 'trivial talker' that it has today, and conversely, *boy* was used for a servant of some kind – a sense it still retains in colonial settings, but which it has lost in British English. And finally, **transference**: this is one of the most common ways by which new senses are created, and, as such, is described by linguists as a **productive** process. It involves terms being transferred from one setting to another so avoiding the need for entirely new words. For example, all the terms which we use to refer to railways, such as *track*, *rail*, and *switch*, started their existence elsewhere. A *track* is a small path, *a rail*, a piece of wooden fencing, and a *switch*, a long slender twig or branch. As for *train*, it originally referred to a convoy of people.

But one particular form of transference – metaphorical transference – remains the most significant contributor to semantic change. We have touched on metaphor a number of times during the course of this book and it is now time to say a little more about it. Linguists sometimes tend to gloss over the subject of metaphor partly because it's associated with literary devices, and partly because, until recently, they weren't entirely sure about how to account for it in linguistic terms. But it is one of the principal ways in which we exercise our creativity in language. At the beginning of this chapter we discussed some of the limitations of language. I suggested to you that the principal one was the gap between the world of experience, inarticulate and formless, which comprises much of our existence, and the formal constraints of the linguistic system. I want to suggest to you now that metaphor is both a recognition of that gap and also the chief way in which language seeks to overcome it. In their book *Metaphors We Live By* (1980), the linguists George Lakoff and Mark Johnson argue that the formation of metaphors is not, as is sometimes thought, just an extra function of language, but an integral part of how all language works. And this, they suggest, is because our mental processes, that is, the way in which we reason and think, are metaphorical in character.

Just why this is so should be clearer if we consider a few linguistic examples. Take the following, for instance:

(a)   *The bus is coming to take me to town.*
(b)   *The time is coming for me to leave.*

In both cases the verb *come* signifies the arrival of something. It's a material verb of action (see Chapter 4). However, in (b) it has a different sense from (a) – although we recognise a relationship between them. It is this relationship which linguists refer to as 'metaphorical transference'. Time is visualised in (b) as an approaching object, not necessarily a bus, of course, but an object nonetheless, moving through space. The underlying metaphor here, then, could be expressed as 'time is a moving object'. We know that it isn't, but that is how we often experience it to be. We feel ourselves to be stationary, unchanging, whilst time moves inexorably past us. This is the source of expressions such as *time flies* and *time passes*. There is nothing inevitable about this way of perceiving time. Another culture might well perceive time to be stationary whilst people do the moving. As Lakoff and Johnson are at pains to point out, a culture's metaphors are an invaluable guide to its values and outlook. And in the case of time, because of the complexity of the concept, we use a variety of metaphors to express its significance for us. In the following example the process of transference centres on the verb *spend*, to give us the underlying metaphor time is money:

(c) *How do you spend your money?*
(d) *How do you spend your time?* (Cf. *don't waste my time; this will save you time*)

A majority of these metaphors are an indelible and integral part of our language which we take on board quite unconsciously. And perhaps we can now see why. Metaphors provide an essential means of articulating what would otherwise remain inarticulate. Much of our experiential life is inward and intangible, whether it be of love, joy, suffering, or time. All of these are complex dimensions involving elusive states of being, or modes of awareness. Metaphors allow us, by a process of transference, to make the intangible, tangible; to translate the inexpressible into the expressible. Characteristically, metaphors take material verbs and transfer their sense to non-material situations. In so doing they exploit the associative senses of words and create fresh collocations. Something is always lost in the process of translation since no single metaphor can express the whole of an experience, but language gets round this by providing a variety of metaphors for any one concept. Here is a selection from Lakoff and Johnson of metaphors for love:

(e) *His whole life revolves around her* (love is a physical force)
(f) *She drives me out of my mind* (love is madness)
(g) *He's bewitched by her* (love is magic)
(h) *She fought for him* (love is war)

These metaphors are what we can call 'structural metaphors', that is they structure our experience in some way. In addition to these, however, we also have two other types of metaphor: orientational metaphors and ontological metaphors. The first sort – orientational ones – are concerned with the way in which we give a transferred sense to physical space and movement. Consider the way in which the prepositions, *up, down, in, out* take on metaphorical meanings in the following examples:

(i) *I'm looking up the chimney* → *Things are looking up*
(j) *I'm going down the road* → *I'm feeling down*
(k) *I'm staying in the house* → *Count me in/out*

With these transferences we are using our bodies and our spatial awareness to construct metaphors. They reflect the importance we attach to standing up as opposed to lying down, and the priority we give to the inside of our bodies as against our exteriors. As a consequence, *up* becomes associated with conditions which are positive, *down* with those which are negative, and *in* with those which are seen as privileged in some way. In other words, we could argue that there is a physiological basis to these metaphors. And finally, ontological metaphors. These are the most subtle of all the three groups distinguished by Lakoff and Johnson. Our language works by translating experiences such as events, activities, and states, into concrete entities so that they can be talked about. For example, a judge at the end of a court case sums up the evidence. This is an activity, or event in time, not an object. Language allows us, however, to turn it into one, and talk about *the summing up*, as in *the summing up was severe*. Similarly, even to talk about such things as life and love, we need to treat them as objects, whether containers, as in *he's in love*, or substances, as in *he's got a lot of life left yet*. We don't really register these as metaphors, however, except when a new twist is given to them by a poet or novelist. In his poem 'The Love Song of J. Alfred Prufrock', for example, the poet T. S. Eliot takes the 'life as substance' metaphor a stage further when Prufrock says of himself 'I have measured out my life with coffee spoons'.

I have spent some time on metaphor because there is every possibility that it holds at least one of the keys to the way in which words mean. Lakoff and Johnson define metaphor as 'understanding and experiencing one kind of thing in terms of another'; in other words, as representation. But isn't this what all language does? Using the sound string /tri:/ to refer to the thing growing in the garden is precisely 'understanding one kind of a thing in terms of another'. Could it be that what we term metaphor is a specialised instance of a more general semantic property, that all language is a form of representation? I'm raising these questions here not with any expectation that we might pursue them now but because they offer fruitful lines of enquiry. Linguistics is still in the process of coming to terms with the challenge offered by metaphor, but there is every possibility that what we have termed 'creative competence' is more central to the generation of linguistic structures than has always been recognised.

5.2.4   The role of reference

I have spent a fair amount of time on ways in which words signify because this is the area that modern semantics is most preoccupied with. But it is important to bear in mind that language is not insulated from the real world. We can't hope to account for the meaning of words simply by studying the systematic relationships they have with each other by means of their senses. A vital part of their meaning comes from the way we use them to refer to things in the real, or extra-linguistic, world. Sense and reference are mutually dependent on one another. I said earlier that before we could confidently call something a /tri:/ we had to have the concept 'tree' in our minds, that is, we had to understand the word's sense. At the same time, however, we would need to have seen a large number of individual trees before the concept, or sense, would have any meaning for us. Could we truly be said to know the meaning of the word if we had simply looked up its sense in a dictionary without ever having seen a single one? We should be in the position of those inhabitants of hot countries who had never seen snow, and for whom it was simply a fiction.

Sense is really an abstraction from reference. If you looked up tree in a dictionary, it wouldn't list every single characteristic of trees. To do that would take ages and be quite unhelpful; after all, what we are looking for are the defining features of tree, that is, its essential characteristics. As a consequence, most dictionaries restrict their definitions of trees, dogs, houses, and so forth, to prototypes. **Prototype theory**, as it's known, has been very influential in modern semantic approaches in helping to account for how the mind stores and processes the senses of words. It does so by concentrating on typical, rather than marginal, usages. If we were asked for the sense of *bird*, for example, we should probably base our answer on a robin or sparrow, that is, a central member of the species, rather than on an ostrich or a penguin, which are more marginal. None the less, as with our original example of tree, we should need more than prototypical knowledge in order to identify correctly a particular creature as a bird.

Reference knowledge is essentially extra-linguistic in character. I mean that it's concerned with knowledge about the world. We can distinguish two types: general and specific reference. If I say *I like trees*, I am using the sense of the word *tree*, or its sign value, to refer to a group of objects which have something in common, that is, 'treeness'; if, however, I were to say *this is a tree*, my purpose is simply to identify a particular object as having the sense 'tree'. But in either case I need a certain amount of knowledge about the object(s) in addition to my linguistic knowledge. The problem with reference knowledge is that there is no end to it: it's encyclo-pedic. If you consider all the facts about actual trees, or birds, which it is possible to know and which would be helpful in identifying a particular member, the list would be endless. And you could also argue that the more reference knowledge you had, the richer the sense of a particular term would be. The word *tree* probably has a richer sense to a botanist than it does to those of us who simply know the basic facts about them.

What I am saying, then, is that to understand a particular usage we need more than linguistic knowledge. This is common sense really. If it's the case, as I have been arguing, that words refer to activities, events, processes, and objects in the world around us, then the more of this knowledge we have the more likely we are to understand the sense of the words appropriately. Reference knowledge is fuller and more resistant to systematic analysis than sense knowledge, but we rely on it a good deal to determine whether statements are acceptable or not. We would reject the statement *dogs have three heads*, for example, because it violates what we know to be true about them. More particularly, it violates what linguists call a **synthetic truth**. Something is synthetically true if it reflects a fact about the real world. As a consequence, such truths are contingent, that is, they are not absolute. If, for example, we came across a rare breed of dogs with three heads the statement would no longer be untrue. But under no conceivable circumstances could the statement *dogs are cats* be true (unless we understood the senses here as associate rather than conceptual). This violates an **analytic truth**, or 'truth by the very nature of language' (Leech, 1981, p. 77). The problem with *dogs are cats* is that the senses are in opposition to each other. You might say 'what if we discovered a breed of animals which was half cat and half dog?' Well in that case we should have to invent a new word to express that fact – as in *zedonk*, 'half zebra and half donkey'. The senses of the existing words simply wouldn't be expandable enough to cope. In practice, the dividing line between the two sorts of truth is not always so straightforward, nevertheless most people do recognise a distinction, and it seems to correlate with that between sense and reference.

5.3   Studying pragmatics

Earlier on in this chapter we distinguished between 'sentence meaning' and 'utterance meaning', and I said then that semantics was concerned with the first, and pragmatics with the second. You may well find, in practice, that – as with the distinction between analytic and synthetic truth – it's not always easy to separate the two, and opinions may differ over the boundary. None the less, it is a useful distinction to make. Broadly speaking, the difference can be seen in the two ways in which we use the verb 'mean'. As I pointed out in Chapter 3, if we don't understand something we usually ask either *what does it mean?*, or *what do you mean?* In the first case our concern is with the sense of what has been said, whilst in the second, it is with the speaker's attitude, or viewpoint. We have called this latter type of meaning the 'force' of an utterance rather than its sense. Establishing utterance force is essential to determining the full, contextualised, meaning of any communication. To do this successfully we have to be able to interpret utterances, not simply decode them. This is the area of meaning to which it is now time to turn.

And straightaway we encounter a problem, because, as we saw at the start of the chapter, considering the force of something opens up the whole issue of meaning in a way which is difficult to account for in terms of linguistic rules. There is no rule, for example, which can tell us whether or not someone is being sincere, or has an ulterior motive. Linguistics can only take us so far in determining this layer of meaning. The first thing we need to do then is to delimit the area of enquiry. We have to say that the kind of meaning which we are studying is that which is open to inspection, that is, acknowledged to exist by the parties who are communicating. There is no way we can determine concealed, or hidden, meanings by purely linguistic criteria.

It should be fairly easy to see why this is so. When we listen to someone speaking to us we assume that they are wishing to communicate – it's called the **communicative intention** (see Chapter 2). As I said when we briefly discussed this issue in Chapter 2, if this were not the case we wouldn't waste our time listening. Similarly, if we are speaking, we assume that our audience wishes to understand us. In other words, communication is based on cooperation between speaker and listener. The idea that someone may be misleading us in some way, either intentionally or unintentionally, seems alien to this concept. Of course, people often do mislead us in all sorts of ways, but the fact that we recognise this as a misuse of language is an indication that communication has as its *raison d'être* a strong social, and moral, basis. We referred to this in Chapter 2 as the **cooperative principle**, and I shall have more to say about it in a moment. Learning to cooperate is part of our communicative competence. It involves developing strategies for making ourselves understood, as well as strategies for interpreting the utterances of others. The fact that these may break down on occasions, or be only partially successful, doesn't negate the principles or processes involved. Indeed, if anything it simply reinforces them, and makes us try harder next time.

As we argued earlier, the 'force' of an utterance is the meaning it has in a particular situational setting, or social context. In other words, it is contextual meaning, as opposed to sense, which is largely decontextualised meaning. The difficulty here of course is that the range of contexts in which something can be uttered is seemingly infinite. Fortunately, however, there are various clues which we can utilise to help us determine the meaning of an utterance. One of these is tone of voice, or intonation. **Intonational force**, as we may call it, is an important contextualiser of meaning. On occasions it may even enable us to reverse the apparent sense of something. For example, we could imagine a playful lover saying *I hate you* in a low, intimate tone, suggesting not hatred at all, but desire.

In this case the appeal of the utterance lies in the way force is ␣
against sense. This opposition is basic to a great deal of irony. If s␣
says to you *I like your hat* in a tone indicating mockery then you␣
that *like* is being used ironically, that is, its force is the reverse of its s␣
And in between, of course, there are a whole range of tones ranging f.␣
awe to indifference. Another important clue is **thematic force**. This kr␣
of force is concerned with the way we announce to our audience what ␣
is that we are principally concerned about. As we saw in the last chapter,
this is often reflected in the syntactic organisation of our communication.
Putting an item first in a sentence, for example, is a good way of drawing
attention to it and letting someone know what it is that we wish them to
focus on. Poets, also, frequently rearrange items syntactically in order to
stress or emphasise the significance of something. In the following line
from Milton's *Paradise Lost*, the famous seventeenth-century poem about
the fall of man, Milton is describing the dramatic way in which God threw
Satan out of heaven: 'Him the Almighty hurled headlong down'. In so
doing, Milton switches 'Him' from its position after 'hurled', where it's the
unmarked object of the verb, to the front of the sentence, where it precedes the subject 'the Almighty'. As a consequence, the status of Satan as
central protagonist in the drama is heightened, and correspondingly, the
power needed to defeat him is also emphasised. Literary critics sometimes refer to this process of thematising as **foregrounding**, that is, bringing something from the background of an utterance into the foreground
by syntactic rearrangement. But, in addition, you might note that putting
'Him' at the front of the line means that it now receives a heavy stress. As
we observed earlier, when we speak we choose to stress certain syllables, or words, rather than others. What we are doing is promoting the
principal parts of our utterance and giving them greater prominence, or
force. The phenomenon which we call rhythm is fundamentally a way of
organising utterances to maximise their force. To a certain extent we
could say that all language, even written language, is performed in some
way. And this has clear implications for meaning. Just consider the
following simple statement for example and think about how stressing a
different word might alter its force: *I can't drive there.*

    (i)   *I can't drive there* (but s/he can)
   (ii)   *I **can't** drive there* (it's out of the question)
  (iii)   *I can't **drive** there* (but I can walk there)
  (iv)   *I can't drive **there*** (but I can drive somewhere else)

All we have done here is consider how the stress pattern of an utterance
can contribute to its force, but if we were also to consider how these

...night be combined with different tones of voice, so combining
...onal and thematic force, then the possibilities for extra meanings
be increased immeasurably.

...t important as intonational and thematic clues are in determining
...erance meaning they would be of little value if we were not able to
...late them to an appropriate context. To a considerable extent interpreting the utterance meaning of sentences depends upon the degree of
shared knowledge which exists between speaker and hearer. This
assumed, or shared, knowledge is called by philosophers **presupposition**. If someone said to you *your room is a pigsty,* they would be pre-
supposing that you knew what a pigsty was, and more importantly, what
was characteristic of them in our culture. If you had no knowledge of the
term *pigsty*, or perhaps, belonged to a culture where such places were
revered, you couldn't understand the speaker's meaning. Having made
the right presupposition, that is, 'pigsties are messy places', we can then
draw the correct inference – 'your room is messy'. Presupposition and
inference are part of the logical machinery we use to interpret utterances. But they don't work in a vacuum. They need the raw material of
shared knowledge and cultural understanding on which to operate. This
is because when we communicate we don't explicitly state everything
that we mean, not unless we are talking to someone from a totally different culture. To do so would be enormously time consuming as well as
very boring. As a consequence, a good deal of our meaning is implied:
we assume the listener can draw the correct **inference**. Just consider
how much is implied in the following utterance: *the picnic was ruined.
Someone forgot the corkscrew.* On the face of it there is no necessary
connection between these two statements, but the speaker is implying a
link and assuming we have enough prior knowledge to make the right
inference. To do so we have at least to know what picnics are, that wine
is often taken on them, and what function corkscrews perform. This
would allow us to arrive at the inference 'the picnic was ruined because
we couldn't have any wine'.

So far so good. The only problem with this logical process, however, is
that there is no absolute way of determining the limit of what we can
infer. We might think, for example, from the way the speaker is emphasising *someone* and looking at us that they are accusing us of forgetting
the corkscrew. In which case we would draw an extra inference – 'you
have ruined the picnic'. In other words, because so much of utterance
meaning, or force, depends on implication, or **implicature**, as linguists
call it, we can never be entirely certain of the full extent of meaning. Most
of us know people who read all sorts of meanings into what seem to be

apparently innocent statements. In a sense there is no way, linguistically, of proving whether they are right or wrong, because it is we who are the arbiters – it is we who decide on the pragmatic meaning. I might feel you are over-reacting in thinking yourself accused of forgetting the corkscrew. Who is to say whether I'm right or not? We are back again to a point I made at the start of the chapter about the essential indeterminacy of meaning.

5.3.1 The cooperative principle

It is because of the sheer volume of possible meanings which could be inferred from utterances that we depend most crucially on the principle of cooperation in our everyday exchanges. There is an unspoken pact that we will cooperate in communicating so as to understand and be understood. This pact may be broken, but it exists as a norm against which violations, such as lying, or deviations, such as exaggerations, can be measured. As we saw in Chapter 2, the philosopher most associated with the cooperative principle is Paul Grice. He defined it as an imperative to 'Make your contribution such as is required, at the stage at which it occurs, by the accepted purpose or direction of the talk exchange in which you are engaged' (Grice, 1991, p. 26). This sounds rather legalistic and bureaucratic to be of much use. Indeed it is arguable that all attempts to give the principle the force of a commandment in this way are bound to be unsatisfactory. It is after all a principle, not a rule; in other words we are talking about a convention of communicative practice. But if we bear this in mind it can provide a useful starting point for considering the unconscious assumptions which lie behind the determination of pragmatic meaning.

Grice enumerates the following four maxims which, according to him, characterise the cooperative principle:

(i)   maxim of quantity
(ii) maxim of relation
(iii) maxim of manner
(iv) maxim of quality

The first of these, **the maxim of quantity**, is concerned with the amount of information which we expect from any conversational exchange. When we speak to someone we feel obliged to give them enough detail to enable them to understand us. If we don't, we are not really being cooperative. At the same time, however, we have to avoid providing too much information and obscuring the point we are making. Being able to judge the boundary between too little and too much is part of our communicative competence. If you ask someone whether they have any pets and receive the reply *I've got a budgerigar*, you are entitled to assume that is the limit. But if you then discover they have several other pets you would feel misinformed. The reply is simply not detailed enough. Learning to provide sufficient information is a skill which has to be acquired. Knowing what counts as an answer is not something we are born with, and young children, in particular, find it difficult to be sufficiently informative. At the same time, however, once we know the convention about quantity, it is possible to use it to our own advantage. Being 'economical with the truth', as we might term it, is a frequent phenomenon in everyday life. Politicians, for example, frequently under-report issues in order to avoid embarrassment. And so do all of us on occasions. Consider the following exchange:

> A: *Who's eaten the biscuits?*
> B: *I've had some.*

If *some* is indeed the limit of B's consumption then the reply is appropriately cooperative, but not if s/he has eaten all of them. In this case, by witholding information, s/he is violating the maxim of quantity. On the other hand, if B were to give us a complete account of everything eaten that day s/he would be providing us with too much information and be guilty of violating the maxim in a different way. Most of us know people who are over-circumstantial in their conversation and weary the listener with excessive detail.

The **maxim of relation** directs us to organise our utterances in such a way as to ensure their relevance to the conversational exchange. People who change the subject abruptly, or who go off at a tangent, are usually considered rude or uncooperative. We normally feel under an obligation to link any new contribution to the existing topic to preserve some sense of continuity. At the same time, however, utterances can be relevant in a variety of ways. So strong is our assumption of cooperativeness that we will try our utmost to wring some meaning out of a reply before deciding that it is irrelevant. In so doing, we draw heavily on presupposition, implicature, and inference. Consider the following exchange for instance:

> A: *Where's my chocolates?*
> B: *The children were in your room this morning.*

or

> B: *I've got a train to catch.*

In neither case are B's replies explicitly relevant But they can easily be made so by relating them inferentially to the context. Indeed, so powerful is the maxim of relation that some recent theorists, notably Dan Sperber and Deirdre Wilson (1986), have seen it as subsuming the others. They argue that all of them can be seen in terms of the requirement to relate our utterances to the situational context, whether by direct, or indirect, means. Indeed, one source of humour lies in deliberately mistaking the relevance of a remark, as in the following:

LECTURER: *You should have been here this morning.*
STUDENT: *Why, what happened?*

The lecturer's statement is capable of being interpreted in two different ways, either as an exclamation or a reproof. It is only the situational context which enables us to decide which is correct. The humour here lies in the student choosing not to interpret it as a reproof whilst knowing that it is. As a consequence s/he is being deliberately irrelevant.

The **maxim of manner** obliges us to organise our utterances in an orderly manner, that is, to provide information in a way which can be assimilated by the listener. We have only to imagine what recipes, car manuals, and other sources of information would be like if instructions and details were not provided in a chronological order. But even in less functional contexts there is an assumption of orderliness. This is even the case where the natural sequence is disrupted in some way. Many novels, for instance, change the natural order of events by flashing back, or anticipating the future, but underlying these disruptions there is usually, except in the most experimental works of fiction, a chronological framework which is being departed from and returned to. Orderliness is, of course, one of the first things to go out of the window when people are upset or angry. But again, we could say that the violation of the manner maxim is precisely one of the ways in which strength of feeling is communicated. In other words, without the underlying cooperative convention we would not be able to register deviations.

The **maxim of quality** in a sense underlies all the other maxims in that it assumes that we are speaking what we believe to be true. Lying is an obvious violation of the cooperative principle. If you know someone is lying to you there are a number of options open to you. You can confront them with the fact and force them to cooperate, or withdraw your own cooperation and go through the motions of communicating. Difficulties arise, however, when it seems necessary to lie in order to preserve the cooperativeness – so-called 'white lies'. We may well feel obliged to say nice things about a neighbour's art work, for example, even if we really think it's terrible. Because of this, the linguist Geoffrey Leech (1983) has proposed a politeness principle in addition to Grice's. This would moderate the force of the quality maxim, and allow for cooperative departures from it, by enjoining people to be tactful unless there was a specific reason not to be.

I have suggested to you that the real interest of the cooperative principle lies in the variety of ways which speakers, and writers, find to obey it, even whilst apparently flouting it. As a consequence, a useful distinction we can make is between apparent and real violations. A real violation of the cooperative principle might involve a sudden change of subject (violating the maxim of relation), indicating that our contribution had been completely ignored. But this could easily become cooperative and thus only an apparent violation given a different set of circumstances. As in the following exchange:

A: *Wasn't that a boring lecture?*
B: *Did you remember to feed the cat this morning?*
[A looks up and sees the lecturer standing beside her]

There are a great number of apparent violations, or floutings, as some writers call them, ranging from the deliberate but cooperative irrelevance above, to simple exaggeration, as in *I've told you a million times* – an apparent breaking of the maxim of quality. In other words, we have a choice over how we cooperate; we can choose to do so directly, or indirectly, depending on the circumstances and our individual disposition. And it is the way we choose to cooperate which is responsible both for the rhetorical strategies we employ as addressers, and the interpretative difficulties we experience as addressees.

5.3.2 Speech acts

We considered speech acts briefly in Chapter 2 and now is an appropriate moment to return to them again. If you recall, we said that speech act theory sees all exchanges as events of some kind: they are intended to accomplish something, whether the straightforward acts of informing and requesting, or the more complex ones of giving pleasure and warning. Speech act theorists refer to these as **illocutionary** acts – acts performed through the medium of language – as opposed to **locutionary** acts which are those we perform by the mere fact of speaking. Any utterance is a string of words in a certain order – a locutionary act – and also a means of accomplishing something – an illocutionary act. One way of approaching illocutionary acts is via the principle we have just been looking at. We can see them as different ways in which cooperativeness is realised in any exchange.

At the extreme end we have utterances which are so directly related to their context that saying the words actually brings about a real change. These are called **performatives**, because in these cases saying is doing:

act of marriage	*I hereby pronounce you man and wife*
act of naming a ship	*I name this ship the 'Saucy Sue'*
act of closing a meeting	*I declare this meeting closed*
act of a wager	*I bet you a fiver*
act of apology	*I apologise*

In order for these utterances to count as performatives various conditions have to be met. Only certain people can pronounce you man and wife, for example, whilst if you apologise and clearly don't mean it you have not really apologised. The right context has to be matched with the right form of words. And you might also notice that in each case the statement is in the present tense. This has to be so for it to qualify as a performative. If we change the statement *I name this ship the 'Saucy Sue'*, to *I named this ship the 'Saucy Sue'*, the act of naming vanishes completely since all we are doing is reporting the event, a different act entirely. A number of verbs can have performative functions: *affirm, allege, assert, forecast, predict, announce, insist, order*.

Performatives are a special case of what we have earlier termed **direct speech acts**. Once we move away from them we get increasing degrees of indirectness and indeterminacy. Many direct acts, for example, omit the performative verb and leave it to the nature of the utterance to alert us to the act being performed. Usually the situation is enough to tell us this. So we can assume, for instance, that *get off there* is an order even without the initial part, *I order you to*, whilst *mind the step* is a warning even though *I warn you to* is missing. But, of course, without a performative verb to tell us what act is being performed the possibility for ambiguity is increased enormously. There is no way of knowing simply from the form of the words whether the utterance *see you tonight* is a threat, a promise, or an order. In fact it might be more than one of these since utterances can fulfil several different functions. But difficult as it may be, one of the principal things we do when trying to interpret an utterance is that of deciding on the particular act or acts which are being performed. Only then can we judge how to respond.

And in deciding on the particular act we automatically draw on the cooperative principle. In other words, we assume the utterance is intended to be relevant, orderly, sufficiently informative, and not misleading. Direct speech acts are directly cooperative in nature. The obvious answer to the question discussed earlier, *where's my chocolates?*, would be *I don't know*, or *you've eaten them*. Both are immediately relevant and perform the act of information. But a view of language which saw it simply as the performance of direct acts of this sort would be greatly impoverished. We have already noted that a great deal of meaning is elusive, individual, and non-determinable. Much of what we communicate is done through indirect speech acts. As I said in Chapter 2, an indirect speech act is one which we perform whilst performing a direct one. So, for example, the reply *you've eaten them*, in addition to being a direct statement of information, might also be functioning indirectly as a complaint: 'you haven't left one for me'. *Where are your boots?* said by a parent to a child in addition to being a question (its direct speech function), might also, indirectly, be an order: 'put them on'. And going back to the mysterious *see you tonight*, we can now say that the source of the ambiguity lies not with the nature of the direct act being performed since this is a simple statement of intention – an announcement – but with the *indirect* act(s).

Indirect acts are indirectly cooperative. They depend on us being able to pick up the relevant clues from intonational and thematic force, together with the context of utterance, in order to arrive at a correct interpretation of the speaker's meaning. Not surprisingly, indirect speech acts often involve deviations from the cooperative principle. The student who asks her indiscreet friend whether she fed the cat is only uncooperative in terms of the direct act she is performing – that of enquiry; but the indirect act – that of warning – is fully cooperative. Similarly, the statement *I've told you a million times* only breaches the maxim of quality as a direct act – that of reporting – whereas, indirectly, as a complaint, it is fully compliant. So one way of looking at apparent violations of the cooperative principle is to see them as indirect speech acts. This could extend even to metaphor and irony. Statements such as *you are the sunshine of my life*, and *it's a bit small* (said of Mount Everest), are apparent violations of the maxim of quality since literally they are not true. But part of the point of them lies in the very fact of their deviation, because they function as indirect acts.

5.4   Final conclusion and summary

What we have returned to here is the gap which exists between language and the world, or human experience. We have many more meanings than we have exact syntactic forms to express them. In an ideal world perhaps every possible speech act, whether direct or indirect, would have its own corresponding syntactic form. Ambiguity, confusion, and misinterpret ation would then be eliminated from our language use. But so would much of what makes us human. The endless diversity of human nature, its capacity for generating a plurality of meanings, which can be experienced simultaneously, makes any simple correlation between linguistic forms and meaning impossible. Language struggles to keep up with the sheer complexity of thought and emotion which it represents. We put an enormous semantic burden on utterances. In return, language maximises the resources which are available to it: the lexis, with its complex web of sense relations; syntax with its diversity of structural forms generated for making statements and asking questions; and paralinguistic features such as stress, intonation, and punctuation.

We have seen that there are three dimensions to the way in which words and utterances signal meaning. These are 'reference', 'sense' (or signification), and 'force'. In practice, the exact division between these is not always easy to establish, but in general we can distinguish them in the following way:

reference: meaning in relation to exterior world
sense: meaning in relation to linguistic sytem
force: meaning in relation to situational context

Reference and sense are largely the province of semantics, which is concerned with the 'sentence' meaning of words, whilst 'force' is the pursuit of pragmatics, or the utterance meaning of words. The study of sense involves us in examining the various sense relations which words have within the linguistic system, and also with looking at the ways by which new senses are generated. We have seen that of principal importance here is the process of transference, or metaphor. The study of force, on the other hand, is more concerned with the nature of interpretation, and the processes of inference and presupposition which allow us to provide contextual meanings for utterances. We have seen that these can only operate within conventions about communication involving the importance of cooperation. On the basis of these it is possible to see utterances as the performance of various kinds of acts.

And lastly, we might surmise how it is that we reach any kind of collective agreement on the meaning of particular utterances. You may be operating the same interpretative procedures as me, but how do I know that you will come up with the same answers? Well, of course, there can be no guarantee of this, and as we have seen, we can't always point to language as the final arbiter, since to a certain extent it means what we agree it means, or rather, it means what we can convince other people it means. This is the whole point about argument and debate, which in the final analysis is often a debate about the meanings of words. The literary critic Stanley Fish (1980) has argued that we live in 'interpretive communities' which operate tacit agreements about interpreting utterances. What he seems to mean is that we exist within various kinds of groups – academic, domestic, personal, occupational – which have a common way of expressing themselves and through which understanding of utterances is mediated. It remains a contentious idea, but at least what Fish is pointing us to is the need to envisage some larger entity, which can authenticate the process by which we attach meanings to particular words, and function as the guarantor of individual speech acts.

Further reading

Aitchison, J. (1994) *Words in the Mind: An Introduction to the Mental Lexicon* (Oxford: Blackwell).

Blakemore, D. (1992) *Understanding Utterances: An Introduction to Pragmatics* (Oxford: Blackwell).

Goatly, A. (1996) *The Language of Metaphors* (London: Longman).

Green, G. (1988) *Pragmatics and Natural Language Understanding* (New York: Erlbaum).

Grice, H. P. (1991) *Studies in the Way of Words* (Cambridge, Mass.: Harvard University Press).

Hofman, T. R. (1993) *Realms of Meaning* (London: Longman).

Hudson, R. (1995) *Word Meaning* (London: Routledge).

Hurford, J. R. and Heasley, B. (1983) *Semantics: A Coursebook* (Cambridge: Cambridge University Press).

Jackson, H. (1988) *Words and their Meanings* (London: Longman).

Lakoff, G. and Johnson, M. (1980) *Metaphors We Live By* (Chicago: University of Chicago Press).

Lakoff, G. and Turner, M. (1989) *Beyond Cool Reason* (Chicago: University of Chicago Press).

Leech, G. (1981) *Semantics*, 2nd edn (London: Pelican).

Leech, G. (1993) *Principles of Pragmatics* (London: Longman).

Levinson, S. (1983) *Pragmatics* (Cambridge: Cambridge University Press).

Lyons, J. (1981) *Semantics* (Cambridge: Cambridge University Press).

Palmer, F. R. (1981) *Semantics*, 2nd edn (Cambridge: Cambridge University Press).

Ricoeur, P. (1986) *The Rule of Metaphor* (London: Routledge).

Saussure, F. de (1966) *Course in General Linguistics* (originally published 1913), ed. C. Bally and A. Sechehay, trans. W. Baskin (New York: McGraw-Hill).

Thomas, J. (1995) *Meaning in Interaction: An Introduction to Pragmatics* (London: Longman).

Thomas, O. (1969) *Metaphor and Related Subjects* (New York: Random House).

Tsohadtzidis, S. L. (1994) *Foundations of Speech Act Theory* (London: Routledge).

Waldron, R. A. (1979) *Sense and Sense Development*, rev. edn (London: André Deutsch).

6 Studying Linguistics Further

6.1   Introduction

We have now looked at the three main levels of linguistics: phonology, syntax, and semantics. Let me remind you what these are. Phonology is concerned with the sound structure of the language, in particular with the way in which sounds can form words. Syntax explores the organisation of these words into units such as phrases and sentences. And semantics examines the ability of words to signal meaning through the relationships they have with each other, and with the world of experience. Taken together, these levels constitute what we have termed the **grammar** of the language. Each is governed by a set of rules, or principles, and in Chapters 3, 4, and 5 we have examined some of the ways in which linguists attempt to describe these. As Jean Aitchison puts it in *Teach Yourself Linguistics* (1992, p. 8), they constitute the 'bread and butter' of linguistics. We can represent this grammatical model in the following way:

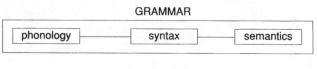

GRAMMAR

| phonology | syntax | semantics |

FIGURE 6.1

There are two other points which I hope have emerged from our discussion so far. First, these three levels are not isolable areas of the language. None of them could exist without the others. And second, the system is not watertight. Words circulate all the time through the linguistic system, like blood around the body. But at every stage of their

GRAMMAR

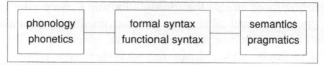

FIGURE 6.2

existence they are constantly being renewed by transfusions from the non-linguistic world. These transfusions might be phonological – words can change their pronunciation form; or syntactic – words may change their class, for example, nouns may become verbs; or semantic – words may change their meaning. It is a dynamic not a static system. And because of that, we have identified in each case a more abstract, and a more concrete, dimension of these levels. So a revised diagram would look like Figure 6.2.

Having established some of the groundwork for studying linguistics we can now begin to consider some of the ways in which we can extend our knowledge. There are two possibilities here. Either we can deepen our knowledge of the levels themselves, or we can explore some of their applications within branches of linguistics such as sociolinguistics, psycholinguistics, and stylistics. The first part of this chapter will be devoted to the process of deepening, and will consider the topics of 'sound', 'syntax', and 'meaning' again; and the second will be devoted to the process of extending and will consider ways of studying some of the principal branches.

6.2 Studying more sound

6.2.1 Distinctive feature analysis

In Chapter 3 ('Studying Sound') we spent the majority of our time demonstrating the need for a phonemic alphabet and exploring the principles on which one could be constructed. We saw that the physical characteristics of individual sounds, which constitute their phonetic existence, are utilised by the linguistic system in the generation of phonemic contrasts, for example the difference between *sue* and *zoo* rests solely in the fact that the initial sound in *sue* is unvoiced, whereas in *zoo* it is voiced. The particular configuration of characteristics which a phoneme has are referred to as its 'distinctive features'.

One way in which we can deepen our understanding of speech sounds is by exploring more closely the interrelationship between the phonetic and the phonemic level of sounds. We can do this by examining the operation of the distinctive features in actual speech. Take the feature **nasal**, for example, which Chapter 3 identified as a property of the phonemes /n/, /ŋ/ and /m/. All of these sounds are produced by the lowering of the soft palate at the back of the mouth, as a consequence of which the sound comes out through the nose. What sometimes happens, however, is that the soft palate lowers early, in preparation for the nasal sound, with the result that the nasality spreads on to the preceding sound. This is typically so when a vowel precedes the nasal. In such cases the vowel may have a slightly nasal twang to it. Most English speakers will nasalise the vowel in the word *man*, where /æ/ is sandwiched between two nasals:

   man = [mæ̃n]

The small sign, or **diacritic**, over the [æ̃] is there to tell us that the vowel has been nasalised. So we have two allophones of the phoneme /æ/, one nasalised, and one not. Some accents, notably American, allow more nasalisation than others. This sometimes results in the complete omission of the nasal consonant. The word *can't*, for instance – /kænt/ in American English – is often pronounced [kæ̃t], the nasal sound being provided by the vowel. This is not systematic enough for us, however, to say that American English has created a new phoneme. But if we were studying French it would be another matter. Here, nasalisation has proceeded even further and phonemic nasal vowels are common. In the word *un*, for example, /n/ has been dropped completely, except when followed by a word like *homme*, and the preceding vowel is heavily nasalised.

Examining a feature such as nasality allows us to track some of the ways in which pronunciation changes occur. Characteristically, the presence of a particular feature becomes more, or less, marked, giving rise to fresh variants of a phoneme. In some instances, as in the case of French above, entirely new phonemes are created. This is how the phoneme /ŋ/ seems to have entered the phonology of English. It's a nasal sound which only occurs before velar plosives – /k/ and /g/. We noticed its occurrence in our discussion of *charming* in 'Studying Sound' (Section 3.3). The feature at issue here is 'velarisation'. What appears to have happened is that the n of *charming* has become velarised, that is, the back of the tongue has been raised to the velum, or soft palate, in preparation for the articulation of the plosive g. In initial stages this was probably just an allophone of /n/ – as it still is in Midland accents. But eventually the /g/

was dropped and [ŋ] developed full phonemic status. We can test this because it contrasts with /n/ in the following minimal pair:

sing = /sɪŋ/
sin = /sɪn/

All of the distinctive features which we listed in Chapter 3 provide useful starting points for exploring and describing variations in pronunciation. Variations in voicing, lip rounding (in the case of vowels), and palatalisation all result in variant sounds for each phoneme. In order to capture these, linguists have to employ an extensive system of diacritics. These are phonetic symbols which tell us how an individual phoneme is pronounced in different phonetic environments. We have seen some of them already. Once you have mastered the phonemic alphabet the next stage is learning to use these symbols. But you may be wondering just how many allophones there are. Unfortunately there is no simple answer to this because the language is changing all the time. It is also the case that some phonemes allow more variation than others. At the same time, however, some variation is rather trivial and not worth bothering about – for example, the slight alterations we make in the pronunciation of /s/. Phonologists tend to be interested only in those which are systematic enough in their occurrence to allow the formulation of pronunciation rules. A pronunciation rule for the nasalisation of /æ/, for example, would take the form shown in Figure 6.3. But we can in fact improve on this because as a general rule all vowels become nasalised before a nasal consonant, not just /æ/ (see Figure 6.4).

The construction of pronunciation rules is the end of a long process of investigation and identification on the part of the phonologist. An essential part of that process consists of finding out which variant sounds belong to which phonemes. Phonologists use a number of criteria here,

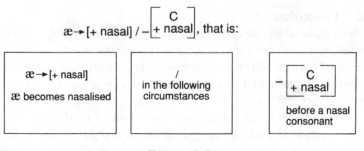

FIGURE 6.3

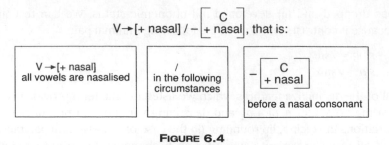

FIGURE 6.4

two of the most important of which are **complementary distribution** and **free variation**. We'll consider these briefly. Complementary distribution states that if two sounds, or to use the term we introduced in Chapter 3, 'phones', never occur in the same environment, that is, the same position in a word, they may be members of the same phoneme. So, for example the two *l*s which we identified in Chapter 3 – clear *l* and dark *l* – are in complementary distribution. Clear *l*, or [l], occurs before vowels – for example, *lip*, *lead* – and dark *l*, or [ɫ], occurs before consonants and word finally – *milk*, *mill*. Many allophones fulfil this criterion of complementary distribution but there are some which do not. These are the ones which are covered by the second criterion of free variation. This states that if two or more phones occur in the same environment, but without changing the word in which they occur, they may belong to the same phoneme. A good example of this is the consonant phoneme at the end of *bid*. Like many other voiced plosives at the end of words it sometimes loses its voicing due to the fact that sounds in these positions are weakly articulated. Sometimes, then, we may pronounce this word with a devoiced /d/ – [d̥], and sometimes with the normal voiced variant – [d]. It doesn't matter which, because however we pronounce it the sounds are not contrastive – the difference does not produce a new word. So [d] and [d̥] are in free variation.

6.2.2　Intonation

Another way in which we can extend our study of sound is by considering the relationship between the sound system and the levels of syntax and semantics. To do this involves examining a unit larger than the phoneme: the syllable. Have a look back at what we said about the syllable in Chapters 2 (Section 2.2.1, vii), and 3 (Section 3.2). I suggested there that the best way to view the syllable was as a unit of rhythm, indeed, the smallest we have in the language. All language is rhythmically organised. We stress certain syllables more than others in our utterances and in so doing create little rhythmical patterns. One of the things which this affects is the pace of our delivery. Stressing every syllable in the following utterance, for example, would slow it down to the point where its message would be unmistakable:

IF/ I'VE/ TOLD/ YOU/ ONCE/ I'VE/ TOLD/ YOU/ TWICE

Clearly, the stress pattern here is part of the meaning, or more strictly, the force of the utterance. One could, for instance, imagine an adult at the end of his/her tether saying this to a naughty child. In the following version, however, with a different stress pattern, the force is different again:

if/ i've/ TOLD/ you/ ONCE/ i've/ TOLD/ you/ TWICE

In this version the unstressed, or weak syllables contrast with the stressed, or strong, ones to produce a much more interesting and more varied rhythm. What the rhythm does is to pick out the central bits of the message and make them more prominent. In other words, the stress pattern has an information value; stressing something is a way of saying 'notice this, it's important'. But also, if you look at the line again you will see that after the first two weak syllables we have an alternating pattern of strong/weak. We tend to organise our utterances in alternating patterns of this kind, with one or more weak syllables counterpointing a strong one. If you listen to newsreaders on the radio or television, you will notice that the stresses tend to fall at fairly regular intervals. English is sometimes referred to as a 'stress-timed' language, and, although it isn't strictly true, it is noticeable that most speakers will speed up or slow down their delivery to avoid too long a gap before a stress. Try, for example, saying the following sentences, clapping your hands on the stressed syllables and keeping the same time throughout.

JOHN STANDS
JOHNny STANDS
JOHNny underSTANDS
JOHNny misunderSTANDS
JOHNny doesn't misunderSTAND

You should have found that as the sentences got longer you wanted to introduce an additional stress because of the difficulty of fitting in all the weak syllables.

The rhythmical patterning of English speech is usually referred to as **prosody**. Linguists who are interested in this area of linguistics talk of **feet** and **metrics**, and in some cases the analysis of particular patterns can be highly technical. But it has to be said that despite a good deal of interest in prosody the discovery of a complete set of rules which speakers obey in distributing stress is still some way off. At the same time, however, there is more to prosody than simply the distribution of stresses. When we speak our voices are rising and falling continually; to speak all on one level would be extremely boring. What we are doing is altering the pitch level of our utterances, a bit like a pianist running up and down the notes in a particular key. As we noted in Chapter 3, speaking is similar in some ways to singing. This variation of pitch is referred to as **intonation**. As with stress, attempts to provide a set of rules for intonation are still some way from completion. However, many linguists accept that speech is organised in some way into what are called **tone units**. These are stretches of speech over which a particular tone operates. Each tone unit is normally viewed as having a 'head' or **nuclear syllable**. We can think of this as the most prominent, or salient, bit of the tone unit because it's the syllable where the greatest movement of pitch occurs. It also coincides with the syllable which receives the most stress in an utterance. But bear in mind that stress and intonation are not the same thing. Syllable stress has to do with our perception of emphasis, usually connected with a sense of volume, although there is no clear correlation here, whereas intonation is concerned with movement of pitch, rather than any sense of emphasis. Because of this it's useful, when discussing intonation, to talk about prominent, rather than stressed syllables, of which there may be many in any tone unit.

There is no real agreement amongst phonologists about the exact number of tones in speech, but all agree on at least four. These are:

1. Fall ➘
2. Fall-rise ➘ ➚
3. Rise ➚
4. Rise-fall ➚ ➘

The chief problem which most people have in working with intonation patterns is that it's extraordinarily difficult to hear yourself speak. As soon as you try and imitate a tone, the fact that you are deliberately listening to yourself gets in the way. You can avoid this, either by taping yourself saying sample sentences, or by using the services of a friend to listen to you. But another way of simply registering the presence of pitch variation in your voice is to play the game which children sometimes do: make up a short sentence and try and communicate its message simply by humming it. If you do this you will discover that some syllables are hummed more forcefully than others; these are the stressed ones. But in addition, there is one which is the target of the utterance; this is the nuclear prominence. You will also be aware of your voice following a contour of rising or falling pitch. If this doesn't work try experimenting with just one syllable, as below, altering the tone each time. As you do this think of the different force which a particular tone might have:

 (definitely not)

 (Are you sure?)

 (Really? Is that so?)

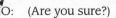 (stop that right now)

Traditionally, tones are linked with particular attitudes or emotions, as above. The most common ones are:

Falling tones: positive, or assertive attitude
                 /that's MINE/,
                 /he's a FOOL/

Falling–rising: doubtful, uncertain attitude
                 /he COULD/,
                 /I'm not SURE/

Rising: enquiring, diffident attitude
                 /COFFee/

Rising–falling: impatient, sarcastic
                 /it's up to YOU/, /how NICE/

In practice, however, it's very difficult to give tones semantic meaning in this way independently of context: /how NICE/, for example, could simply be expressing enthusiasm, not sarcasm, whilst /he COULD/ said with a falling, rather than a falling–rising, tone might equally suggest doubtfulness – 'he could but I'm not sure he would'. Nor is it easy to link tones with particular grammatical structures, although the attempt is often made. 'Yes/no' questions of the type /are you GOing?/ are said to employ a rising, more enquiring tone, whilst 'Wh' type questions (those starting with *which*, *why*, or *when*) have a falling tone – /what's the MATTer?/ But again this isn't invariable. In the following sentence the question could equally well carry a falling or a rising tone.

/it was bob SMITH/ WASN'T it?/

/it was bob SMITH/ WASN'T it?/

So what can we concretely say about the function of intonation and tone units given the uncertainty we have been discussing?

Arguably the most fruitful approaches are those which adopt an interactive approach to intonation. Here is the account outlined by Michael McCarthy in *Discourse Analysis for Language Teachers* (1991).[1] In transcribing tone units McCarthy adopts the following notation. (You'll find that notations vary in sophistication, but the rule for us as beginners is 'the simpler the better'.) A tone unit:

1. is enclosed within slant lines
2. has one nuclear prominence (shown in bold capitals)
3. may have one or more non-nuclear prominences (shown in capitals)
4. may have any number of stressed syllables (not indicated)
5. may have any number of unstressed syllables (not indicated)

McCarthy suggests that we can look upon tones as signalling the 'state of play' in discourse. In this respect a speaker has to decide, when delivering the tone group, whether it should be delivered as open-ended, that is, incomplete in some way, possibly inviting a response from the listener; or as closed, that is, complete in itself and possessing a finality. In received pronunciation open-ended communications are carried by rising tones, whilst closed are carried by falling tones. In the following example it is possible for the utterance to carry either open or closed tones depending on the interaction between speaker and listener:

/IF you LIKE/ we can GO via MANchester/

Here the falling–rising tone on the nuclear syllable **LIKE** indicates that the decision to go via Manchester is still undecided – it is up to the listener to indicate his or her wishes – whilst the falling tone on **MAN** closes the utterance by indicating the extent of the offer, or suggested route. An alternative possibility is for the offer to be made simply with the second tone group, in which case the intonation would be as follows:

/We can GO via M̰A̰N̂chester/ but ONLY if you WA̰NT to/

But let's imagine a different scenario in which the listener has already indicated his/her firm desire to go via Manchester and the speaker is giving in. In this case a falling tone on **LIKE**, indicating closure, reinforced by one on **GO**, would be most likely:

/IF you L̰ḬKE/ we can G̰O via manchester/

In addition to the open v. closed force of tones, however, there is another dimension of interaction to be taken into account, and that is speaker dominance. We have said that falling and rising–falling are closed tones, and that rising and falling–rising are open tones, but within each group there is a more dominant one. In the case of tones which fall, the rising–falling is the most dominant, whilst in the case of those which rise, the rising tone is more dominant. Here is a summary of the possible permutations:

1. Falling: closed, non-dominant
2. Rising–falling: closed, dominant
3. Rising: open, dominant
4. Falling–rising: open, non-dominant

The interactive approach helps to explain why tones have conventionally been linked to certain attitudes or emotions. Open tones, because they often invite a response, and imply incompleteness, frequently accompany polite or friendly feelings, whilst closed tones because they suggest finality and definiteness, more normally accompany assertive ones. It's not surprising then that the rising–falling tone is the least common of all, for not only does it suggest finality but it does so with extra dominance. We might come across this tone for instance in the classroom in the case of a teacher instructing a pupil:

/it's TO͡OK/ TO͡OK/is the past tense of TA͡KE/

Here the rising tone on **TAKE** as an open tone has the force of appealing to the pupil with the sense of 'do you see now'.

6.3   Studying more syntax

6.3.1   Morphology

In our chapter on syntax we explored the way in which words cohere together in phrases, and ultimately, sentences, on the basis of their word class, and we described such an approach as 'categorial'. But whilst this provides us with the core of a modern approach to syntax, there are important areas which our account omitted. One of these has to do with units of analysis which are intermediate between words and phrases. We shall be looking at these in a moment because they have provided the basis for a more sophisticated account of syntactic structure. But another has to do with units below the level of words themselves. This is the concern of **morphology**. In the past, morphology has sometimes been studied separately from syntax, but in recent years it has become more usual to include it within syntax. This is principally because it is vital to the system by which we signal tense and number: in other words, the inflectional system of English. Morphology is concerned with the structure of words – the term itself is of Latin origin and means 'of the structure of things'. If you think about the process whereby we create new words in the language, it is very rare that we actually make up something entirely new. We usually either borrow a word from another language, or, more often, adapt an existing word. One of the frequent ways in which we do this is by adding a suffix on to the word, or in morphological terms, a **morpheme**. Morphemes are the smallest units of meaning, and the smallest units of grammatical analysis in the language. It's important not to confuse them with syllables, which are units of sound, and essentially meaningless. Adding a morpheme on to an existing stem will always change the meaning in some way (even if it's only 'grammatical' meaning). Consider the effect of adding the suffix *ify* to the following words:

1.   *code* → *codify*
2.   *beauty* → *beautify*
3.   *simple* → *simplify*
4.   *ugly* → *uglify*

There are superficial differences here, like the disappearance of a grapheme from the spelling. But the principal change is that all the words, whether they are nouns, like *code* and *beauty*, or adjectives, like *simple* and *ugly*, have all been turned into verbs and acquired fresh meanings. The suffix *ify* is a verb morpheme and it has the capacity to transform any word it is attached to. Clearly it can only do so, however, where the stem makes this semantically possible. We couldn't add it on to *window*, for example. There has to be a degree of cooperation between stem and suffix. Having said that, of course, there will be differences of opinion as to what is acceptable. You may well feel that *uglify* is itself an ugly word, but it is perfectly acceptable to some people.

As well as verb morphemes we have morphemes which can create new nouns, adjectives, and adverbs. Here is a selection:

1. *readable*: *read* + *able*, verb → adjective
2. *sandy*: *sand* + *y*, noun → adjective
3. *authorship*: *author* + *ship*, noun → noun
4. *informant*: *inform* + *ant*, verb → noun
5. *happily*: *happ(y)* + *ily*, adjective → adverb
6. *homewards*: *home* + *wards*, noun → adverb

These small units – *able, y, ship, ant, ily, wards* – which are bolted on to the root word are called **bound** morphemes. They are detachable and can be added on to a variety of words, but cannot stand alone as words in their own right. Occasionally they might look like words; *ship*, for example, is found on its own, but in this case it is an entirely different form. *Ship* the bound morpheme and *ship* the word are homonyms (see Section 5.2.2), or accidental lookalikes. If these movable bits are called 'bound' morphemes we might speculate as to what we might call the root word to which they are attached. Simply to call them words, or lexemes, blurs the distinction between them and the lexemes, which are formed from them. The solution adopted by linguists is to refer to these roots as free morphemes. All the examples above, then, combine a free morpheme with a bound morpheme.

So far we have been looking at what linguists call **derivational** morphology. In other words, the processes by which new lexemes are generated in the language. Suffixation is only one of these processes; there is also **prefixation**, **compounding**, **clipping**, **blending**, and **conversion**. All of them are rich in linguistic interest and studying them will provide you with a good insight into the innovative resources of the language. But altering the shape of a word doesn't always result in an entirely new lexeme. If we alter the word *dog*, for example, into *dogs* we

haven't produced a new lexical item; the only semantic difference here is one of number. All we have done is to put an existing word, in this case, a lexeme, into the plural. And although we have produced a new word, it remains the same lexeme. So, one big difference between this type of morphology and the one we have just been considering is that this second type does not generate new lexemes. Linguists call it **inflectional** morphology. There are very few inflections in English. The elaborate case system which used to be a feature of Old English has all but faded away, leaving us with only a handful of inflectional morphemes. Principal among these are the formation of the plural and the formation of the past tense. The standard morphemes here are *s* and *ed*.

Free morpheme	Plural morpheme
cat	*s*
dog	*s*
badge	*s*

Free morpheme	Past tense morpheme
miss	*ed*
harm	*ed*
sort	*ed*

But notice that although the bits we are adding on are the same, they are not always pronounced identically. There are three different ways of pronouncing the plural, depending on the consonant phoneme which ends the word. In the case of *cats* the plural is pronounced /s/, whereas in dogs it is /z/, and in badges it is /ɪz/. Similarly, there are three different ways of pronouncing the past tense morpheme: /t/ in *missed*, /d/ in *harmed*, and /ɪd/ in *sorted*. Another way of expressing this is to say that both morphemes have three **allomorphs**. Allomorphs are the phonemic, that is, sound form, of morphemes. These particular allomorphs always occur after certain sounds and as such are said to be 'phonologically conditioned'. You might try and work out what the rules governing their pronunciation are: the clue is to look at the voicing of the final phoneme of the free morpheme. There are, however, quite a few plurals and past tense forms which are irregular. The plural of *foot*, for example, is *feet*, not *foots*, whilst the past tense of *bring* is *brought*, not *bringed*. In the vast majority of instances these are survivals from Old English patterns of morphology; they are fossils from the past. As such, the rules governing their formation are no longer productive in English. They are not part of our linguistic competence, in the way that knowing we should add an *s* to *cat*, or an *ed* to *miss*, are. We simply have to learn them individually as exceptions.

All I have done here is to sketch in an approach to morphology and leave you to follow up some of the topics. Matters get more complex when we consider that a lexeme might be subject to a number of morphological processes within the language. Working these out can be fairly involved, but they take us to the heart of the way in which language operates. As an example, take the noun *bomber*. This is derived from *bomb* by addition of the suffix *er*. But *bomb* occurs in the language both as noun and a verb. So which is the root of *bomber*? To determine this we have to track the morphological history of the word. In its first incarnation *bomb* is a noun as in *the plane dropped a bomb on the town*. The verb *to bomb* is derived from the noun by a process of conversion and has the meaning of planting or dropping a bomb; so we can now say *the plane started to bomb the town*. *Bomber* is derived from the verb with the meaning 'something, or someone, engaged in the activity of bombing':

> *bomb* → *bomb* → *bomber*
> noun > verb > noun
> derivational processes = conversion + suffixation

As with other aspects of syntax this can also be shown in the form of a tree diagram (see Figure 6.5).

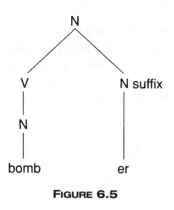

FIGURE 6.5

6.3.2   X bar syntax
In our discussion of phrase structure we saw that phrases were formed out of the five main word classes: verbs, nouns, adjectives, adverbs, and prepositions; and I used the image of a constellation to suggest the way in which various words cluster around the head word either to pre-modify, or post-modify, it. There is nothing wrong with this level of analysis, and

when you are starting out with linguistics It is still the most useful way of approaching phrase structure. But linguists are forever seeking more refined and subtle explanatory frameworks and, for many, what has come to be known as X bar, or $\overline{X}$, theory has greater explanatory power.

X bar theory is a dynamic model of sentence structure and, as a consequence, has changed considerably in the intervening years since its entry onto the linguistic scene. We'll begin by looking at the early model of it before considering, briefly, the current state of the theory. You will remember that in our sample sentence in Chapter 4, *the cat devoured the tiny mouse*, we identified *the cat* and *the tiny mouse* as noun phrases in that they satisfied both the replacement test and the movement test. But let's look again at the phrase *the tiny mouse*. The word *mouse* on its own is clearly not a phrase. At the least it needs a determiner, such as *the*, to give it a phrasal capability. But what of the sequence *tiny mouse*? It seems to be intermediate between the two categories, smaller than a phrase, but larger than a word. One way round this difficulty would be to call it a **noun bar**. 'Very ingenious', you may say, 'but what is the evidence that these two words form any sequence at all?' Well, if we look at our two tests – the replacement test and the movement test – the sequence does seem capable of passing the first of these. In the following sentence, for example, the word *one* stands not just for *mouse*, but for *tiny mouse*:

Which tiny mouse is yours – this one or that one?

If we revisit our diagrammatic representation (in Chapter 4) of the phrase *the tiny mouse* with this new level of structure it would like Figure 6.6.

Nor is this the end of the story; for if we extend the phrase to *the poor tiny mouse* we have yet another intermediate sequence, that is, *poor tiny mouse*. Like the smaller sequence, *tiny mouse*, it will also pass the replacement test:

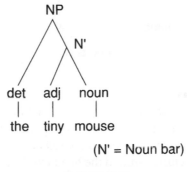

(N' = Noun bar)

FIGURE 6.6

Which poor tiny mouse is yours – this one or that one?

To cope with this we can adapt our diagram by putting in another N bar (N'). And this time, to show that NP is the final rung of the ladder we can call it N" (noun double bar) – see Figure 6.7.

What this diagram tells us is that the complete phrase, or double noun bar, *the poor tiny mouse* consists of a determiner, *the*, plus a noun bar, *poor tiny mouse*, which, in turn, consists of an adjective *poor* plus a noun bar which contains an adjective *tiny* plus a noun *mouse*. This, however, is still not the end of the phrasal possibilities here. We could, in theory, put any number of adjectives and thus noun bars between the starting point of the phrase *mouse* and its terminal point *the*, and end up with an almost limitless phrase. We can express this, in terms of the rewrite rules which we used in Chapter 4, in the following way:

$$N" \rightarrow DET + N'$$

$$N' \rightarrow ADJ + \begin{Bmatrix} N' \\ N \end{Bmatrix}$$

(*Remember – curly brackets indicate that constituents are alternatives.) In this way the N' entry shows the recursive, or repeatable possibilities, of the rule.

But what is the advantage we might ask of refining the rules in this way? There has to be some gain in descriptive terms to make it worth the bother. The answer is that it enables linguists to capture certain similarities between phrases more elegantly. Elegance is not something most people would automatically associate with linguistics, but this is probably because the common understanding of the term derives from the world of fashion and the arts. Like a number of empirically based subjects, however, linguistics is

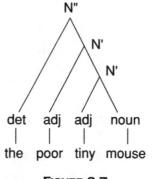

FIGURE 6.7

concerned with the pursuit of 'intellectual' elegance. When mathematicians produce a higher-level formula to express a whole set of lower-level ones, they can justifiably say they have produced an intellectually more elegant explanation. And so it is with linguistics. To see exactly how this is more elegant, however, we need to look more closely at features of commonality between phrases. The first thing to notice is that the structure which underlies the noun phrase also underlies the other phrases, that is, verb, adjective, adverb, and prepositional phrases. What I mean is that they all have the capacity for smaller phrasal constituents, or phrase bars, within them.

Not only that, but they all can be pre- and post-modified in similar ways to the noun phrase. True, they don't all take determiners and adjectives – we can't premodify a verb with *the*, for example – but they can take their equivalents. Just think for a moment of the functions which *the, poor, and tiny* perform in our phrase above. We could say that *the* performs a specifying function – it points to the mouse in question – whilst the adjectives perform an attributive function – they attribute certain qualities to the animal. Once we make this move we can see that the same goes for other phrases. If you remember, we said in Chapter 4 that the simplest verb phrase consisted of a verb. This is the case in the sentence *The cat disappeared*, where *disappeared* is an intransitive verb (it normally doesn't take an object, although see Chapter 1). Here, the verb is acting as a phrase all by itself. However, we could expand it in the following way by saying *The cat has completely disappeared*. In this case *disappeared* is not the full phrase. Using the notation we employed above, it is a V' (verb bar). The word before it, *completely*, is acting as an attribute and expands the V bar into another V bar, whilst *has* performs the vital function of indicating, or specifying, the tense of the phrase (present), and expands the V bar into the full phrase, or V double bar (V").

Specifiers and **attributes** don't account for all the elements which can modify phrases. X bar theorists also distinguish **complements** and

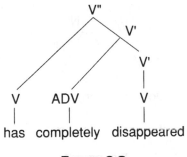

FIGURE 6.8

adjuncts. Complements are more tightly bound to the kernel, or head word, of the phrase, whilst adjuncts have a looser association. In Chapter 4, for example, when we were considering the sentence *The cat sniffed the tiny mouse in the kitchen*, we argued that the noun phrase *the tiny mouse*, and the prepositional phrase *in the kitchen*, were both part of the verb phrase *sniffed the tiny mouse in the kitchen*. But we also said that the sentence could be construed in two ways, that is, either the mouse belonged in the kitchen, or it was sniffed in the kitchen. We are now in a position to say that if the mouse lived in the kitchen then the prepositional phrase forms part of the complement of *sniffed* whilst if the sniffing took place in the kitchen then it is an adjunct.

We haven't the space here to look at adjective, prepositional, and adverb phrases, but if we had we should discover that they could all be described in bar terms with a head word, and various intermediate stages supplied by specifiers and so on, up to the double bar stage. As I hope you can see, the advantage of using terms such as 'specifier', 'attribute', 'complement', and 'adjunct' is that it doesn't tie us down to particular word categories; a specifier, for example, doesn't have to be a determiner. And this is where the X factor comes in. Once we have a common structure for all phrases we don't need separate rules for each type of phrase. It becomes possible to replace N, V, P, A, Adv, by X, where X is a category variable. This means it can represent any major word level category we want. Adopting this principle, we could re-express the rules for our noun phrase above (*the poor tiny mouse*) in the following manner:

$$X'' \rightarrow SPEC + X'$$

$$X' \rightarrow ATTRIB + \left\{ \begin{array}{c} X' \\ X \end{array} \right\}$$

The advantage of these rules is that they will also fit the verb phrase *has completely disappeared*. And if we put SPEC and ATTRIB in round brackets, indicating that they are optional, they will generate an even wider number of phrases, including simply, *disappeared*, on its own. This is just the beginning. We could widen the scope of the rules by including sites for complements and adjuncts as well. So, by using a common set of terms, and employing the full bracketing power at our disposal, it would be possible to arrive at a set of rules which apply to all phrases based on the category variable X. We can see how this might work if we look at a summary of the rules below. To simplify matters we will call adjuncts and attributes **modifiers** since they perform the same function; the only difference is that attributes occur before the head word and adjuncts afterwards:

1. The head of a phrase is X, where X stands for noun, verb, adjective, or preposition.
2. Complements expand X into X-bar.
3. Modifiers expand X-bar into X-bar (X-bar can reiterate as often as one wants, thus figure 6.9 below shows two such nodes).
4. Specifiers expand X-bar into double X-bar, or XP.

We can show this diagrammatically in Figure 6.9.

It should be clear by now that X-bar syntax allows for considerable economy in the description of phrase-structure rules. Instead of having to construct separate rewrite rules for each of the categories, they can all be collapsed into one using X as a category variable. Like most innovative analytic procedures, however, it is constantly increasing in subtlety. The account I have given so far is called the primitive X-bar model. Since its adoption by modern generative linguists it has undergone a number of refinements. We need briefly to consider these because they have far-reaching consequences for the traditional account of syntactic structure.

One limitation of the primitive X-bar model is that although it allows us to describe phrases in a common way, we are still stuck with the conventional rewrite rule for sentences. Remember that our simple rule for sentences was:

S = NP + VP

[A sentence consists of a noun phrase plus a verb phrase]

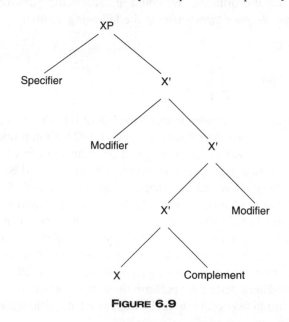

FIGURE 6.9

On the face of it X-bar syntax doesn't help us with this. Employing the category variable X as in,

$$S = XP + XP$$

makes the rule too powerful because it does not specify a value for X. Such a rule would allow sentences to be formed from any type of phrase combination. But what if we stop thinking of sentences as special and consider them as just another kind of phrase? On the face of it this is quite a startling idea, and one which cuts completely across traditional categories. In traditional grammar, sentences have the structure of a clause, not a phrase. The difference is quite significant because, whereas phrases are the result of the projection of a head word (a noun, for example, projects itself by adding on pre- and post-modifiers), a clause is the result of a predication relation between two phrases, i.e. a verb phrase is predicated of a noun phrase (S = NP + VP). But maybe if we looked deeper into the structure of a sentence we might see that it too is generated from the projection of a head constituent.

The question is 'What constituent could that be?' As we have seen, the main lexical categories (nouns, verbs, adjectives, adverbs, and prepositions) already have their own phrasal projections. It's here that X-bar syntax makes a startling leap by suggesting that lexical categories are not the only ones which can form phrases: functional categories can as well. In recent X-bar theory auxiliary verbs, conjunctions, and determiners – classes which provide the framework of a sentence, and with little overt semantic content – are much more important than we had imagined. Far from being just the grammatical hinges linking lexical items together, they become the power-house driving the whole engine.

In the case of auxiliary verbs, this is something which perhaps should not come as a surprise, given what we have seen of their importance elsewhere in framing questions and negations. The auxiliary verb, where it is present, always carries the responsibility for indicating tense and number agreement, as, for example, in the following sentence:

John does like football

Here *does* is in the third person singular present tense, agreeing with John. Were there no auxiliary verb, the task of number agreement and tense would pass to the main verb, i.e.

John likes football

Tense and number are the principal inflections important for sentence construction. A complete sentence needs an appropriately tensed verb agreeing with its subject. We're not always aware of this because English has a very impoverished inflectional system. But here again, X-bar syntax makes use of an important concept in modern theoretical approaches to syntax, namely that properties of inflection can be present in a sentence without being visible. This is not quite so odd as it sounds. We are, after all, used to elements of a sentence being left out through a process known as **ellipsis**. This often happens in conjoined sentences, as in,

> *Jane can't buy the books but John can*

Here the sequence *buy the books* is deleted from the second sentence, but is none the less understood by us to be there, even though unpronounced. Similarly, we could say that although English doesn't spell out all its inflectional information in the way some languages do, it is still present as part of the grammatical structure. Native speakers are aware of its presence as part of their linguistic competence. In the sentences below the word *buy* has exactly the same form but its **case** is entirely different in (b) from (a):

(a) *I buy books*
(b) *I can buy books*

In (a) *buy* is first person singular present tense, whereas in (b) it is an infinitive. We can see this if we put both sentences into the third person, which is the only person where inflectional properties are marked:

(c) *He buys book*
(d) *He can buy books*

The form of *buy* stays the same in (d) as in (b), despite the third person, because it's in infinitive case whereas in (c) it changes, as we would expect, because its case is present tense

So, when we say that English has an impoverished inflectional system, what we really mean is that its system of **marking** inflections is impoverished. This insight has the capacity to revolutionise our understanding of what a sentence is. But the question now is 'if inflectional information is invisibly present in sentences where is it located?' Initially, a number of linguists focussed attention on auxiliary verbs and posited the existence of an auxiliary phrase, or AUXP. This means detaching the auxiliary from the verb phrase, something which would seem to make sense. We might notice in our sentence illustrating ellipsis, *Jane can't buy books but John can*, that the auxiliary *can* is already so detached. This would suggest it is not part of the verb phrase. At the same time, however, not all sentences have auxiliary verbs. We could posit the existence of an invisible auxiliary, but this would make things very difficult since auxiliaries do carry some semantic meaning in addition to inflectional information. Including them, even invisibly, would have consequences for the meaning of a sentence. A more radical solution, adopted by current X-bar theory is to create an **inflectional phrase**. The head of this phrase is a category called **I**. This forms an I bar by merging with a verb phrase and then is raised to full IP (or I") by merging with subject elements acting as specifiers. Where there is an auxiliary in the sentence I will be located there. Where it isn't present it will be invisibly located in front of the verb phrase. Illustrations of both possibilities are given in Figures 6.10 and 6.11.

If you have followed the argument so far it should be apparent that what this new level of syntactic description has accomplished is to incorporate sentences within regular X-bar processes. A sentence is now an inflectional phrase, or IP. Within this phrase the verb phrase acts as the complement of the head I, so producing an I-bar. The specifier for this I-bar is the subject of the sentence: *he* in Figures 6.10 and 6.11. We can now replace our old formula for a sentence (S = NP + VP) with a new one:

IP = NP + I'
I' = I + VP

There are two further refinements to X-bar theory which we briefly need to consider. They concern the other two functional categories mentioned

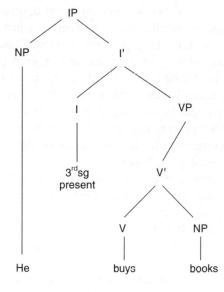

FIGURE 6.10

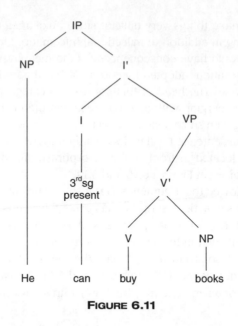

FIGURE 6.11

above: determiners and conjunctions. First of all, determiners. Most traditional syntactic analysis will treat these as part of the noun phrase. This is the approach we have taken throughout. So in the case of our phrase *the tiny mouse* we have argued that *tiny mouse* is a N' raised to a full NP by *the* acting as a specifier. Recent X-bar approaches, however, have given much greater significance to determiners, just as they have to auxiliary verbs. In a sense they perform a related function; auxiliary verbs, or more correctly I, serve to locate the verb phrase in time; similarly, determiners locate nouns and their accompaniments in space, whether actual or textual (THIS = near me, THE = this particular one). Accordingly, many linguists now argue that a phrase such as *the tiny mouse* is really a determiner phrase with *the* as its head and *tiny mouse* as its noun phrase complement. This would mean the complete phrase having the structure shown in Figure 6.12.

Such a diagram may at first seem disconcerting, and it has to be said that there isn't complete agreement among grammarians about the structure of such phrases. The evidence for determiner phrases is quite complex and detailed. But it looks as though what X-bar theory is highlighting is that there may be two kinds of phrases in sentences: the lexical kind with nouns, verbs, adjectives, adverbs and prepositions as their heads (which provide the inner semantic core), and the functional, or grammatical kind, with categories such as inflection and determiner as

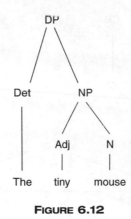

FIGURE 6.12

their head (which provide the superstructure). Into this second kind we can also put conjunctions. Consider the sentences below:

(a) *Mary will meet her friend at the station*
(b) *I was wondering whether* **Mary will meet her friend at the station**

(cited in Poole, 2002, p. 63)

Clearly (a) is a sentence and thus qualifies as an IP. It must also qualify as an IP in (b) where it is a subordinate sentence. The question is where does *whether* belong in the structure? Traditionally, such words are called subordinating conjunctions, since they serve to subordinate one sentence or clause to another. A more recent term for them is **complementisers** since they indicate to us that the second sentence is a complement of the preceding verb. So, *Mary will meet her friend at the station* is the complement of the verb *wondering*. It tells us what I am wondering about. But *whether* doesn't seem to belong either to the first bit *I was wondering* or the second, *Mary will meet her friend at the station*. At the same time we can't leave it out:

*I was wondering Mary will meet her friend at the station

As with determiners and auxiliaries, the solution would seem to indicate another level of structure. In this case a complementiser phrase, or CP. This phrase has a complement as its head word and an IP, or inflectional phrase as its own complement. As such the sequence *whether Mary will meet her friend at the station* will have the structure shown in Figure 6.13 (cited in Poole, 2002, p. 64). (Note that there is no specifier on this occasion although complementiser phrases can occur with them.)

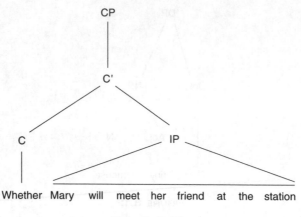

FIGURE 6.13

It has to be acknowledged that X-bar theory is a complex and sophisticated area of syntax. Its method of analysis is not always easy to grasp, particularly to students unaware of the process by which it has developed. If you have found this introduction too difficult to follow just

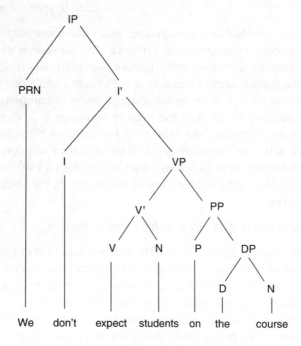

FIGURE 6.14

bear in mind, first, that it is an advanced analytic approach, and second, like most cutting-edge methodologies, it is still the subject of debate and controversy. It will repay close study, however, for it offers, arguably, the most radical approach to syntax in recent years, and looks set, in one or other of its incarnations, to become the standard model of theoretical analysis. One possible gain of X-bar theory is that it has necessitated a simplification in the diagrammatic representation of sentences. Because of the proliferation of different kinds of phrases and intermediate bar states there is no way any tree diagram could bear the weight of all this descriptive information. If it was difficult before, it would be impossible now. Consequently, linguists take to heart the new 'minimalist' approach recommended by Noam Chomsky, according to which representations are 'required to be minimal... with no superfluous steps in derivations and no superfluous symbols in representations' (cited in Radford, 1997, p. 149). I shall close this section with an example of how such a minimal representation might look (See Figure 6.14).

6.3.3 Transformational grammar

In Chapter 4 we looked at the rules for generating simple sentences of English. I pointed out to you then that the examples we were using were 'idealised', kernel sentences of English of the kind which formalist syntacticians habitually use. However, we are all aware that these kinds of sentences only account for a small part of our output as speakers and writers of the language. There are all sorts of ways in which we manipulate sentences in order to ask questions, give commands, or alter thematic emphasis. Consider for a moment some of the following permutations on our original sentence, *The cat devoured the tiny mouse.*

   (i)   *The cat hasn't devoured the tiny mouse.*
  (ii)   *Has the cat devoured the tiny mouse?*
 (iii)   *The tiny mouse has been devoured by the cat.*
 (iv)   *Which tiny mouse has the cat devoured?*

Clearly, the meaning of any one of these is different from our original. But there is, none the less, a semantic relatedness between them. The animal doing the devouring is always the same, as is the animal being devoured. A conventional phrase structure grammar of the sort we outlined in Chapter 4, even with its X bar refinements, wouldn't really capture that relatedness. We should simply end up with five different tree diagrams. So, in addition to a phrase structure grammar, we need another kind of grammar, one which can show how these variants are derived from each other. This is where transformational grammar comes to the rescue.

Perhaps all of these sentences derive from a common original, or **deep structure**, represented most nearly in the sentence *the cat devoured the tiny mouse*. The deep structure could be said to be the propositional core of the sentence. Linguists usually represent it in the following way:

> *devour (cat, tiny mouse)*

This representation means that there is a verb *devour* which has as its subject *cat*, and as its object *tiny mouse*. To get from this rather abstract mental proposition to our starting sentence we have to imagine a minor transformation involving the addition of tense to *devour* and determiners to *cat* and *tiny mouse*, plus some reordering. To derive the passives, negatives, and interrogatives, above, however, would involve more complex transformations.

Chomsky's argument, then, is that we all possess two grammars as part of our linguistic competence. First, a phrase structure grammar which consists of the rules governing idealised sentence formation, and second, a transformational grammar, which enables us to manipulate sentences to produce the full range of sentence types. As a consequence, every sentence has a surface structure – a post-transformational stage – as well as a deep structure – a pre-transformational stage. To see how this works in practice let's briefly consider sentence (iv) *Which tiny mouse has the cat devoured*? Transformational grammarians would argue that this derives from the sentence *The cat has devoured which tiny mouse*? First of all there has to be a rule which allows us to use *which* as an interrogative determiner replacing *the*. This may seem a bit odd to begin with, but it isn't impossible to encounter it here in ordinary conversation, for example, *the cat has devoured which tiny mouse, did you say*? Then there are two major transformations. First, the interrogative transformation which switches round the auxiliary verb *has* and the subject *the cat* (known as 'I' (inflexion) movement) and second, a 'wh' transformation (known as 'wh' movement) that moves the noun phrase *which tiny mouse* to the front of the sentence:

The cat <u>has</u> devoured <u>which tiny mouse</u>

'I' movement

'wh' movement

There are all kinds of evidence which are put forward for the occurrence of transformations, but probably the most important piece has to do with trace theory. According to this, constituents which are moved leave behind a trace, or echo of themselves in the surface structure. If you think about the verb *devour* for a moment, it is one of those verbs which require an object – you have to devour something – and we know that objects in English normally follow the verb. But in our sentence *which tiny mouse has the cat devoured* there is nothing following the verb at all. It must be that the object which was generated there in the deep structure has been moved out of its normal slot. We can test this by trying to insert an object in that slot – *which tiny mouse has the cat devoured the rat* – which results in nonsense. Transformational grammarians argue that the reason we can't insert an object there is that the moved constituent leaves behind an invisible mental trace of itself to indicate that this slot has already been taken, a bit like leaving a reserved notice on a table whilst we make our way to the food counter.

Transformational grammar has been enormously influential in recent years and has effectively changed the way in which most linguists approach syntax. But it has also been the subject of a great deal of debate, and revision. In the beginning linguists tended to treat every sentence variation as a transformation with the result that anyone studying it encountered a plethora of complicated movement rules, but nowadays these have been streamlined to a few central operations, of which 'wh' movement is one. Not only that, but the terminology has changed. 'Deep' and 'surface' structure have become 'D' and 'S' structures, principally because the original terms seemed to imply some sort of qualitative evaluation; 'deep' suggested 'profound' whilst 'surface' was too close to 'superficial'.

Before we leave syntax, then, let's just recap as to where we have now got to. We are saying, in formalist terms, that everyone, as part of their linguistic competence, has a mental blueprint for the construction of well-formed sentences. This blueprint is what we are terming 'D' structure. Phrase structure rules, of the X bar kind, allow us to generate idealised sentences from this blueprint, drawing on words from our mental lexicon, or dictionary. These words all have their own semantic character and the rules have to be flexible enough to allow for their individuality, for example some verbs need objects, others don't, and so on. But as well as this, our competence also includes a transformational component which allows us to move constituents around to create the full range of sentence types encountered in everyday language. The output of this component is 'S' structure.

But where in all this, you're probably thinking, does the human aspect of syntactic structure figure? Talk of X bars and transformations is all very well but it's a bit remote from our direct experience of the language. The best place to consider this is in relation to meaning.

6.4   Studying more meaning

6.4.1   Meaning and syntax

In Chapter 5 we looked at the two principal dimensions of meaning in relation to linguistics – semantics and pragmatics – and we distinguished different ways of talking about meaning: sense, reference, and force. In the case of semantics we said that words acquired their meaning from their place in the linguistic system, whilst with pragmatics meaning was a question of contextual and situational relevance. We didn't, however, consider the relation between semantics and the other levels of linguistics. As we saw in Chapter 3, meaning is important in the determination of phonemes because phonemes are partly semantic entities ('A phoneme is the smallest segment of sound which can distinguish two words'). And equally, meaning is important in the realm of syntax. We encounter words, not as isolable units, but as parts of phrases and clauses. Formal syntax tends to treat these structures as bits of Meccano which are assembled according to a pre-set pattern. But, as we discovered in Chapter 5, this is only half the story. There is a functional dimension to syntax which is ultimately semantic in character. A useful way of extending your knowledge of linguistic meaning is to consider this relationship more closely.

For an example of how we might do this, let's look again at the noun phrase. In Chapter 4, 'Studying Syntax', we examined some of the ways in which nouns are pre- and post-modified, and I pointed out that the closeness of the modifying item to the noun was linked to its semantic function. It does indeed seem to be the case that the physical proximity of items strengthens the bond between them. This is a phenomenon we encounter with many constructions, not simply noun phrases. Consider for a moment the difference in meaning between these apparently synonymous pairings

not possible/impossible
not considerate/inconsiderate
not happy/unhappy

In each case the form in which the negative is firmly attached to the adjective has a stronger and more permanent meaning. It's as if the syntactic glue is a register of a difference in force. It is similarly so with the modification of noun phrases. In a phrase like *the black dog*, the adjective, *black*, is semantically different from its appearance in the clause *the dog is black*, where it comes after the noun and separated by the verb. In the first case blackness is being identified as a characteristic, or permanent feature of the dog, whereas in the second it is an extra or additional one. The difference is signalled by the position of the adjective. Many adjectives, like *beautiful*, *big*, and *lovely*, can occur in both positions. They are what we think of as prototypical adjectives. Linguists call them central adjectives. Others, however, can only occur in one position. They are termed peripheral. Some peripheral adjectives only occur after the noun, for example:

> *the man was afraid/asleep/ready* → **the afraid/asleep/ready/man*

The properties being denoted here are inherently temporary. Being afraid, asleep, or ready are not qualities which typify the man. They cannot therefore be included in the noun phrase. This is not to deny, however, that we might on occasions wish to treat a temporary quality as something more permanent, or typical; compare, for example, *the man was frightened* and *the frightened man*. Other peripheral adjectives can only occur before the noun. Adjectives such as *mere*, *utter*, *principal*, and *major* are only found in this position:

a mere lie →	**the lie is mere*
an utter rogue →	**the rogue is utter*
the principal actor →	**the actor is principal*
the major reason →	**the reason is major*

If you think about these adjectives, they all indicate permanent features of their respective nouns.

The point is, then, that the position of an adjective in relation to the noun depends, to a large extent, on semantic criteria. Not only that, but the noun phrase itself has a semantic structure. This is evident if we look at the characteristic way in which pre-modification occurs. Closest to the noun come those items which classify it in some way, as in *country church*, *village store*, *hunting dogs*. Classifiers are never central adjectives; we can't say **the church was country*, **the store was village*. And although we can say the *dogs were hunting*, *hunting* is acting here as a verb, not an adjective. Indeed, classifiers are not really adjectives at all. We call them so in this position for the sake of convenience, because they are performing an adjectival function, but *country* and *village* are nouns, whilst *hunting* is a verb. They are co-opted adjectives and as such their 'adjectiveness' is limited. They can't be graded, for example, as most central adjectives can: we can say *very beautiful*, and *very clever* but not **very country*, **very village*, or **very hunting*. In some cases the classifier gets so close to the noun that it becomes part of it, and from this merger we derive compound nouns, for example, *daydream* and *brainwave*.

After classifiers we get a range of central adjectives attributing various qualities to the noun. They characteristically occur in the following order, working outwards: colour, size, evaluation – for example *lovely big black hunting dogs*. What this gives us is a descriptive priority based on a semantic ordering in which colour, followed by size, are seen to be more essential features of the animals than the speaker's evaluation. In the outer ring of pre-modification, after central adjectives, we find numerals, one, two, three, and so on. Like classifiers these are co-opted adjectives and don't have the full range of adjective-like qualities: we can't say *very one* or *very two* or *the lovely big black hunting dogs were three*. So it seems that the unmarked semantic structure of noun phrase pre-modification is as follows:

> *six lovely big black hunting dogs*
> (number, evaluation, size, colour, classification, head noun)

A corollary of the argument so far is that formal classifications such as adjective, noun, verb, and so forth, are not really precise enough to describe the semantic reality of word classes. There are degrees of 'adjectiveness', and also of 'nounness'. A word like *eating*, which is a present participle of the verb *to eat*, becomes a noun in the sentence *eating is forbidden*. But it's restricted in its noun-like qualities: it can't be put into the plural *eatings are forbidden*, or be pre-modified by the: *the eating is forbidden* (except in certain constructions, for example, *the eating of food is forbidden*). This is an indication to us that semantically it isn't naturally a noun. And if you look at the various subclasses of nouns you will see that they are all slightly different in their syntactic behaviour. This is one of the things which makes it difficult to define what a noun is in formal terms: there is no one thing which they have in common. The underlying reason for this is not syntactic, but semantic. Consider, for example, the division between **mass** and **count** nouns. This is a very broad categorisation which separates nouns that indicate countable entities, for example, *tables*, *chairs*, and so on, from those which indicate uncountable entities, such as *music* or *sincerity*. In terms of morphology, count nouns can be put into the plural, because you can have more than one of them, whereas mass nouns can't: *musics*, *sincerities*. On the other hand, mass nouns can occur without a determiner – *music is good for you*, *sincerity is a virtue* – whereas count nouns can't: *table is wooden*, *chair is broken*. This neat categorisation is upset, however, by the fact that a good many nouns can operate as both mass and count. Many people, when they start studying language find this degree of flexibility frustrating. But this is usually because they have too formalistic a view of syntax.

If, however, you treat the problem as a semantic one, it becomes less of an irritation and more of an insight into the way in which language relates to experience. We encounter objects in the world in two principal ways: as items and as substances. As items they can be individuated and counted, whereas as substances, they can't. So, for example, a noun like *tea* can refer to a substance in which case it behaves as a mass noun – *tea is good for you* – but it can also refer to a single item, and then it behaves as a count noun – *three teas please*. Some nouns, like *table* and *music*, are less flexible and only occur as one or the other, but all we are saying is that we haven't yet developed an alternative sense for them yet (although the current expression *popular musics* suggests we may have in the case of *music*). This is one of the areas in which language is constantly evolving. In Britain, for example, *accommodation* is a mass noun – we think of it as a substance, even of an abstract kind – so we don't encounter *accommodations*. In America, however, we would do, because there it can be treated as an item.

The point I am making is a natural consequence of Nelson Francis' argument, which I quoted in Chapter 5, 'Words do not have meanings; people have meanings for words.' I suggested to you in Chapter 1 that all the classifications which grammar imposes on language are inevitably rough and ready. You will encounter them all the time when studying syntax: transitive *v.* intransitive, finite *v.* non-finite, gradable *v.* non-gradable, mass *v.* count. Words move around in this system precisely because the world of experience which they represent is infinitely varied and changeable. If there is irregularity in language it is because we are irregular. I am suggesting to you then that the way to get a real handle on syntactic categories is to penetrate the semantic reality they encode. It's never too early to start this, but it's advisable to do the elementary syntactic spadework involved in learning about these classifications first.

6.4.2 Meaning and logic
As with the other levels of linguistics, semantics also has its more abstract reaches. In Chapter 5 we discovered that a principal difficulty we face in accounting for meaning is that it's very difficult to formulate precise rules about it in the way in which we can for syntax and phonology. One way in which some linguists attempt to fill that gap is by pursuing the relationship between language and logic. We know that interpreting sentences involves us in making presuppositions and drawing inferences. These are part of what is termed 'natural logic'. But in addition to this, the discovery by syntacticians of a deep, or propositional, structure to language suggests that utterances do have a more formal logical basis.

You may be wondering how this can be so after what we said about the essential indeterminacy of utterances. It's all a question of what sort of meaning we are exploring. Imagine the situation where I ask my daughter to fetch my car keys. At the semantic level the meaning of this derives from the sense the words have in the linguistic system together with the particular pragmatic speech act I am performing. And as we have seen, a full understanding of the latter depends on the situational context of utterance – 'who', 'when', 'where', and 'why'. But we could say that prior to all of this there is a propositional level of meaning which makes any kind of communication possible. Two basic propositions here would be: 'there are objects in the world to which the phrase "my car keys" refers', and 'there is an activity in the world to which the term "fetch" refers'. The concern here is with determining the truth value of utterances: with the conditions that we mentally demand in order for us to accept an utterance as meaningful.

Truth conditional semantics, as it is sometimes called, is not bothered about the pragmatic uses to which we put utterances but with uncovering the logical basis of language. The central question it sets out to answer is 'How do we map word strings onto the real world?' Knowing how to determine truth and falsity is regarded by truth conditional semanticists as the foundation of being able to use language meaningfully. So, for example, knowing what a sentence like *The sun is shining today* means, involves knowing what situation in the world this would correspond to, or fit. On the basis of such knowledge we could judge the statement to be either true or false. Examining the logical foundation of language necessitates using the **metalanguage** of formal, or propositional, logic in the description of sentences. Not surprisingly, this is a highly complex and difficult area of semantics, and really requires some training in the use of logical symbols. Sentences are translated into mathematical type formulae and then subjected to rigorous truth tests.

The simplest and most basic propositions are **atomic propositions**. These consist of a name plus a predicate (a predicate, as we said in Chapter 4 is a claim being made about a subject). For example,

Fido barks

Here *barks* is the predicate with the name *Fido* as its subject. The significant point about names is that they have no descriptive content. As we said in Chapter 5, they have reference but no sense. Names just denote things in the outside world. So, the **semantic value** of *Fido* is simply 'Fido' or, in logical form,

Fido   SVal (*Fido*) = Fido

Barks, however, is not a name. It describes an activity in the real world. When we use it to refer to something we have in mind the set of things to which it can refer. Unlike *Fido* it is capable of sense as well as reference. As a consequence, its logical form is different:

Barks   SVal (*barks*) = the set of things that bark

Using *barks* to refer to a specific event of barking is called its **extension**. So the extension of a predicate is the set of things to which the predicate actually applies. In the case of *Fido* the extension is simply the referent, i.e. the actual animal. However, both words can also be used repeatedly in many different contexts. There is no law of copyright on actual words. Someone might use *Fido* to refer to a fox, or even a human being. Similarly, *barks* can be used to refer to a wide range of barking events, some of which might invite varying interpretations ('Was it a bark or a growl?'). This range of possible uses is called a word's **intension**. So, the intension of a predicate is the set of all the things the predicate is true of in all possible worlds. By the same token, the intension of a name is the actual referent wherever it occurs in any possible world.

Putting all this together we can describe the truth conditions of the sentence *Fido barks* in the following way: 'The semantic value of *Fido barks* is true if and only if the semantic value of Fido is a member of the semantic value of barks. Or, in logical formulae:

Sval(S) = true iff Sval (NP) ∈ Sval (VP)

(S) =	Fido barks
(NP) =	Fido
(VP) =	barks
∈ =	'is a member of'

Understanding the sentence entails being able to access the **principle of compositionality** which informs it. We can state this as,

> The interpretation of a sentence is determined by the interpretations of the words occurring in the sentence and the syntactic structure of the sentence.
> (Cited in Radford et al., 1999, p. 358)

So, if we know what *Fido* and *barks* refer to in the actual world and if we know that *Fido* serves as the subject and *barks* as the predicate then we are equipped to understand this particular sentence. In the language of this kind of linguistics *Fido* is an **argument** of the predicate *barks*. Verbs vary in the number of arguments they require. Some, like *hit* and *like* require two arguments – we hit, or like, something or someone, and others, such as *give* and *show*, require three – we give, or show, something to someone. We might omit some of these arguments in natural language but the logical form requires them all to be present.

The simple propositions we have been considering of a name plus a predicate can be made more complex by combining them together using the logical connectives *and*, *or*, *if*, and *if...then*. These function as hinges linking together two or more propositions and stating the terms under which the combined proposition can be considered true. Here, truth conditional semanticists use a number of symbols to represent some of the logical operations of English. The formulae in the table below will capture the logical relations of the following sentences:

1. *John arrived late and missed the train*
2. *Either John will go to the meeting or I shall*
3. *Either John will go to the meeting or he won't*
4. *If John passes his driving test I'll eat my hat*
5. *John will go to the meeting if he is able to*

One of the advantages of logical formulae is that they capture differences between apparently similar usages. The *either/or* connectives in (2), for example, are logically different from (3) because they allow for the possibility of both propositions being true, that is, 'John will go to the meeting **and** I shall go to the meeting'. Similarly, *if* has a different meaning in (4) as opposed to (5). In (4) it is logically possible for me to eat my hat even if John fails his driving test, whereas in (5) it is a necessary condition of John going to the meeting that he is able to.

It is important to recognise, however, that logical connectives are interpreted differently in formal semantics from the way they are in ordinary discourse. In normal conversation, for example, (4) would be taken to imply that I would only eat my hat if John passed his test. And similarly, the propositions in (2) would usually be taken by most people to be mutually

	Connective	Syntax	English
1.	$\vee$	$p \wedge q$	p and q
2.	$\wedge$	$p \wedge q$	p and/or q
3.	$\vee_e$	$p \vee_e q$	p or q but not both
4.	$\rightarrow$	$p \rightarrow q$	if p then q
5.	$\equiv$	$p \equiv q$	p if and only if q

[**p, q** stand for sentence constants, or propositions]

exclusive. There is a distinction, in other words, between natural logic and formal logic. In terms of natural logic, for example, we should assume in (1) that John's being late caused him to miss the train, but in fact the truth value of the propositions doesn't depend on that. There is nothing in the sentence which necessitates that logical link other than the mere fact of lineal order. Formal logic doesn't aim to capture all the meaning of utterances. It is simply concerned with their abstract propositional core. As a consequence, no distinction is made between the following sentences, all of which use the conjunction connective, as in (1):

6. *Jane was poor and she was honest*
7. *Jane was poor but she was honest*
8. *Although Jane was poor she was honest*

Again, the truth value of these propositions is independent of the particular conjunction being used despite the fact that the sentences do not mean the same.

What we have been considering is something called **first order logic**. This consists of propositions which apply to named referents in the real world. But there are many propositions which are not of this kind at all. Think for a moment of the following sentence:

Every cat is purring

The difficulty with this statement is that we can't identify any one thing in the world which corresponds to *every cat* in the way we can for subjects like *Jane*. This means we can't give it a truth value. To determine its truth we would have to identify each cat in turn and see if it was purring. None of the cats on their own would correspond to *every cat*. In other words, the entity denoted by this phrase has variable reference: it applies to any cat, but not exclusively to one. First order logic sorts out this problem by introducing into the logical formulae symbols, such as x, y, and z, which can stand for individual variables. The scope of the variable is then indicated by linking it to a quantifier. In this particular case logicians use the **universal quantifier** – ∀. So we can express the logical form of the proposition contained in *Every cat is purring* in the following manner:

∀x (CAT (x) → PURR (x))
'For everything x, if x is a cat then x is purring'

The universal quantifier doesn't express **existential commitment**, that is, *Every cat is purring* can be true even when there aren't any cats. Logically it means the same as 'There is no non-purring cat'. What the formula does is to state the truth conditions which apply in making such a statement.

The other main logical quantifier is the **existential quantifier**. This is used for noun phrases which have as their determiners *a/n* or *some*. It is written as ∃, and applied to a variable like x it means 'there is an x' or 'there is at least one thing x'. An existential proposition is basically asserting the existence of at least one thing of the kind being talked about. As a consequence, it does entail existential commitment, unlike the universal quantifier. Here are a couple of examples:

> *A cat purred*
> ∃x (CAT) (x) & PURR (x))
> 'There is an object x such that x is a cat and x purred'

> *Some cows are mooing*
> ∃x (COW (x) & MOO (x))
> 'There is an object x such that x is a cow and x is mooing'

As is usual with expressions in logical form no account is taken of tense. The logical truth or falsity of statements does not depend on when the event described occurs. In addition, the existential quantifier is neutral between singular and plural. The advantage here is that the same logical form can represent the core propositions in a variety of actual sentences.

As well as the universal and existential quantifiers, English also has restricted quantifiers, *most*, *many*, *several*, and *few*. These in turn have their individual logical forms. But the one which has caused most debates among logicians is the simple determiner *the*. From one point of view a phrase such as *the man* could be taken as a substitute for a name since it picks out a particular individual in the way that a name does. So we could say that descriptive noun phrases with the determiner *the* should be logically treated in the same way as names. But this runs into a difficulty. Clearly, when we use the phrase *the man* we have in mind one particular individual, just as we have when we say *Kevin*. To use a term we employed earlier, both expressions have the same extension. But the difference is that we can use *the man* to refer to any number of particular individuals, whereas we can't with *Kevin*. In other words, *the man* has a different intension. The solution suggested by the philosopher Bertrand Russell is to view *the* as a **generalised quantifier**. He argued this using what has since become a much-cited example:

> *The king of France is bald*

The noun phrase *the king of France* picks out a single individual in the manner of definite descriptions and on first sight we could substitute a name and retain the same meaning. But this won't do for the simple reason that there isn't a king of France. As a proposition then, the statement is false. However, it isn't meaningless. We could imagine a situation where the monarchy was restored to France and the king was indeed bald. So, whilst *The king of France is bald* is false in the actual world, it isn't necessarily so in a possible world. Putting it another way, the intension of *the king of France* is different from its extension. What Russell and those following him suggest we do when we compute the truth of statements is to map the intensions of definite descriptions onto their extensions. In the case of the baldness of the king of France, Russell argued that two kinds of requirements were built into the use of *the*: the existential commitment (there is such a thing) and the uniqueness requirement (there is only one). Accordingly, the *king of France is bald* has within it three kernel propositions, the first two of which express logical expectations contained in all other uses of *the*:

(a) 'There is a king of France' (existential commitment)
(b) 'There is only one king of France' (uniqueness requirement)
(c) 'He is bald'

(after Kearns, 2000, p. 94)

The logical form of this is as below:

$$\exists x \, (\text{KING OF FRANCE } (x) \, \& \, \forall y \, (\text{KING OF FRANCE } (y) \rightarrow y = x) \, \& \, \text{BALD } (x))$$

'There is an x such that x is a king of France, and any y which is a king of France is the same object as x, and x is bald'

(cited in Kearns, 2000, p. 94)

Russell's analysis of *the* as a generalised quantifier has been revisited and refined over the years, to take account of singular and plural uses, but what it illustrates is the considerable logical computation which goes into the apparently simplest of words. For some linguists, particularly those more interested in pragmatics, the failure to take account of natural logic is a limitation of truth conditional semantics. But for others it is a necessary simplification in the process of laying bare the logical skeleton of language. The fact that we rarely encounter it simply in skeleton form doesn't matter. Most of the operations which we perform in language, from the employment of tense and modality to the use of terms such as *all*, *every*, and *some*, have as their basis a formal logical structure. The attempt to capture this, albeit in the abstract language of symbolic logic, is one of the most exciting developments of contemporary semantics. But for the beginner, it is one to be explored with caution. Symbolic logic is like strong medicine – a little of it will go a long way.

6.5   Studying linguistic branches

There are two main ways in which most students encounter linguistics: either in courses on phonology, syntax, and semantics – what we have termed 'the bread and butter' of linguistics; or, in the context of some particular branch of the subject. These have become more numerous over the years as the subject has grown, but the principal ones are **sociolinguistics** (the study of language and society), **stylistics** (the study of language and literature), **psycholinguistics** (the study of language and mind), **applied linguistics** (the application of linguistics to language teaching), **computational linguistics** (the simulation of language by the use of computers), **comparative linguistics** (the study of different languages and their respective linguistic systems), and **historical linguistics** (the study of language change over time). You will find that these branches overlap and that linguists may not always distinguish between them clearly. Stylistics and comparative linguistics, for example, are sometimes treated as aspects of applied linguistics.

Fortunately, for students beginning any of these areas of study there are now a range of books available which presume little, or no, prior knowledge, of the subject. As with all linguistic study, however, you will find them more rewarding the more you know about the 'bread and butter' levels of the language. Probably, the three fastest growing, and most innovative of the branches, are sociolinguistics, stylistics, and psycholinguistics. The remainder of this chapter will suggest ways of studying them.

6.5.1   Studying sociolinguistics

Language is above all a social phenomenon. It's arguably the most significant of all the mediums by means of which we establish relationships with others, and make ourselves understood. Studying it, therefore, involves studying society. Despite the impression which people sometimes have of linguistics, it can never be an ivory tower pursuit. Indeed, modern sociolinguistics is in part a reaction against what has sometimes been termed 'armchair linguistics' – the notion that all the linguist need do is dream up sentences and analyse them. That may work very well if all we are interested in is idealised sentences and grammatical competence, but it's insufficient if we are studying actual utterances and communicative competence.

So the first thing we need to get clear is what sociolinguists are up to. Sociolinguistics is the radical wing of the discipline. It's less purist and desk-bound than the Chomskyan variety. Sociolinguists are field researchers: they go out collecting data from ordinary people about their actual language use, and on the basis of that evidence they construct theories as to how and why language changes. A good way to begin thinking about sociolinguistics, then, is to list all the factors which you consider might affect your own language use. Here are some which affect mine:

(a) *social class*
    I include here, education, parental background, profession. These all have an effect on my pronunciation and choice of words.
(b) *social context*
    I adjust my speech to the different social contexts I find myself in. I speak more formally in meetings than to my friends.
(c) *geographical origins*
    As a native of the Midlands I still preserve some features of a regional accent.
(d) *ethnicity*
    As a native speaker of English I use the language in ways that a non-native speaker wouldn't.
(e) *nationality*
    As a native inhabitant of Britain I speak differently from an American or Australian.
(f) *gender*
    My voice quality is male – pitch, intonation patterns – and I am aware that some of my linguistic habits are typically male.
(g) *age*
    As a middle-aged person I know that my vocabulary, pronunciation, and manner of expression are different from someone in their teenage years.

As the list above shows, the factors which contribute to my own language variety are very extensive. To make it even more complicated, they are all in a dynamic relation with each other. My regional accent, for example, is affected by my social class. I have lost many features of it, either consciously or unconsciously, because it is socially stigmatised in the circles in which I move. At the same time, however, it is also affected by social context: some regional features, for instance, will frequently appear when I'm with friends and family. This is because I am sometimes anxious to speak in a way which will be socially approved. All of these factors contribute to what linguists call my **dialect**. 'Dialect' is a rather slippery term in linguistics, simply because it covers so much territory. As a consequence you mustn't be surprised to see it used with a degree of latitude. You will usually encounter it in connection with regional varieties, thus 'regional dialects', but it is sometimes used in relation to social class, thus 'social dialects'. The simplest way to think of 'dialect' is as a variety of the language, distinguishable in terms of vocabulary and syntax (and sometimes pronunciation). **Accent** refers to varieties which are distinguishable in terms of pronunciation alone. As you can see, there is a degree of overlap between the two terms, thus the brackets round pronunciation. This is another reason for the slight fuzziness which surrounds 'dialect'. When used on its own by linguists it often includes accent, but when used in conjunction with 'accent' as in 'accents and dialects', it excludes it. Despite the fuzziness, however, it's useful to distinguish between them because it's perfectly possible to speak in a non-regional dialect, that is, using the vocabulary and syntax of standard grammar, but with a regional accent. And just to complicate matters further, there are also features of my language variety which are particular to me. I am, after all, an individual, not simply the representative of a certain class or geographical region. As a consequence, the choices I make, whether to use standard or non-standard English on certain occasions, for example, are particular to me. They represent my own personal way of using the language. These constitute what linguists call my **idiolect**. This is unique to me.

It's important to recognise, then, that everyone, ourselves included, has a dialect, and an accent. Many people when they first start to study sociolinguistics still cling to the idea that accents and dialects are what other people have. Not so. Even standard English is a dialect, that is, it's a variety of the language distinguishable in terms of vocabulary and syntax. Correspondingly, received pronunciation (r.p.) is an accent, albeit a non-regional one. It's an indication of the influence of standard English that its dialectal nature has become invisible to us. This in itself is an aspect of language development which is of sociolinguistic interest. But apart from the normative power of standard English and received pronunciation, it's probably also the case that many students, initially, have a very dated view of sociolinguistics. This is partly a leftover from traditional dialectology.

Traditional dialectologists used to carry out their field research in remote rural areas of the country, well away from the growing urban sprawl of the cities. They studied the speech of non-urban rural males ('nurms') in an effort to provide a record of historic dialects before they died out. A consequence of this was that a large area of linguistic innovation and change went relatively unnoticed. By contrast, contemporary sociolinguistics is concerned with modern dialects. These are frequently, though not exclusively, urban in origin. The significant factor which distinguishes them from traditional dialects is that they are on the increase, or, in linguistic terms, productive. Many of the innovations in speech habits which are occurring currently are dialectal in origin. When people talk of *doing a runner* or something being *out of order* they are drawing on Cockney, or London dialect, and when people describe something as *well wicked* they are reflecting the impact of Caribbean English. Peter Trudgill (1990, p.5) illustrates the difference between traditional and modern dialects with the following examples:

> *Hoo inno comin* (traditional dialect)
> *She ain't comin* (modern non-standard dialect)
> *She isn't coming* (modern standard dialect)

Once you have a clear idea of what sociolinguists are interested in and some understanding of basic terms such as 'dialect' and 'accent', the next step is to investigate your own speech and that of people around you. Develop the habit of listening closely to how people say things and of noticing recurring features of pronunciation and expression. You can begin with just a few basic features and then widen the net as your knowledge of the subject grows. The best features to start with are those which are most productive across a range of varieties. Try listening for *h* dropping and the fronting of *th* (see Section 3.3). Both of these are very much on the increase. Fronting is the substitution of /f/ for /θ/ in words like *thief* (fief) and /v/ for /ð/ in words such as *brother* (bruvver). When listening for these features ask yourself the following questions:

1. At what places in a word are they likely to occur, at the beginning, the middle, or the end, that is, what is their distribution?
2. Is their production affected by speed of delivery, formality of occasion, gender or age of speaker?

Similarly with dialect. Select a couple of non-standard features, such as the use of the past participle *done* instead of the past tense *did*, as in *I done it yesterday*, and the use of the double negative, for example, *I haven't got no money*, and ask yourself how consistently they appear in the speech of your informants and whether their production is affected by any of the factors mentioned in (2) above. And finally, do the same thing with one or two vocabulary items: select words particularly prevalent in your locality and investigate their occurrence. You could begin, for example, by considering the occurrence of any dialectal variants used for gym shoes, such as *pumps, plimsolls, daps, gollies, sandshoes*, and testing their frequency against the more commercial term *trainers*.

If you try the experiment above you will be thinking as a sociolinguist. Practitioners in the field begin with selecting linguistic variables: these are forms which are variably found in people's speech. Variables are usually enclosed in round brackets, for example, (h), (f/v), (done). They then collect data randomly from people, called 'informants', in a particular area, and build up a picture of the occurrence of the variable and its correlation with the age, social class, and gender of the population. Most of the classic sociolinguistic studies, such as Peter Trudgill's study of (ng) (variably pronounced /n/ or /ŋ/), in Norwich, and William Labov's study of (r) in New York speech, have used this method. Once this has been done for a range of variables across the country it's possible to build up maps which show the frequency and spread of certain accent and dialect forms, nationally. In Figure 6.15, for example, you can see Peter Trudgill's map of the distribution of children's truce terms (the words they use for making-up). The lines which show the boundaries of individual terms are called **isoglosses**, and it is on the basis of these that linguists can reach conclusions about the way in which the language is changing.

I have probably made this sound rather cut and dried: in fact it is anything but. One of the things you will discover if you set about collecting data in the manner I have suggested is that there are a number of difficulties in the way. In the first five chapters of this book I urged on you the importance of defamiliarising language, and its associated levels, in order to see it through fresh eyes. This also goes for sociolinguistics. It's a useful exercise to reflect on the problems which beset the researcher in his/her attempt both to get reliable data, and then to analyse it. You will probably discover, for example, that people adjust their speech if they think they're being observed. It's known as the 'observer's paradox', formulated by Labov as 'the aim of linguistic research in the community must be to find out how people talk when they are not being systematically observed; yet we can only obtain this data by systematic observation' (Freeborn *et al.*, 1993, p. 152). Similarly, most people speak differently to a stranger than they do to a friend, or in a meeting than in the street. Not only that, but a majority of us alter our speech if we are reading something out loud, or talking over the telephone. Linguists refer to all of this as **style-shifting**, and it's a phenomenon we have to take into account when observing people. As a general rule people will adopt more socially prestigious forms of speech, both in accent and dialect, on those occasions when they feel judgements are being made about them.

There is an important lesson to be learnt from this: none of us has a uniform accent or dialect. We all mix together different varieties of the language to a greater or lesser degree. Everyone has their own idiolect. As sociolinguists we are not simply concerned with tabulating data but with uncovering the reality of human speech in social communities. This has consequences both for how we go about the task and the conclusions we draw from it. Standard type research has often consisted of the random interview, supplemented with various tasks, and utilising a range of techniques, designed to compensate for accent and dialect fluctuation. In recent years, however, a different type of research, employing participant observation, in which an observer becomes attached to a group for a period of time, has become more fashionable. This has the advantage of allowing a closer and more intimate study of particular social groups. But whichever method is used, the questions being pursued are ultimately the same: what are the reasons for linguistic change? What influence do factors such as class, age, gender have on the way we speak and use language? These are all areas on which there is now an abundant literature, but the best way to start, as always, is, as I have suggested, with your own speech.

FIGURE 6.15 Children's truce terms

6.5.2 Studying stylistics

Stylistics is concerned with using the methodology of linguistics to study the concept of 'style' in language. Every time we use language we, necessarily, adopt a style of some sort; we make a selection from a range of syntactic and lexical possibilities according to the purpose of the communication. The study of style has traditionally been the preserve of literary criticism. People appreciating novels, poetry, and drama, characteristically examine the way in which those particular forms use different language styles to represent human experience. The ultimate concern of such activities is usually with evaluation: with being able to say how, and in what ways, texts succeed, or fail, as works of art. Stylistics has a different focus, however, and it's important, to have a clear idea of what that is, from the outset. To begin with, stylistics does not discriminate between literary texts and any other texts as worthwhile objects of study. What I mean is that it doesn't give them privileged status. Linguists are just as happy studying the styles of recipes and car manuals as they are *David Copperfield* or *King Lear*. Not only that, but stylistics also doesn't privilege the written over the spoken word. In many respects it overlaps with discourse analysis, in that it is equally interested in spoken varieties of the language. Sports commentaries, sermons, chat shows, are all grist to its mill.

As a consequence, if you are coming to stylistics from a background of literary criticism you may well find the omnivorous nature of stylistics a little disconcerting. How is it that we can give as much serious attention to a recipe as an established work of art? The answer is that it depends what you are looking for. As I suggested above, linguists have a different agenda from literary critics. Their concern is with the text (whether spoken or written), as a linguistic entity, that is, as a piece of language, and with the communicative dynamics that are encoded there. In this respect, an advert for perfume is as complex as a poem. Whether it's as valuable as a representation of human experience is not the issue. Having said that, however, there is a sub-branch of stylistics – literary stylistics – which is more concerned with utilising stylistic approaches as an aid to evaluating literary texts more precisely. But even here, linguists do not attempt to account for literary value. Indeed, there is a growing consensus among critics of both literary and linguistic persuasions that such valuations are the output of communal agreements about ways of reading and interpreting texts, rather than qualities which inhere in the texts themselves.

Like sociolinguistics, then, stylistics covers a very large territory. But unlike sociolinguistics, the conceptual framework within which individual linguists work is comparatively fuzzy. Attempting a linguistic description of stylistic effects involves having a very secure functional model of the language. So far, the most detailed we have is that of Halliday, outlined in Chapter 4 (it might be a good idea here to look back at this section). This is the one which most linguists employ, but despite its usefulness it is not always easy to work with. In addition, the way a text communicates also has to do with a host of variables, such as the context, the relationship between the participants, the topic of discourse, the mode of discourse (spoken or written), the channel (telephone, letter, face to face), and the underlying ideology. And if we take any of these they divide into yet more variables; context, for instance, can mean social, cultural, situational, or linguistic context.

None the less, despite the rather heterodox nature of the subject, studying stylistics can be a liberating experience. Freed from the burden of evaluation we can look with a fresh and almost naïve eye at texts, and ask some very basic, but ultimately searching questions about the distinctive ways in which they communicate. These involve investigating our communicative, creative, and textual competencies. As a way into the subject you can do no better, as with sociolinguistics, than start from what you know, and work to build on and extend that knowledge. There are three main stylistic levels which you can begin by investigating. The first has to do with the linguistic form, or substance of texts – we'll term this the 'micro' level; the second, with the discourse dimension of texts – we'll call this the 'intermediate' level; and the third, with the communicative situation of texts – we can call this the 'macro' level.

Macro level – communicative situation

Intermediate level – language as discourse

Micro level – language as form

You can begin at the micro level by taking any text which comes to hand, preferably something short – a recipe or a magazine advert – and seeing if you can describe its surface linguistic features. Clearly, the more you know about the levels of linguistics, phonology, syntax, and semantics, the more you will be able to observe. Ask yourselves the following questions as an aid to your description:

(i) What kind of word strings are present? Phrases, sentences? If sentences, are they minor (incomplete), or major (complete), simple (one clause), or complex (using embedded or subordinate clauses)? Are the phrases simple or heavily modified?

(ii) What kinds of constructions are present? Passive, active, transitive, intransitive? What tenses are represented? Are the verbs lexical, auxiliary, modal?

(iii) What kind of words are used? What is the register? Formal, technical, slang? Is there any use of polysemy – exploitation of multiple meanings? Any figurative language?

(iv) What is the mood? Interrogative, imperative, declarative? Are there any indications of possible intonation patterns?

(v) How is the text laid out graphically? What is the size of print, spacing? Is the text medium dependent, that is, does it need an illustration?

The first aim, then, is to give as full a grammatical description of the text as possible. You will notice that I have included graphical information as well as purely linguistic. This is because stylistics is concerned with the text as a whole – its physical, as well as its verbal, structure. And although I am speaking as though the text is written, the same will apply to a spoken 'text'. Once you have described the surface features of the text, the next task is to use this as a way of informing the text's discourse level. We can regard this as the 'message' level of the text. This is where Halliday's framework is most useful. He argues that any text has three principal messages. First of all the text is a message in itself. That is, the sentences follow one another in a certain order and cohere together to make a unified entity. This is its **textual** message. Second, it seeks to represent reality (not necessarily physical). This is its **ideational** message. And third, it creates a relationship with its audience. This is its **interpersonal** message. At the discourse, or intermediate level, then, stylistics attempts to relate the linguistic substance of texts to certain central functions. Again, there are a number of questions which we can link to each function:

(i) *Textual function*
How do the linguistic units cohere together to make a text? How do sentences refer backwards and forwards? Texts have a range of devices such as **substitution**, **ellipsis**, and **repetition** which enable them to be **cohesive** and **coherent**. The result of this is said to be their **textuality**.

(ii) *Ideational function*
How do texts represent reality? Important here is the participant –
process–circumstance model from Chapter 4. What verbal
processes are present (material, verbal, relational, and so on)?
How are the participants represented? Are they actors, recipi-
ents, or existents? And what is thematically important in the
arrangement of the clause?

(iii) *Interpersonal function*
What speech acts are being performed? What do the tone,
mood, and syntactic patterns tell us about the relationship the
text is seeking to establish with us? Are the pronouns personal
or impersonal, the constructions passive or active, the syntax
reduced or full?

The macro level is where stylistics is probably most open-ended. At this
level we are considering the broader communicative situation of texts.
This entails taking account of all the constraints which bear on the creation of the text. As I have said, the difficulty here is with the fluidity of the
terms, and you may find that linguists understand them differently. Here
are some of the principal terms used by linguists:

Context
Tenor
Field of discourse
Setting
Code
Mode/medium
Channel

We can begin our investigation at this level by asking what the situational
context is in which the text is embedded. Linguists often distinguish
between 'immediate context' and 'wider context'. In the case of an adver-
tisement, we could say that the immediate context is the commercial one
of selling, in that the purpose of the advert is to persuade us into buying
something. This has consequences for the language used. The wider context might be the ideological context of consumerism, in that adverts
address us as potential consumers with the requisite needs and desires.
Also important is the relationship, or **tenor**, between the person initiating
the text, the **addresser**, and the person for whom it is intended, the
addressee. Again, linguists introduce various refinements here and frequently distinguish between **formal tenor**, relationships like seller/cus-
tomer, boss/employee, doctor/patient, consultant/client, and **informal**

tenor, which describes relationships involving friends and relatives. It's a technique of adverts, for instance, to disguise the formal tenor as an informal one: to pretend the salesperson is a friend. Similarly, we could distinguish the addressee, the person who is targeted to receive the message, from the person who simply happens to notice it, the **recipient**; and the person, or body which initiates the message, the addresser, from the body which actually sends it, **the sender**.

As you can see, the macro framework is already getting fairly complex. But we also have to add in the **field of discourse** – what the subject matter is (the weather, the state of the economy); the **setting** – where the text is encountered (the pages of a magazine, the side of a bus); the **code** – verbal or non-verbal; the **mode** – written or spoken; and the **channel** – the physical means of communication. At the macro level, then, we are trying to set the specific text within a communicative framework which could apply to any and all communicative acts. It's not surprising when you consider the extent of the descriptive task which stylistics has set itself that there is still some way to go before we can feel confident of a model of communication which can take us all the way from the micro level of linguistic form through the conceptual categories of functional linguistics to the general level of the communicative situation.

6.5.3 Studying psycholinguistics

Psycholinguistics is concerned with the relationship between language and the mind. This distinguishes it from sociolinguistics, on the one hand, where the focus is on the social dimension of language, and stylistics, on the other, where it is on the expressive functions of language. Psycholinguistics explores the psychological processes involved in using language. It asks how we store words and syntactic structures in the brain, what processes of memory are involved, and how we understand and produce speech. These are all of considerable practical importance when it comes to understanding language disorders. But above all, psycholinguists are interested in the acquisition of language: with how children learn.

Many linguists feel that if we can understand the internal mechanism which enables children to learn language so quickly we shall have penetrated one of the deepest secrets of the mind. To what extent are humans programmed from birth to acquire language? Is there such a thing as a language gene? Or is it simply that we have a general cognitive, or mental, ability that enables us to pick up language quickly? All of these issues are part of an ongoing debate within linguistics. Currently, the genetic view of language ability holds the field. A recent book by the psycholinguist Steven Pinker, entitled *The Language Instinct* (1995), makes a strong case for considering the elements of linguistic knowledge to be innate. This fits in very neatly with the Chomskyan concept of universal grammar: the idea that there is a common underlying structure to every language, the knowledge of which we are born with.

Psycholinguistics, then, is at the theoretical cutting edge of linguistics and, as such, is pretty heady stuff. So the question is, how can we begin studying it? First of all, we can be encouraged by the fact that much of the recent literature on the subject is very accessible. There is a strong tradition within linguistics of popularising the results of research in ways that demand little previous knowledge. The work of Pinker, mentioned above, and, in particular, Jean Aitchison, provide excellent ways into the subject. In these works you will find discussions of the various methods by which psycholinguists gather their evidence and how they set about analysing it. Secondly, as with sociolinguistics, you can carry out simple observational tasks yourself.

The most effective way to do this is to observe and monitor the speech of one or two young children over a period of time. You need to have in mind, of course, what you are looking for and the purpose of the activity. Your initial concern is to identify distinctive usages, either in sounds, syntax, or word meanings. You will be surprised in doing so how much of children's speech you have hitherto taken for granted. The next stage is to establish what kind of rule your informants are following in producing these usages. Psycholinguistics proceeds on the principle that children's use of language is **rule-governed**. You could start with observing how children form the plural and the past tense. These probably comprise the most conspicuous 'errors' in childhood speech. Young children will frequently say *tooths* and *mouses*, instead of *teeth* and *mice*, and *holded* and *finded*, instead of *held* and *found*. These are examples of **over-generalisation**: the extension of a rule beyond its proper limits. In these cases the child knows the regular rule for forming the plural and the past tense but doesn't know that these particular words are irregular. Having established the presence of this phenomenon, you can then test to see whether all irregular forms are regularised or only some, and how long it takes a child when corrected to acquire the correct form. It's on the basis of experiments like these that psycholinguists form hypotheses about how children memorise forms and self-correct.

Over-generalisation is a frequent phenomenon in language development. It can be found not only in syntactic usage but also in word meanings. Many young children will sometimes refer to all animals as *dogs* or call all vehicles *cars*, and perhaps more disconcertingly, all men, *dad*. Discovering the limits of these words, what they do, and do not, apply to, is a useful way of penetrating the child's semantic system. It can take time, for example, for children to learn that words can refer to separate things. When a child refers to *milk*, for instance, does s/he mean the whole process of pouring it into a mug and placing it down, or does it have the restricted meaning we are used to? Children also under-generalise; indeed, undergeneralisation is probably a more frequent phenomenon than its counterpart. A child may often only be able to use words in a particular context. It's not uncommon for children to call their own shoes *shoes* but not know what someone else's are called.

What I am suggesting, then, is that an initial way into psycholinguistics is to carry out some field research of your own into the acquisition of language, using a couple of basic concepts as your guides. On the basis of this, you can speculate about the kinds of lexical, syntactic, and semantic knowledge which your informants possess. If you do this it will enrich your understanding of the linguistic literature which you read. You will also find that it adds to your knowledge of how language changes; because all of us under- and over-generalise. Over-generalisation is one of the processes behind the loss of inflections from Anglo-Saxon times; we used to have many more irregular forms then than we do now. The morphology of modern English has developed as a consequence of generalising particular ways of forming the plural and past tense into regular paradigms. And it is also a key process in dialectal change. People who say *I loves him* are generalising the rule for the third person singular to cover all forms of the present tense. And in using a word like *deer* with its modern meaning we are under-generalising it: its Anglo-Saxon original, *deor*, meant an animal.

Having begun in a fairly simple way you can extend the process and consider more complex aspects of language acquisition: the formation of the negative, for instance. It takes some time for children to acquire the specific rule about attaching the negative to the auxiliary verb. Initially they will tend to put it at the beginning of the word string: *no Jenny have it*. Later the child decides to put the negative after the first noun phrase: *cat no drink; he no throw it*. The interesting thing about these rules is that the child cannot have acquired them from listening to adult discourse. They have been generated from scratch. And yet they are commonly followed by most children. Are they then a representation of some internal grammar in the child's brain? Does the child start out with a set of possibilities for the formation of the negative and narrow them down as s/he encounters confirmation or disconfirmation from the speech of others? Questions like these form the basis of much psycholinguistic enquiry. It's impossible to see directly into the brain so all we have is the second-hand evidence of language to work on. Over the years psycholinguists have amassed a good deal of observational data and case history analysis, all of which you can work through in time, but it is no substitute at the outset for making your own observations, and for using your linguistic knowledge to speculate about how we manage what is, arguably, the most amazing learning feat of our lives.

Further reading

Adams, V. (1976) *An Introduction to Modern Word-Formation* (London: Longman).

Aitchison, J. (1989) *The Articulate Mammal* (London: Routledge).

Arts, B. (1996) *English Syntax and Argumentation* (Basingstoke: Palgrave Macmillan).

Bauer, L. (1988) *Introducing Linguistic Morphology* (Edinburgh: Edinburgh University Press).

Brown, G. (1990) *Listening to Spoken English* (London: Longman).

Carter, R. (1982) *Language and Literature* (London: Routledge).

Carter, R. and Simpson, P. (eds) (1988) *Language, Discourse and Literature* (London: Routledge).

Chierchia, G. and McConnell-Ginet, S. (1990) *Meaning and Grammar: An Introduction* to *Semantics* (Cambridge, Mass.: MIT Press).

Chomsky, N. (1986) *Knowledge of Language: Its Nature, Origin and Use* (New York: Praeger).

Cook, G. (1992) *The Discourse of Advertising* (London: Routledge).

Coupland, N. and Jaworski, A. (eds) (1997) *Sociolinguistics: A Reader and Coursebook* (Basingstoke: Palgrave Macmillan).

Coulthard, M. (1985) *An Introduction to Discourse Analysis* (London: Longman).

Crystal, D. (1973) *Investigating English Style* (London: Longman).

Fasold, R. (1990) *The Sociolinguistics of Language* (Oxford: Blackwell).

Ferris, C. (1993) *The Meaning of Syntax* (London: Longman).

Freeborn, D. (1996) *Style: Text Analysis and Linguistic Criticism* (London: Longman).

Haynes, J. (1993) *Introducing Stylistics* (London: Routledge).

Haynes, J. (1995) *Style* (London: Routledge).

Holmes, J. (1992) *An Introduction to Sociolinguistics* (London: Longman).

Horrocks, G. (1987) *Generative Grammar* (London: Longman).

Jackson, H. (1990) *Grammar and Meaning* (London: Longman).

Katamba, F. (1993) *Morphology* (Basingstoke: Palgrave Macmillan).

Kearns, K. (2000) *Semantics* (Basingstoke: Palgrave Macmillan).

Knowles, G. (1987) *Patterns of Spoken English* (London: Longman).

Matthews, P. H. (1991) *Morphology*, 2nd edn (Cambridge: Cambridge University Press).

Milroy, J. and Milroy, L. (1993) *Real English* (London: Longman).
Montgomery, M. (1995) *An Introduction to Language and Society* (London: Routledge).
Peccei, J. S. (1994) *Child Language* (London: Routledge, 1994).
Poole, G. (2002) *Syntactic Theory* (Basingstoke: Palgrave Macmillan).
Radford, A. (1988) *An Introduction to Transformational Grammar* (Cambridge: Cambridge University Press).
Radford, A. (1997) *Syntactic Theory and the Structure of English: A Minimalist Approach* (Cambridge: Cambridge University Press).
Salkie, R. (1995) *Text and Discourse Analysis* (London: Routledge).
Short, M. (1996) *Exploring the Language of Poems, Plays and Prose* (London: Longman).
Stenberg, D. (1993) *An Introduction to Psycholinguistics* (London: Longman).
Stenstrom, A. (1994) *An Introduction to Spoken Interaction* (London: Longman).
Trudgill, P. (1983) *Sociolinguistics: An Introduction to Language and Society*, rev. edn (London: Penguin).
Trudgill, P. (1990) *The Dialects of England* (Oxford: Blackwell).
Trudgill, P. (1991) *Dialects of English* (London: Longman).
Trudgill, P. (1994) *Dialects* (London: Routledge).
Wales, K. (1990) *A Dictionary of Stylistics* (London: Longman).
Williams, G. (1992) *Sociolinguistics* (London: Routledge).
Wright, L. and Hope, J. (1995) *Stylistics* (London: Routledge).

Note

1. I am indebted to Michael McCarthy for some of the following examples of intonation patterns. His approach follows on from the work of Brazil (1985) and Crutenden (1986).

7 How to Write a Linguistics Essay

For most of us this is where the crunch really comes. Reading about the subject is OK but having to write something intelligible about it is another matter. All that terminology, those diagrams! Well it isn't so difficult provided you bear in mind a few basic rules. It's the purpose of this chapter to say what these are.

First and foremost, in terms of importance, is **good preparation**. As far as linguistics is concerned this means approaching the subject with the **right mental attitude** – something I stressed at the outset. This is true of writing well about anything, of course, but nowhere more so than linguistics. In particular, I have been emphasising all along the importance of thinking linguistically. If you think **linguistically** then you should write linguistically. As we have seen, thinking linguistically means studying language, and language use, not with the intention of making socially derived judgements about 'correctness', but in a spirit of pure enquiry. The pretensions of linguistics to be a science exist in the importance it places on developing just such a neutrally enquiring attitude. Curiosity is the driving force of most scientific investigation; so be curious. Don't be frightened to ask what may seem to be very basic questions. Most scientific discoveries have been made from going back to first principles, and whilst no one is expecting you to come up with any startlingly new insights, the same procedure holds good whatever the level of your enquiry. You have been asked to write an essay on word classes, for example. Well, before you begin doing anything, ask yourself why we bother to put words into classes at all – why don't we just have words? What does it mean to call something a 'noun' or a 'preposition'? And then you can proceed to the issue which is probably at the heart of the question you have been set – 'how do we determine which class a word belongs to?' You may not put all of this thinking into your essay but it is important in laying the groundwork from which your essay will emerge.

Why is this so? The simple answer here is that most essay questions on linguistics will require you to consider a problem of some kind. They may not directly state what that is, but it's there none the less. It's important, therefore, to develop a **problem-solving attitude**. In the case of word classes there are a number of problems to consider. To begin with, there is the difficulty of deciding what the criteria are for putting a word into a particular class. As we saw in the previous chapter, there is no single criterion which all nouns fulfil, nor is there for most classes. Not only that, but many classes contain subclasses within them, all of which are characterised by different kinds of behaviour. And then again, many words belong to more than one class – similar to dual nationality – while others, those with visitor's status, may just be co-opted into another class. You won't be expected to invent a foolproof system for sorting all these issues out but it's important to show, firstly, that you are aware of what's involved and, secondly, that you are actively considering linguistic solutions. Avoid the kind of answer which simply takes the conventional framework from a textbook and just illustrates it. You'll end up with something which just looks like a set of instructions or a list of examples. Pretty dull stuff.

Remember also, that whilst you're looking at language as if through a microscope, what you are examining is a living organism, which is changing even as you are examining it. This is crucial, because most grammars which you consult will be out of date. Steven Pinker, in talking about intransitive verbs says quite categorically 'Some verbs, like *dine*, refuse to appear in the company of a direct object noun phrase'. So we can't say '*Melvin dined the pizza*' (1995, pp. 112–13). True enough, but it's not uncommon to come across *the boss dined his secretary*. Don't be frightened, then, in your essays, to challenge what you read. The raw material on which all language study is built is your own inheritance. And this brings me to another important tip: try and **use your own examples**. This isn't always possible because there are certain standard examples in the literature to which most people refer. But there's a significant differ-ence between an essay which relies on examples from textbooks, whether it's types of phrases, synonyms, or tone groups, and one where the writer has taken the pains to generate, and analyse, his or her own examples.

Once you have done your investigating and gathered your material, the next task is to organise it. First of all, **make sure you know what is expected of you**. This may seem fairly obvious, but it's very easy to allow your attention to wander in an essay and stray into areas of irrelevance. This is usually a sign that the writer doesn't know how to answer the question, or conversely, has become so interested in one small area as to get sidetracked. Keep your eye always on the central issue. If you are answering a sociolinguistic question on the chief accent innovations which are currently productive, make sure you keep to the issue of accent and don't stray into dialect. And be sure that you are comfortable with the terms 'innovations' and 'productive'. Don't assume that a rough idea of what they mean will do. The best way to approach a question like this is to make a list of the main innovations you are going to cover and use this to structure your essay. But a word of advice here – don't over-organise. You don't want your essay to seem mechanical. Any kind of writing has to have an element of creativity about it if it's going to be lively and interesting. Indeed, if you have done your preparatory thinking about the subject you may well have generated a lot of ideas which you can only sort out in the process of writing. Try and think of your essay as an opportunity to do just that rather than just another hurdle and you will end up with a more interesting piece of work.

More particularly, try and consider the question you are writing about in terms of both **form and function**. I have been stressing this as a crucial distinction in linguistics, and it's as well to keep it in mind when writing about the subject. We can consider language as a system, which is largely the way many linguists approach it, or as a way of fulfilling certain functions. These are really two sides of the same coin, but the view is different according to which side we are contemplating. This is inevitably so: without a formal, systematic side to language, communication would be impossible, but at the same time, without the vast, inarticulate world of human intentionality, communication would have little point. Clearly the type of question you are tackling is important here. If you are writing about some aspect of X bar syntax then there is not going to be very much to say at the functional level, whereas if your topic is intonation the issue of function is inescapable. But a great many topics in linguistics are not so easily categorisable. We have already seen, in the case of the noun phrase, that it has a formal and a functional structure. As a formal entity we can express its structure as a tree diagram, whereas functionally we need to consider the semantic roles which the various words are fulfilling.

Let's imagine, for instance, that you have to write on the tense system in English. You could acquire all the relevant information from a current grammar text and produce a decent summary of the rules for assigning tense in verb phrases, but this wouldn't necessarily demonstrate any understanding of the significance of tense as a category. To do this you would also need to consider the functional dimension of tense: in other words, time. It's very easy to get tense and time mixed up and think they are the same thing: but they aren't. So one of the ways in which you could begin is by disentangling them. Let's have a go at this. Tense is a syntactic category: at S level (surface level) it refers to the way in which we inflect verbs to indicate past and present. Strictly speaking then, it's part of the morphology of English. Most grammars tell us that there is no future tense in English. This is because we have no way of inflecting a verb to show the future. We tend to use the verb *will* with a future sense, but grammatically it's the present tense of *would*. The difficulty with English is that it has to express the complex world of time with only two tenses at its disposal. At this point in our discussion we might briefly consider some of the problems this poses. Young children, for instance, don't always use the present/past distinction with the same functional sense as adults. The present can be used for activities which happen repeatedly and the past for those which happen only once. An account of a boy kicking a football and falling over might go *he **kicks** the ball and he **fell** over*. And then there is the problem of expressing imagined, or hypothetical, time. The traditional way in standard English of indicating some hypothetical possibility is to say *if I **were** you*. . . . This is the past tense form, but abnormally so, because it's the plural of the verb *to be* being used here, not the singular. This usage is referred to as the **subjunctive**, the death of which has been confidently predicted for some time now. It still remains in educated usage, however, despite the more popular tendency to use the regular past tense form, *if I **was** you*.

The relationship between time and tense is a fascinating one because of the various hoops the language has to go through to accommodate the mobility of our existence in time. Observing and commenting on these hoops is a useful way of enriching our discussion. An important point which should emerge from this is that tense is used to convey other things than simply time. We saw in Chapter 4, for example, that in the case of words like *can* and *could*, tense can be used modally to express a subtlety of politeness, without any necessary direct reference to time. So a conclusion we might come to, then, from our initial attempt to disentangle tense and time is that the tense system of English, in morphological terms, is rather impoverished and, as a consequence, overworked. We rely on a simple distinction between past and present to serve a number of expressive needs.

Having observed some of the anomalies of the tense/time dimension we can proceed to describe the syntactic ways in which English tries to compensate for its impoverished system. One tactic English employs is to use combinations of verbs to capture what we can think of as 'complex time'. For example, instead of saying *he lived here*, we might choose to say *he has lived here*. We have now modified the past form *lived* with the present form *has* and, as a consequence, can express a particular nuance of the time continuum. If you think about it, the phrase *has lived* suggests the continuing significance of *lived*, either because it's still going on, that is, he's still living here, or because the fact of the occupation has a present relevance. In other words, important here is not only location in time (when something happened) but duration (how long it happened for). The combination of duration and location in the verb phrase is achieved only by using auxiliary verbs in conjunction with lexical ones. In so doing, the language is able to refine tense by including what linguists call **aspect**. We can refer to any modern grammar at this point in the discussion, to indicate the different kinds of aspect and the way they are represented in the verb phrase. The permissible combinations of auxiliaries and lexical verb are a bit like sequences in chess games – the order is fixed and any change in the permutation alters the relationship between duration and location.

At this stage, having given some indication of the complexity of the tense system in descriptive terms, we can move on to consider a further, and more interesting point arising from our examples. I said at the outset that tense was 'strictly speaking ... part of the morphology of English'. But this now needs some restatement. Adding *has* to the sentence *he lived here* changes the tense of the string from past to present, even though lived remains the head word of the verb phrase and has the correct past tense morpheme. We can test this by continuing both sentences with 'tag' questions:

*He lived here **didn't** he?*
*He has lived here **hasn't** he?*

In the first sentence the question form clearly uses the past tense of the auxiliary verb, whilst in the second, it uses the present. This suggests that tense is not a property of morphemes, that is, it's not the case that the past tense is somehow contained in the morpheme 'ed', but rather that it's an abstract category and as such belongs to the phrase as a whole, not the individual verb. Morphology is used as a way of signalling tense, but it's not the only way: also important is syntactic order. At this point we are now moving into the realm of modern transformational linguistics. At the heart of this is the conception of categories such as tense as slots in the blueprint sentence, properties of D structure, which attach themselves to particular items according to the syntactic requirements of the language.

From my brief overview of the tense system you might have noticed a difference in the kinds of information I provided. Some was simply at an observational level, commenting on anomalies in the relationship between tense and time, some was more descriptive, outlining the structure of the verb group, and some was explanatory, trying to say what sort of category tense is at D level. This conforms to Chomskyan methodology for linguistic enquiry – **observation, description**, and **explanation** – and it's one which I recommend to you as a way of intellectually structuring your own essays. The virtue of it is that it's fairly flexible and can accommodate any level of linguistic investigation. You may, for example, be writing an elementary essay about tense, in which case the majority of your essay will be spent observing the surface features of English with some description and no explanation. At a more intermediate stage, however, you might be concerned with giving as full an account as possible of the structure of the verb group in descriptive terms. On the other hand, if you are at an advanced stage in your linguistic studies you might be concentrating heavily on exploring possible explanations for tense at D level. But, whatever stage you are at, there is a common denominator to all your enquiries. In any linguistics essay, what you are fundamentally exploring is the variety of ways in which language systematically encodes aspects of our experiential life in order to fulfil the functions which we discussed in Chapter 2. We can look at these from various sides of the spectrum and within the different branches of linguistics, but it is the fit between language and life which occupies the central core.

Having got the structure, methodology, and purpose of a linguistics essay clear, however, it's time to consider more closely ways of proceeding with the actual task of writing. I said, earlier, that linguistics has a scientific side to it – this should be evident from what we have established about its methodology. Make sure that you reflect this in your essay. To begin with, **use your opening paragraph to state exactly what it is you are going to do, and then make sure that you do it**. If, for example, you are intending to write a stylistics essay about football commentaries, set out clearly the scope of your study, the types of evidence you are considering, and the linguistic levels you will be discussing. Let's say you are comparing a football commentary from the radio with one from television. You will need to make clear to your audience what the purpose of the exercise is. You might say, for example, that you intend to analyse the principal grammatical features, and that to do so you will be considering the structure of each in terms of phonology, syntax, and semantics. This will be the 'bread and butter' of the essay and will involve a substantial amount of observation and description. In addition, however, you might also be exploring, at a more explanatory level, how these grammatical features relate to the ideational, interpersonal, and textual functions of the extracts, and the communicative situations which give rise to them.

If you set out what you intend to do in this way then the rest of the essay will take shape naturally. After the **introduction** comes the **development** section. This is where you develop those areas which you have already highlighted in your introduction. In the case of our hypothetical stylistics essay this will mean a section on the grammatical features of the extracts, in which you discuss, in turn, intonation pattern, syntactic structure, and semantic aspects. Once you have established a grammatical description of the extracts you can follow this with another section in which you relate these to the communicative functions mentioned above. To do this you will need to take account of their respective communicative situations, that is, the particular channels employed, the tenor, and the situational context. The final part of the essay is the **conclusion**. Here you will do two things: first, you will bring together the main stylistic comparisons and contrasts between the two extracts, making them sharper; and second, you will comment on them as examples of the genre of sports commentary to which they belong.

Let's just recap on what we have said so far. First on the list is the importance of **good preparation**. This means approaching the topic with the **right mental attitude**, in particular, developing a **problem-solving attitude**, being curious, and **using your own examples**. In other words, **thinking linguistically**. Next, when you come to write your essay, **make sure you know what is expected of you**, that is, keep to the terms of reference of the question set. Bear in mind the two dimensions of linguistic study – **form and function** – and try and address both. In terms of the intellectual structure of your essay use the Chomskyan division of **observation**, **description**, and **explanation**, as a guide to the organisation of your argument. And finally, lay your essay out using the broad divisions of **introduction, development**, and **conclusion**.

And what style should I use in my essay? Well, the main danger to avoid here is overloading your essays with technical terms. This is usually a sign that your work is derivative. Only use terms whose meaning you are absolutely sure of and can use with confidence. Having said that, however, if you do manage to master the essential terms relevant to your topic you will find it enormously helpful in your writing. Basic words like 'constituents', 'nodes', 'lexeme', and 'register', will enable you to avoid loose phrases, and will signal to your informed reader exactly what you mean. Not all jargon is bad, and in the case of the more specialised reaches of linguistics it is essential. But it is to be used sparingly and only as an aid to the elucidation of your argument. The other main danger to avoid is making your essay too factual. This is a very common failing. If you are writing an essay comparing American English with British

English, for example, it's not enough just to document the chief differences. It's true that the 'bread and butter' will again be a descriptive account of differences in phonology, syntax, and semantics, but these need to be set within the context of a wider explanatory discussion. You will need to discuss the cultural and historical factors which are responsible for the differences between the two varieties, as well as discussing which are the most distinctive and productive in terms of distinguishing them. And make sure that whatever examples you provide are fully used. Don't simply decorate your essay with them. If you are discussing synonymy in English, make sure that you give enough time to discussing the examples, and elaborating, with sample sentences if need be, on the linguistic processes involved.

The principal requirement for a linguistic essay, then, is that it should be clear, well illustrated, but uncluttered, with a developing argument which balances information against discussion. As far as referring to critical literature is concerned, this will depend very much on the subject you are writing about and the level at which you are writing. Linguistics essays are usually different from literary ones where you are frequently asked to debate the viewpoint of a particular critic. More often than not in linguistics you are presented with a topic and asked to consider, or explore, some aspect of it. This will inevitably involve reading the accounts of other linguists in order that your own may be properly informed, but only in the case of more advanced essays will you be expected to debate these. What examiners are really looking for is the quality of your understanding and the care you have taken in organising and presenting your material. The amount of critical reading you have done and can quote from is only of incidental importance.

And lastly, to end on an encouraging note, linguistics is one subject where it's possible to make your own contribution. As I said at the beginning, no one is expecting you to invent a new theory, but there are always fresh usages, and new bits of linguistic structure, which are continually emerging. In contrast with literary texts, the 'text' of linguistics is continuously evolving. It's not fixed and finite but endlessly fertile and self-renewing. In studying it you are studying not only something you possess, but something you are possessed by. As I suggested to you at the beginning, if we want an image of a truly democratic entity we could do worse than seek it in the power of language.

The International Phonetic Alphabet
[revised 1993]

CONSONANTS (PULMONIC)

	Bilabial	Labiodental	Dental	Alveolar	Postalveolar	Retroflex	Palatal	Velar	Uvular	Pharyngeal	Glottal
Plosive	p b			t d		ʈ ɖ	c ɟ	k ɡ	q ɢ		ʔ
Nasal	m	ɱ		n		ɳ	ɲ	ŋ	N		
Trill	ʙ			r					R		
Tap or Flap				ɾ		ɽ					
Fricative	ɸ β	f v	θ ð	s z	ʃ ʒ	ʂ ʐ	ç ʝ	x ɣ	χ ʁ	ħ ʕ	h ɦ
Lateral fricative				ɬ ɮ							
Approximant		ʋ		ɹ		ɻ	j	ɰ			
Lateral approximant				l		ɭ	ʎ	L			

Where symbols appear in pairs, the one to the right represents a voiced consonant. Shaded areas denote articulations judged impossible.

CONSONANTS (NON-PULMONIC)

Clicks		Voiced implosives		Ejectives	
⊙	Bilabial	ɓ	Bilabial	ʼ	as in:
ǀ	Dental	ɗ	Dental/alveolar	pʼ	Bilabial
ǃ	(Post)alveolar	ʄ	Palatal	tʼ	Dental/alveolar
ǂ	Palatoalveolar	ɠ	Velar	kʼ	Velar
ǁ	Alveolar lateral	ʛ	Uvular	sʼ	Alveolar fricative

VOWELS

```
        Front          Central          Back
Close    i • y ———————— ɨ • ʉ ———————— ɯ • u
            ɪ  ʏ              ʊ
Close-mid    e • ø ——— ɘ • ɵ ——— ɤ • o
                          ə
Open-mid       ɛ • œ — ɜ • ɞ — ʌ • ɔ
                   æ       ɐ
Open               a • ɶ ——————— ɑ • ɒ
```

Where symbols appear in pairs, the one to the right represents a rounded vowel.

OTHER SYMBOLS

ʍ	Voiceless labial-velar fricative
w	Voiced labial-velar approximant
ɥ	Voiced labial-palatal approximant
ʜ	Voiceless epiglottal fricative
ʢ	Voiced epiglottal fricative
ʡ	Epiglottal plosive

ɕ ʑ Alveolo-palatal fricatives
ɺ Alveolar lateral flap
ɧ Simultaneous ʃ and x

Affricates and double articulations can be represented by two symbols joined by a tie bar if necessary

k͡p t͡s

SUPRASEGMENTALS

ˈ	Primary stress	ˌfoʊnəˈtɪʃən
ˌ	Secondary stress	
ː	Long	eː
ˑ	Half-long	eˑ
̆	Extra-short	ĕ
.	Syllable break	ɹi.ækt
ǀ	Minor (foot) group	
ǁ	Major (intonation) group	
‿	Linking (absence of a break)	

TONES & WORD ACCENTS

LEVEL		CONTOUR	
e̋ or ˥	Extra high	ě or ˇ	Rising
é ˦	High	ê ˆ	Falling
ē ˧	Mid	e̋	High rising
è ˨	Low	e̎	Low rising
ȅ ˩	Extra low	ẽ	Rising-falling
↓ Downstep		↗ Global rise	etc.
↑ Upstep		↘ Global fall	

DIACRITICS

Diacritics may be placed above a symbol with a descender, e.g. ŋ̊

̥	Voiceless	n̥ d̥	̤	Breathy voiced	b̤ a̤	̪ Dental t̪ d̪
̬	Voiced	s̬ t̬	̰	Creaky voiced	b̰ a̰	̺ Apical t̺ d̺
ʰ	Aspirated	tʰ dʰ	̼	Linguolabial	t̼ d̼	̻ Laminal t̻ d̻
̹	More rounded	ɔ̹	ʷ	Labialized	tʷ dʷ	̃ Nasalized ẽ
̜	Less rounded	ɔ̜	ʲ	Palatalized	tʲ dʲ	ⁿ Nasal release dⁿ
̟	Advanced	u̟	ˠ	Velarized	tˠ dˠ	ˡ Lateral release dˡ
̠	Retracted	i̠	ˤ	Pharyngealized	tˤ dˤ	̚ No audible release d̚
̈	Centralized	ë	̴	Velarized or pharyngealized	ɫ	
̽	Mid-centralized	ĕ̽	̝	Raised	e̝ (ɹ̝ = voiced alveolar fricative)	
̩	Syllabic	l̩	̞	Lowered	e̞ (β̞ = voiced bilabial approximant)	
̯	Non-syllabic	e̯	̘	Advanced Tongue Root	e̘	
˞	Rhoticity	ə˞	̙	Retracted Tongue Root	e̙	

Glossary

abstract nouns: nouns which have no physical reference (*sincerity*, *luck*), as opposed to concrete nouns which do (*table*, *chair*).

accent: features of pronunciation which show regional or social variation.

acceptable/unacceptable: terms which indicate native speakers' intuitions about the 'correctness', or otherwise, of any usage.

accommodation: adjustments speakers automatically make to their speech when conversing with others.

actor: in functional grammar, the 'doer' of an action. Also referred to sometimes as the 'agent'.

addresser/addressee: respectively, the 'author', and intended 'recipient' of any communication.

adjective: a class of words, comprising items which typically refer to a property, quality, or attribute.

adjunct: a sentence element which gives circumstantial information.

adverb: a class of words, comprising items which typically refer to the circumstances or manner in which an action is done, and frequently marked by the suffix 'ly'. Adverbs can also occur as modifiers of adjectives (*very*, *quite*), and as sentence connectors (*hopefully*, *moreover*).

adverbial: used by some linguists as an equivalent to 'adjunct'. See **adjunct**.

affricates: manner of articulation in which air is released with friction after closure of the speech organs.

agent: see **actor**.

agreement: grammatical relationship in which the form of one element requires the corresponding form of another (*I was*, *they were*).

alliteration: rhyming of initial consonants in a sequence of words.

allograph: written form in which a grapheme is realised.

allomorph: phonetic form in which a morpheme is realised.

allophone: phonetic form in which a phoneme is realised.

amelioration: semantic process by which a word loses an unpleasant sense. Cf. **pejoration**.

analytic truth: truth established by word sense (*cats are animals*) as opposed to synthetic truth where it is established by experience (*cats have four legs*).

antonymy: opposition between the senses of words (*good/bad*, *husband/wife*). See **complementary antonyms**, **gradable antonyms**, **relational antonyms**.

applied linguistics: the study of language and linguistics in relation to practical issues, e.g. speech therapy, stylistics.

approximants: consonants in which the speech organs approach each other but without closure or friction. See **glides** and **liquids**.

aspect: the duration of an activity denoted by the verb, involving the use of the auxiliary verbs 'be' or 'have'.

assimilation: influence exercised by one sound on another making them more alike.

associative sense: the sense which becomes attached to a word because of its use but which is not part of its core meaning.

assonance: rhyming of vowel sounds.

attribute: 1. in functional grammar a role played by a complement in a clause with a relational verb; 2. an adjectival pre-modifier in a noun phrase.

auxiliary verb: a verb used in conjunction with a main, or lexical verb, to make grammatical distinctions of aspect, or mood.

behaver: in functional grammar a role played by the subject in a clause with a behavioural verb.

blending: a process in morphology in which two words are fused to form a new one (*smoke* + *fog* > *smog*).

breaking: phonological process by which a diphthong separates into two monophthongs. **Smoothing** is a term given to the reverse process.

case: a grammatical feature of nouns which applies to the functions they may fulfil in clauses, e.g. nominative, or subject case; accusative, or object case.

carrier: in functional grammar a role played by the subject in a clause with a relational verb.

central adjectives: adjectives which can both pre-modify a noun and occur after it as the complement of a linking verb, such as 'to be'. See **complement**.

channel: the physical medium selected for communication (e.g. telephone, letter).

citational: the form of a linguistic unit when produced in isolation for purposes of discussion.

clause: a structural unit intermediate between **phrase** and **sentence**.

clipping: a process in morphology by which a new word is produced by shortening an existing one (*refrigerator* > *fridge*).

close: in phonetics vowels which are made with the tongue in the highest possible position are described as 'close'. Cf. **open**.

coda: consonants which follow the nucleus of a syllable (*ox*, *pots*).

code: a signalling system for sending messages, e.g. morse code, semaphore. More specifically, however, a language, or language variety.

coherence: refers to the way in which texts, or utterances are internally consistent in meaning, i.e. sense and reference.

cohesion: the formal demonstration of coherence through precise syntactic links (*It* is cohesive in *the man threw the ball. It bounced*).

collocation: the tendency for certain words to occur together. The number of contexts in which a word can be found are referred to as its 'collocational range'.

communicative intention: the intention to convey a message to another speaker, consequently a prerequisite for successful communication.

comparative linguistics: the study of the relationship between languages, particularly those considered to have a common origin, e.g. English and German.

competence: the understanding which users of a language have about its internal system of rules. Distinctions can be made between various types of competence, especially **grammatical competence**, our knowledge of the grammatical system, and **communicative competence**, our ability to use language appropriately in different situations.

complement: a clause element that completes what is said about some other element, such as the subject.

complementary antonyms: a form of sense opposition in which the contrast between the terms is 'either/or' (*alive/dead, married/single*).

complementary distribution: sounds which only occur in mutually exclusive environments are said to be in complementary distribution. In a majority of cases it indicates that they are allophones of the same phoneme.

complementiser: a subordinating conjunction such as *if, while* and *that,* which marks an embedded sentence.

compounding: 1. a process of word formation in which two words combine to form a new one (day + dream > daydream). 2. the joining of two or more clauses by coordination.

computational linguistics: the use of statistical and computer-aided methods in the study of linguistic issues.

concrete nouns: see **abstract nouns**.

constituent: a linguistic unit which is an element of a larger construction.

context: the background situation within which a communicative event takes place.

convergence: a tendency for the accents and dialects of speakers to become more like each other in the process of conversation (see **accommodation**).

conversion: a process of word formation whereby a new word is formed by an existing word changing its class (*a table* [noun] > *to table* [verb]).

cooperative principle: an implicit agreement by speakers that they will obey certain conventions or maxims when communicating. The principal maxims are those of 'quantity', 'relation', 'manner', and 'quality'.

core/non-core: words which are fairly neutral in respect of positive or negative associations are said to be core items, as opposed to those which have marked associations (*thin/wasted*).

declarative: a syntactic structure used in making a statement (*the boy laughed*).

decontextualised: communications which are not dependent on the situational context in which they are produced for their meaning are said to be 'decontextualised' – more typical of written than spoken language. In Chomskyan grammar decontextualised sentences exhibit complete grammatical structures.

deep structure (now **D structure**): the underlying syntactic structure of sentences, capable of being represented by a tree diagram. See **surface structure**.

denote: the objective, i.e. dictionary, relationship of a word to its sense.

determiner: the class of words which co-occurs with a noun to express such things as number, quantity, etc. (*the, some, a*).

diachronic: from diachrony, the historical perspective involved in studying the way a language has changed over time. See **historical linguistics**.

diacritic: a mark, or symbol, which, when added to a phoneme indicates a variation in its pronunciation. Some graphemes can also act as diacritics, e.g. final <e> after a consonant in monosyllabic words (<fade>).

dialect: a regional, or social, variety of the language with distinct syntactic forms and vocabulary items.

digraph: two letters pronounced as a single sound (*churn, ship*).

diphthong: a vowel phoneme which changes its quality in pronunciation.

discourse analysis: the study of linguistic organisation in speech and writing.

distinctive features: phonetic properties of speech which are capable of differentiating between otherwise identical sounds.

distribution: the range of linguistic environments in which a sound, or word, can occur.

dominance: a hierarchical relationship in which syntactic constituents contain within them other constituents.

duality of patterning: the structural organisation of language into two levels whereby meaningless units, e.g. sounds, letters, can function as meaningful units, e.g. words.

dynamic verbs: verbs which express activities and changes of state, characteristically allowing the progressive (*she's arriving*). Cf. **stative verbs**.

elision: the omission of sounds in connected speech.

ellipsis: the omission of parts of a sentence where the meaning is understood, as in a telegram.

embedding: putting one phrase or clause within another.

euphony: sequence of sounds which gives pleasure.

existent: in functional grammar the role played by the subject in an existential clause.

extension: a semantic process in which a word expands in meaning. See **limitation**.

field: also termed **semantic field**. An area of meaning containing words with related senses.

field of discourse: subject area which features as the topic of communication in speech or writing.

figurative: the use of words in a non-literal way, e.g. metaphor, simile.

focus: an element in a sentence to which the speaker wishes to draw special attention.

force: the contextual meaning of a linguistic item, frequently signalled by intonation.

free variation: the substitution of one sound for another without causing any change of meaning.

fricatives: a manner of articulation in which air is released continuously with friction.

general American: the variety of English spoken by the majority of Americans, in use from New York State to the West Coast.

generative grammar: a grammar which aims to describe all and only the grammatical sequences of a language.

glides: /j/ and /w/ are described as 'glides'. They are a subset of 'approximants'. See **approximants**.

goal: term in functional grammar to describe the role performed by the person or thing acted upon by the verb. Similar terms are **medium, affected**, and **patient**.

gradable antonyms: a form of sense opposition in which degrees of oppositeness are possible between the terms (*hot/cold*; *old/young*).

grammar: 1. the study of syntax. 2. an account of the rules governing linguistic behaviour with particular reference to phonology, syntax, and semantics.

graph: the smallest physical segment in a written or printed sequence of words (m, M, *m*).

grapheme: the smallest contrastive unit in the writing system of a language (m, l, t).

historical linguistics: the study of language development over time. See **diachronic**.

homophones: words which are pronounced the same but which are otherwise not related.

hyponymy: relationship between a general and a specific word in which the latter is included in the former (*red* is included in *colour*).

ideational: in functional grammar the ideational function is concerned with the linguistic representation of experiences, especially mental and emotional.

illocution: an act performed through the process of uttering a locution, i.e speaking, and thus a 'speech act'.

imperative: a sentence type normally used to give a command.

implicature: an extra meaning beyond what is explicitly stated in an utterance. See **inference**.

incompatibility: a feature of items in a semantic field where the choice of one excludes the other (*this instrument is a piano* entails *this instrument is not a violin*).

inference: the process of working something out which is not explicitly stated in an utterance. See implicature.

intension: the defining properties of a word; roughly synonymous with **sense**.

interpersonal: in functional grammar the interpersonal function is concerned with the communicative use of language, especially in establishing and maintaining relationships.

interrogative: a type of sentence normally used to ask questions.

intonation: the pitch contour of speech.

intonational force: those meanings in an utterance conveyed by intonation rather than simply the lexical senses of the words.

isogloss: a line on a map which shows the area in which a linguistic feature is used.

kernel clause: a clause in simple declarative, i.e statement form, which has not been transformed.

langue: Saussure's term for the abstract system of language which native users employ. See **parole**.

level: a major dimension of the structural organisation of language (semantic level, syntactic level, phonological level).

lexeme: a word as an abstract entity, distinct from the forms in which it appears through inflection (*broken*, *broke*, and *breaks*, are all forms of *break*).

lexical sense: the definition of a word normally found in a dictionary. See **sense**.

lexical verb: a 'content' verb expressing a state, event, or action and normally the head of a verb phrase.

lexicon: the vocabulary of a language to which native speakers unconsciously have access.

liaison: the process by which a consonant sound is introduced between two words for ease of pronunciation.

limitation: semantic process in which a word contracts in meaning. See **extension**.

liquids: /l/ and /r/ are described as 'liquid' consonants. They are a subset of 'approximants'. See **approximants**.

locution: the physical act of speaking. See **illocution**.

manner of articulation: the configuration adopted by the speech organs in articulating a sound.

marked/unmarked: linguistic features which are prominent, unusual, or 'deviant', are said to be 'marked', as opposed to those which are normative, or non-prominent, and so 'unmarked'.

medium: 1. the manner in which a message is transmitted, i.e spoken or written. Sometimes referred to as **mode**. 2. another term for the **goal** in functional grammar.

metalanguage: language used for talking about language.

metaphor: a figurative use of language in which the senses of words are transferred (*the ship ploughed the ocean*, where *ploughed* has the transferred sense of 'sailed').

metonymy: a figurative use of speech in which the name of a referent is replaced by the name of something associated with it ('the Monarchy' – *the Crown*; 'the Government' – *Number 10*).

monophthong: a vowel in which there is no noticeable change in quality. See **diphthong**.

mood: a grammatical category which relates to different sentence types. In functional grammar these are closely linked to the interpersonal component of grammar (declarative, interrogative, imperative, exclamative).

morpheme: the smallest distinctive unit of grammatical analysis. Cf. **word**.

morphology: the study of word structure.

motor difficulty: a difficulty in coordination, typically of hand and eye.

nasals: sounds made by lowering the soft palate and allowing air to pass through the nose.

node: point on a tree diagram where two branches join.

nomenclaturism: the belief that the relationship between words and things is natural rather than conventional.

non-verbal communication: communication which takes place other than through words. It may be vocal (**paralinguistic**), e.g. intonation, or non-vocal, e.g. gesture.

normative: a socially approved linguistic usage.

noun: a class of words, comprising items which typically refer to entities of some kind. See **abstract nouns**.

nuclear syllable: the syllable in a tone group which carries the maximum pitch variation.

object: a clause element which normally follows the verb and is dependent on it.

onomatopeia: a word formation in which the sounds are said to echo the sense, as in *buzz*, *cuckoo*, and *crash*.

onset: the optional initial sound(s) in a syllable.

open: in phonetics vowels which are made with the tongue in the lowest possible position are described as 'open'. See **close**.

orthographical fallacy: the belief that the spelt form of a word predicts its pronunciation.

orthography: the writing system of a language. In English, the alphabet.

overgeneralisation: extending a word meaning or grammatical rule beyond its recognised use.

paradigmatic: the relationship between words which allows substitution to occur (*give me your/his/the bike*). See **syntagmatic**.

paralinguistic: see **non-verbal communication**.

parole: the verbal behaviour of individuals in speech and writing. See *langue*.

peak: the central sound, or 'nucleus' of a syllable.

pejoration: a semantic process in which a word takes on a negative evaluation (gossip, originally 'god-relative'). Cf. **amelioration**.

performance: what we do when we actually use language, i.e the physical process of speaking and writing. See **competence**.

performative: said of speech acts which not only 'say' something but 'do' something verbally (*I name this ship*). See **speech act**.

peripheral adjectives: adjectives which can occur in only one of the two main 'adjective' sites. See **central adjectives**.

phatic communion: sociable talk with little meaningful content the main purpose of which is to establish or maintain contact.

phenomenon: in functional grammar the role played by the object in a clause with a mental verb.

phone: the smallest perceptible segment of speech sound.

phoneme: the smallest contrastive segment of speech sound.

phonetics: the technical study of the way in which speech sounds are produced, transmitted, and received.

phonology: the study of the sound system of a language, in particular, the identification of phonemes and their linguistic organisation.

phonotactics: the study of permissible sound sequences in a language.

phrase: a sequence of words, smaller than a clause, which behaves as a syntactic unit.

phrase structure grammar: the rules which define how words are grouped into phrases, and phrases into higher units.

place of articulation: the point in the vocal tract where the speech organs restrict the passage of air in some way so producing distinctive speech sounds.

plosives: consonant sounds made by the sudden release of air after complete closure of the speech organs. Also called **stop consonants**.

polysemy: the existence of multiple senses of a word.

post-modify: the elements in a phrase which are subordinate to the head word and occur after it are said to 'post-modify' it.

pragmatics: the study of the situational and interpersonal factors which affect the meaning of utterances.

predicate: the verb phrase in a major clause.

predicator: the main verb in a clause.

prefixation: the process of adding an affix to the beginning of a word (dis + please). See **suffixation**.

pre-modify: the elements in a phrase which are subordinate to the head word and which occur before it are said to 'pre-modify' it. See **post-modify**.

preposition: a class of words which comprises items that typically refer to temporal or spatial relationships (*in, through, before*).

presupposition: an assumption implictly made by speakers and listeners which is necessary for the correct interpretation of an utterance.

productive: linguistic rules which are capable of producing many instances of the same type are said to be 'productive'.

proper noun: a noun which is the name of a unique place, person, or thing (*London, William*).

prosody: the study of rhythm and intonation in speech.

prototype: a representative type or exemplar (thrush is a prototype of bird).

psycholinguistics: the study of the mental processes involved in language production and reception.

quantifier: a term such as *some, much, most, several, all,* and *each*, which expresses contrasts in quantity. In semantic theory there are two main types: the universal quantifier (*all*) and the existential quantifier (*some, each*).

received pronunciation(r. p.): the most socially prestigious form of pronunciation in British English, belonging to no particular region.

reduction: in phonology the substitution of a weak central vowel for a strong vowel in unstressed syllables.

reference: the relationship between words and the things, activities, properties, relationships, etc. in the outside world, to which they refer.

register: a socially defined style of language such as religious or medical language. The term is also used to distinguish different levels of formality in communication. A domestic chat, for example, normally employs a different register from a business letter. See **style-shifting**.

regularisation: part of the process of producing idealised sentences and involving the omission of any non-fluency elements such as hesitations or slips of the tongue.

relational antonyms: a form of opposition in which one term asserts the converse of the other (*buy/sell*).

rewrite rule: a rule in generative grammar of the form 'A → B', that is, 'replace A with B'.

rounding: a configuration of the lips in the production of some vowel sounds and allowing a contrast between rounded and unrounded vowels. See **spread**.

sayer: in functional grammar the role played by the subject in a clause with a verbal verb. See **target**.

schwa/shwa: an unstressed vowel – /ə/ – made in the centre of the mouth and heard in weak syllables such as *about, banana*.

semantic features: an element, or component of a word's meaning (doe → + adult + female + animal).

semantics: the study of the way in which words 'mean' in a language.

sense: the meaning a word has within a language. Limited by some linguists to a word's conceptual or propositional meaning.

sensor: in functional grammar a role played by the subject in a clause with a mental verb.

sentence meaning: the sense an utterance has apart from the context in which it is uttered. Cf. **utterance meaning**.

setting: the situation in which communication takes place and which provides a contextual frame for it.

signification: the process by which the sound form of a word is united with a mental image to provide a stable meaning.

signified: the mental image a word conveys to our minds.

signifier: the sound form of a word, i.e. its pronunciation form.

simile: a figurative comparison, *as old as the hills*, as opposed to a literal comparison, *as old as his brother*.

sociolinguistics: the study of the relationship between language and society.

sonority: a feature in phonetics which measures the relative resonance of a sound in the vocal tract.

speech act: an act performed using language as a medium. Usually divided into direct acts where a single act is being performed, and indirect, where one act is performed by means of another, e.g. requests framed as questions (*Can you open the window?*).

spread: configuration of the lips in articulating some vowel sounds in which the lips are stretched sideways. See **rounding**.

standard English: non-regional dialect used as a model for educated written usage.

stative verbs: verbs which express states of affairs rather than actions (*seem, know*). See **dynamic verbs**.

string: permissible sequence of words, whether phrase, clause, or sentence.

style-shifting: the ability by speakers to use more than one register in a communication. See **register**.

stylistics: the study of style in language using a linguistic perspective.

subject: grammatically, a clause element which normally precedes the verb and conditions its form in the 3rd person singular present tense (*he hits*). Some grammars distinguish between different types of subjects, e.g grammatical and logical subjects (in *the ball was hit by the boy* – *the boy* is the logical subject, and *the ball*, the grammatical subject).

subjunctive: a mood in grammar typically used to express doubt or a hypothetical state (*if I were you*).

substitution: a typical cohesive device in texts whereby one element is replaced by another.

suffixation: the process of adding an affix to the end of a word. See **prefixation**.

superordinate: the more general term in a relationship between words involving inclusion. See **hyponymy**.

surface structure (now S structure): the linear arrangement of the words in a grammatical string. See **deep structure**.

syllable: the smallest rhythmic unit of sound.

synaesthesia: interconnection between the senses (*sharp noise* – touch/hearing).

synonymy: sameness of meaning.

syntagmatic: said of the linear relationship between words in a grammatical construction. See **paradigmatic**.

synthetic truth: see **analytic truth**.

tag question: a question attached to the end of an utterance (*he went, didn't he?*).

tenor: the relationship between participants, their roles and status, in a communicative situation.

tense: a change in the form of a verb to mark the time at which something takes place.

textual: in functional grammar a meta-function of language which has to do with the way language is constructed as a text.

textuality: the property exhibited by texts which are coherent and cohesive.

thematic force: the meaning conveyed by an utterance by means of its syntactic arrangement.

theme: the initial element in an uttterance which typically acts as its starting point.

tone unit: part of an utterance over which a distinctive pitch contour extends.

transferred sense: see **metaphor**.

transformational grammar: a grammar which aims to establish rules for the generation of surface syntactic structures from deep structures. See **deep structure** and **surface structure**.

transitive/intransitive: verbs which take objects are said to be 'transitive' as opposed to those which do not, which are 'intransitive'.

truth conditional semantics: the study of the propositional meaning of utterances and the logical conditions for establishing their truth or otherwise.

undergeneralisation: the use of a word or expression to refer to only part of its normal meaning.

universal grammar: the structure underlying the grammars of all languages.

utterance meaning: the meaning an utterance has which derives from the context and manner in which it is uttered. Cf. **sentence meaning**.

value: the range of meaning a word is capable of within the linguistic system

verb: a class of words, comprising items which typically refer to actions or states, and which can show contrasts of tense and aspect.

verbiage: in functional grammar the role played by the object in a clause with a verbal verb.

voicing: vibration of the vocal cords in speech production.

vulnerable: said of sounds which are most susceptible to loss or alteration as a consequence of accent innovations.

well-formed/ill-formed: a pair of terms which express linguistic judgements about the grammaticality of utterances.

word: the smallest unit of grammar that can stand alone. Cf. **morpheme**.

X bar theory: the theory that all phrases in all languages conform to a single plan expressible in terms of the variable 'X' where 'X' stands for any word category.

yod dropping: the dropping of /j/ in the pronunciation of words such as tune (/tjun/).

References

Aitchison, J. (1987) *Words in the Mind: An Introduction to the Mental Lexicon* (Oxford: Blackwell).

Aitchison, J. (1992) *Teach Yourself Linguistics*, 4th edn (London: Hodder & Stoughton).

Attridge, D. (1982) *The Rhythms of English Poetry* (London and New York: Longman).

Austin, J. L. (1962) *How to do Things with Words* (Oxford: Oxford University Press).

Berne, E. (1968) *Games People Play* (London: Penguin).

Brazil, D. C. (1985) *Intonation and its Parts: Melody in Spoken English* (London: Edward Arnold).

Burgess, A. (1993) *A Mouthful of Air* (London: Vintage).

Camus, A. (1948) *The Plague* (London: Hamish Hamilton).

Crutenden, A. (1986) *Intonation* (Cambridge: Cambridge University Press).

Crystal, D. (1987) *The Cambridge Encyclopedia of Language* (Cambridge: Cambridge University Press).

Crystal, D. (1988) *Rediscover Grammar* (London: Longman).

Crystal, D. (1995) *The Cambridge Encyclopedia of the English Language* (Cambridge: Cambridge University Press).

Fabb, N. (1994) *Sentence Structure* (London: Routledge).

Firth, J. R. (1937) *The Tongues of Men* (London: Watts).

Fish, S. (1980) *Is there a Text in this Class? The Authority of Interpretive Communities* (Harvard: Harvard University Press).

Francis, N. W. (1967) *The English Language: An Introduction* (London: English Universities Press).

Freeborn, D., French, P. and Langford, D. (1993) *Varieties of English*, 2nd edn (Basingsoke: Palgrave Macmillan).

Graddol, D., Cheshire, J. and Swann, J. (1991) *Describing Language* (Milton Keynes: Open University Press).

Grice, H. P. (1991) *Studies in the Way of Words* (Harvard, Mass.: Harvard University Press).

Harris, R. (1988) *Language, Saussure and Wittgenstein* (London: Routledge).

Hughes, G. (1988) *Words in Time* (Oxford: Blackwell).

Ingraham, A. (1903) *Swain School Lectures* (London: Kegan Paul).

Johnson, S. (1958) *Samuel Johnson: Rasselas, Poems, and Selected Prose*, ed. B. H. Bronson (New York: Holt, Rinehart & Winston).

Joyce, J. (1960) *A Portrait of the Artist as a Young Man* (London: Penguin).

Kearns, K. (2000) *Semantics* (Basingstoke: Palgrave).

Lakoff, G. and Johnson, M. (1980) *Metaphors We Live By* (Chicago: University of Chicago Press).

Lakoff, G. and Turner, M. (1989) *More than Cool Reason* (Chicago: University of Chicago Press).

Leech, G. (1981) *Semantics*, 2nd edn (London: Penguin).

Leech, G. (1983) *Principles of Pragmatics* (London: Longman).

Locke, J. (1964) *An Essay Concerning Human Understanding*, ed. A. D. Woozley (London: Fontana).

McCarthy, M. (1991) *Discourse Analysis for Language Teachers* (Cambridge: Cambridge University Press).

Ong, W. (1982) *Orality and Literacy* (London: Methuen).

Pinker, S. (1995) *The Language Instinct* (London: Penguin).

Pinter, H. (1968) *A Slight Ache and Other Plays* (London: Methuen).

Poole, G. (2002) *Syntactic Theory* (Basingstoke: Palgrave).

Quirk, R. (1962) *The Use of English* (London: Longman).

Quirk, R. and Greenbaum, S. (1990) *A Student's Grammar of the English Language* (London: Longman).

Radford, A. (1988) *An Introduction to Transformational Grammar* (Cambridge: Cambridge University Press).

Radford, A. (1997) *Syntactic Theory and the Structure of English: A Minimalist Approach* (Cambridge: Cambridge University Press).

Radford, A., Atkinson, M., Britain, D., Clahsen, H. and Spencer, A. (1999) *Linguistics: An Introduction* (Cambridge: Cambridge University Press).

Saussure, F. de (1966) *Course in General Linguistics* (1913), ed. C. Bally and A. Sechehay, trans. W. Baskin (New York: McGraw-Hill).

Searle, J. (1969) *Speech Acts* (Cambridge: Cambridge University Press).

Sperber, H. and Wilson, D. (1986) *Relevance: Communication and Cognition* (Oxford: Blackwell).

Sterne, L. (1967) *The Life and Opinions of Tristram Shandy*, ed. G. Petrie (London: Penguin).

Trudgill, P. (1990) *The Dialects of England* (Oxford: Blackwell).

Wales, K. (1989) *A Dictionary of Stylistics* (London: Longman).

Index

This index lists the main items discussed in the book. Page numbers **in bold** identify the chief discussion of an item.